IRISH HARPING, 1900–2010

IRISH HARPING
1900–2010

'It is New Strung'

HELEN LAWLOR

FOUR COURTS PRESS

Typeset in 11pt on 14pt Sabon for
FOUR COURTS PRESS LTD
7 Malpas Street, Dublin 8, Ireland
www.fourcourtspress.ie
and in North America for
FOUR COURTS PRESS
c/o ISBS, 920 NE 58th Avenue, Suite 300, Portland, OR 97213.

A catalogue record for this title is available
from the British Library.

ISBN 978-1-84682-367-1

Printed in England by
Antony Rowe Ltd, Chippenham, Wilts.

Contents

Illustrations

Acknowledgments

I gratefully acknowledge the assistance given by the following individuals who participated in and facilitated my fieldwork: Siobhán Armstrong, Harry Bradley, Mick Broderick, Eileen Gannon, Mercedes Garvey, Gráinne Hambly, Hammy Hamilton, Ann Heymann, Janet Harbison, Irish Traditional Music Archive, Denise Kelly, Laoise Kelly, Sheila Larchet Cuthbert, Jim McAllister, Úna McSweeney, Máire Ní Chathasaigh, Siobhán Nic Chonaráin, Sarah Noonan, Mary O'Hara, Sr Carmel Warde and Cairde na Cruite.

This research was generously supported by the DkIT Ionad Taighde Ceoil (Music Research Centre) and the DkIT Research Office. Further funding was also given by UCD through an Ad Astra Research Scholarship and a research travel grant from the Society for Musicology in Ireland (SMI).

I thank my colleagues in the department of Music and Creative Media at Dundalk Institute of Technology, Dr Eibhlís Farrell, Adèle Commins, Glen Doyle, Professor Thérèse Smith, Jaime Jones, the staff of the UCD School of Music, Professor Philip Bohlman, my family and friends.

For Norah, Willie, Tomás, Saoirse & Aido

CHAPTER 1

Introduction

This book provides a critical appraisal and analysis of the Irish harping tradition from the beginning of the twentieth century to the present day.[1] The music, cultural context, gender identities and modes of transmission of the Irish harp have undergone several phases of existence, revival and transformation over the past years. In the early decades of the century the harp was identified with convent schools and was used for the playing of instrumental arrangements of popular Irish song airs, such as those popularized by Thomas Moore. From the 1920s to the mid-century the harp experienced its lowest levels of popularity, but from the 1950s revival, the Irish harp was popularized as accompaniment to song. Two further phases are identifiable between the 1960s and the present day: the emergence of art-music style and traditional-music style for the harp, both of which continue to contribute to the contemporary harp scene. A further addition to harping today is the revival of the wire-strung or early-Irish harp, that has been gaining momentum in Ireland, particularly over the last ten years. Musically, the harp is now situated as an art-music, traditional-music and early-music instrument in its various guises. This book will draw primarily on the theory and methodology of ethnomusicology for its theoretical and practical grounding.

The aims of this book are to first, provide a musical ethnography of the Irish harp in the specified time period. While much work exists on early-Irish harping, the more recent history of the instrument has received little attention. Second, the revival of the Irish harp is interrogated from the perspective of revival theory in order to provide a parallel study of the Irish harp to other music revivals. Third, this book appraises key theoretical trends evident in current ethnomusicology, such as transmission, gender studies and identity, as they apply to the Irish harping tradition. By engaging with the critical discourse of ethnomusicology and related areas, trends in the harp tradition in Ireland can be evaluated and synthesized in relation to a broader field of studies. Fourth, musical analysis of several key styles and trends is presented throughout, where relevant to the overarching argument. Musical analysis enables a deeper and more musical interpretation of issues and problems in relation to style and repertoire. Fifth, this book collates important research and information that fills a gap in the current knowledge and provides a significant original contribution to the discourse of Irish harping, Irish musical studies and ethnomusicology.

The overall structure of this book can be divided into two parts. The first part of the book comprises chapters 2 to 6 inclusive. These chapters focus on distinct phases and eras of the Irish harping tradition. Chapters 7 and 8 offer a critique of theoretical issues as they apply to the harping tradition. Chapter 2 provides a re-examination of ideas surrounding harping at the beginning of the twentieth century. The harping tradition did not 'die out', as is commonly thought, but existed in a different format to that which had gone before. Until about the 1920s, there was a strong focus on instrumental music for the Irish harp, with the work of Mother Attracta Coffey and Mother Alphonsus O'Connor being of crucial importance during this period. From around the 1930s onwards there was a stylistic shift towards using the harp for song accompaniment. This shift had lasting repercussions for harp style into the mid century and affected the material that was popularized during the revival. Chapter 3, 'Revival', interrogates the Irish harp revival of the 1950s from the perspective of revival theory, with particular reference to Tamara Livingston's model.[2] This revival involved the use of the harp as accompaniment to song. Visual imagery and notions of 'stage Irishness' are critically appraised with regard to the harp revival. I argue that despite contemporary criticism of the harping tradition, this period in Irish harping cannot be overlooked and offers important insights into song style and the discourse of ideas about Irish music and Irish harping at that time.

Chapter 4 provides a critical commentary and musical analysis of the development of 'art-music' style harping on the Irish harp. The foundation and contribution of Cairde na Cruite (Friends of the Harp) in 1960 to Irish harping is assessed within the framework of revival transformation. The music of this style and period is analyzed, and the musical culture of art-music style harping is examined. Chapter 5 critiques the recent development of 'traditional-style' harping from the late 1970s to the present day. The style and repertoire are analyzed in order to justify the terminology 'traditional-style'. Performance contexts of traditional-style harping are appraised in relation to the processes of globalization and diaspora. Chapter 6, 'The early Irish harp in its modern context', completes the first section of this book, and the early-Irish (or wire-strung) harp is the main focus of investigation in this chapter. The contribution of key individuals is assessed, as are performance contexts, techniques and instrument types.

Chapter 7, 'Transmission and Irish harping', evaluates issues of transmission in Irish traditional music, with a particular focus on the harping tradition. Issues of orality and literacy are central to the debate on transmission and the teaching of an oral tradition in the modern age provides both exciting possibilities and difficulties. A case study of a harp class at Scoil Éigse (2007) and Irish music transmission via the internet are employed here.[3] Chapter 8, 'Gender and identity', explores issues of gender and identity as they apply to the Irish harping tradition. The feminization of the instrument has been a significant factor in the gender associations of the harp throughout the twentieth century. The harp also carries strong ideological and symbolic ideas in its sociocultural capacity. The implications of these issues of identity are critically analyzed

The Irish harping tradition is a unique phenomenon within traditional Irish music and the broader sphere of music in Ireland. The standard 34-string Irish harp, uniquely for traditional instruments, straddles the worlds of aural or oral traditional music and the literate world of Western art music. These two styles can be labelled respectively as 'traditional-music style' (which is broadly aligned with mainstream traditional music) and 'art-music style' (which broadly combines practices of Western art music with some Irish repertoire). The term 'traditional' is an emic term used to describe traditional-style harping. The appendage '-style harping' is not normally used in harping, but is implied. I have adopted the term 'art-music style' in order to classify and discuss a discrete style of harping. This is not an emic term, however; no term is used to describe this particular style.[4] A significant proportion of the repertoire available to an Irish harpist is the traditional dance music repertoire, but there is also a large written repertoire that must be given consideration. Many leading Irish harpists from the 1950s onwards such as Mary O'Hara, Nancy Calthorpe, Gráinne Yeats, Sheila Larchet Cuthbert, Aibhlín Mc Crann, Janet Harbison, Kathleen Loughnane and Denise Kelly have published their own compositions and arrangements in collections such as the 'Sounding Harps' volumes and *Rogha na gCruitirí* published by Cairde na Cruite. The influential *Irish harp book* contains a diverse collection of music from T.C. Kelly's 'Interlude' to Turlough Carolan's 'Farewell to Music', arranged by Sheila Larchet Cuthbert. Kathleen Loughnane acknowledges the duality of sources for harp music: 'With the demise of the harping tradition, some of the tunes lived on in the repertoire of the uilleann pipes and fiddle ... But many lovely harping tunes remained on the page ... On this CD I have included harping tunes both from Bunting's collection and from the aural tradition'.[5] The two styles, 'traditional' and 'art' music-style have different modes of transmission, performance contexts and aesthetics. However, the features that are shared, such as the instrument, repertoire and at times musicians, demands that both stylistic traditions must be given due consideration. In addition to the neo-Irish harping scene, there is a growing number of practitioners of the early-Irish or wire-strung harp.

An emic, or insider, perspective fieldwork enables an interrogation of the music-making practices in Irish harping. My music education began aged seven when I learned tin-whistle from a neighbour, Fidelma O'Brien, wife of well-known piper, Mick O'Brien. Without realizing it, I was living in a community of traditional musicians (itself a relatively unusual occurrence for a Dublin suburb) as almost every child on our street played traditional music. Far from being a childhood pastime, traditional music for three families from one street remained a way of life that characterizes the lifestyle of those involved. I studied the harp from the age of fourteen at weekly classes and summer schools where I was taught by, among others, Michael Rooney, Gráinne Hambly, Laoise Kelly and Janet Harbison. These harpers are considered to be among the finest players and teachers and although I was always well aware of their reputation, I knew nothing about ethnomusicology or bi-musicality as a student attending harp classes. It is perhaps at festivals such as the Fleadh Cheoil when I competed as part of a *grúpa ceoil* and as a harper that I experienced the sociology of Irish music, whereby young musicians could see and hear master musicians playing and learn to respect other people's music. At sessions, in festivals and in Dublin I learned much about the music, its contexts and functions, before I embarked on any research. On entering university to pursue a degree in Music Education, I began playing in the 'art-music style' of Irish harp with Denise Kelly, a classically trained concert-harpist. From this point onwards I experienced a very different harp world to that which I had known previously and over four years learned through participation the repertoire, technique and socio-musical context of this particular branch of harping. My encounters with harping therefore began with a form of understanding through experience and contact with the tradition. Following Rice's model, this experience formed my initial pre-understanding of the harping tradition(s) as a student and performer.[6] My investigations into harping style, history and musical contexts for this book have allowed me to experience a different hermeneutic arc of understanding and experience through study and fieldwork so that my interpretations of the harping tradition are based on emic and etic perspectives, experience, fieldwork and differentiated arcs of under-standing.

Traditional-music style harping

Traditional-style harping is the style of harping aligned with mainstream traditional Irish music. The style and performance contexts are those of that tradition and transmission is often primarily oral-based. The technique sometimes uses a more relaxed hand position and plucking style than that of art-music style. Fixed finger positions are not enforced as ornamentation and variation are key characteristics of this style. The repertoire consists mainly of dance tunes, airs and music of the harper composers. Emic or insider knowledge is essential for research into any traditional music. In the case of Irish traditional music two elements of the tradition – orality and the centrality of participation – demand insider knowledge for any meaningful interpretation. The orality of this tradition is related to the dual intangible processes of ornamentation and variation. Moreover, the characteristic rhythmic emphases used to varying degrees around the country can only be fully experienced through participation. This participation generally takes the form of performance or active listening, whereby participants can experience the processes and aesthetics of traditional music while expressing in performance their individual musicality. Flute player Harry Bradley made the following comment in an interview: 'I think in the past musicians used to play on their own a lot more, which I think was a very good thing'. Here he emphasizes the importance of both performance and listening and, later, advocated that musicians should: 'develop their own voice and become self sufficient'.[7] These issues are also central to the traditional-music style of Irish harping as a discrete element in the broader context of Irish traditional music. The relatively recent development of this style (mainly from the 1980s onwards) has implications for the reproduction of style, technique and repertoire. In comparison with other instrumental traditions such as flute or fiddle, the harp has only a limited number of recordings, tune books and established figures. Thus an increased importance has been placed on harp classes. Local and festival-based classes have therefore become the main site for transmission. Classes such as that described in chapter 7 are now the main forum for the transmission of traditional-music style harping.

Art-music style harping

Unlike traditional-music style, art-music style harping is broadly aligned with the style and context of Western Art music. This is a literate tradition which has developed in Ireland over the past one hundred years or more. One of the central figures, Sheila Larchet Cuthbert, author of *The Irish harp book*, described in an interview her musical education at Loreto Abbey, Rathfarnham as follows:

> And when I went there I was playing cello and piano. I studied both in the Royal Irish Academy of music and the harpist then, Mother Alphonsus, she suggested that I might try the concert harp and that I might like it … So when I left school, I stayed with Mother Alphonsus for about another year and then I eventually went to a French harpist who was in Manchester, Tina Bonifacio.[8]

This type of musical training is very common for harpists trained in the art-music style of Irish harping. Research into this type of music, with arrangements and pieces composed by named authors, is generally from the perspective of historical musicology and is often focused on composers or compositions. I am, however, taking a different approach. By combining my experience as an insider with fieldwork into art-music style harping I can research the practices of music making within this aspect of Irish harping as opposed to concentrating solely on the musical artefacts. The inextricable links between both branches of Irish harping – shared history, repertoire and instrument – demand that any meaningful research engages with both musical traditions. As is the case with traditional-style harping, I already had lived experience of this type of music prior to embarking on any research into it during fieldwork. I gained a fresh perspective on how style is reproduced and how the forum for transmission (solo classes) impacts on subsequent music-making activities. The learning styles, contexts and approaches of art-music style are significantly different to that of traditional-music style. Similarly, the performance contexts, repertoires, techniques and approaches also exhibit strong differences. The terminology used ('art' and 'traditional') is intended to represent and reflect these differing styles of Irish harping.

CHAPTER 2

Irish harping, 1900–50

During the first half of the twentieth century two types of Irish harping can be observed. The first type, art-music style harping, forms the basis of the same style grouping that is in existence today. The second type, singing to harp accompaniment, flourished from 1930 until the 1980s, and is still performed today. The importance of this era in Irish harping cannot be underestimated as the roots of the art-music style of harping lie directly with the musical practices and personnel of the early twentieth century. Art-music style (in Irish harping) focuses strongly on the purely instrumental expression of music. The practices of art-music style, such as the publication of music and the use of 'composed' arrangements, can also be observed. However, the development of the song tradition in the 1930s features a shift away from solely instrumental expression and a growing popularity for harp as accompaniment to song. This type of harping had a lasting legacy, given that the harp revival of the 1950s was inspired and aided by those who practiced this style. The high status of the harp in today's society could not have been achieved were it not for the harp revival. Despite the limited dissemination of harp music before 1950, it is clear that the harping tradition did not die out.

Irish harping in the late nineteenth and early twentieth centuries has only recently attracted scholarly attention, with the work of Mary O'Donnell.[1] Prior to this a common belief existed that assumed a minimal amount of harping during that period. Joan Rimmer advanced this argument, despite the fact that there certainly was evidence of harping activity at the turn of the century:

> There seems to have been little harp–playing in Ireland apart from the visits of foreign virtuosi on the pedal harp, after the third decade of the nineteenth century ... At the end of the century enthusiasts like James MacFall produced instruments such as the

'Tara Harp', made in 1902 for Cardinal Logue. This had a box like a pedal harp set on three little feet, a slim, curved fore pillar with a T-formation copied from the medieval low-headed Irish harp, a high head and elaborate decoration – in all, a charming piece of antiquarian *art nouveau*.[2]

William Henry Grattan Flood paints a bleak picture of harping in Ireland in 1906:

> Then came the famine, and, alas! the harp was allowed to become neglected till the Irish Ireland movement, inaugurated by the Gaelic League, and fostered by the Celtic Literary Society and kindred associations, again galvanized the national instrument into life. However, it is evident that notwithstanding these efforts, as evidenced by the harp competitions at the Feis Ceoil and Oireachtas since 1897, the national instrument is now merely heard 'to show that still she lives'.[3]

Despite the various complaints and laments concerning the lack of harping at the time, there is clear evidence that the harping tradition had not completely died out in the nineteenth century, but did continue to exist, albeit in a very limited context, up until the beginning of the twentieth century. A renewed interest in the Irish harp at the start of the twentieth century sowed the seeds and provided the basic material required for the development of the harp revival in the latter part of the twentieth century. That revival aimed to bring the harp to a much wider audience, to disseminate harp music and to provide formal teaching. The main difference between nineteenth- and twentieth-century efforts was that in the twentieth century, the harp was successfully revived as a popular instrument (in both art music and traditional music), but in the nineteenth century, such levels of popularity were never achieved.

In the last two decades of the nineteenth century the Irish cultural revival began to gather momentum. This revival was concentrated on selected areas of Irish culture, namely language and sport. The Gaelic League was founded in 1893 with the express aim of saving the Irish language from extinction and with the purpose of re-establishing the language as a viable expression of Irish identity through common usage. The League had widespread popular appeal: for example, by 1897, 40 branches were established and by 1904, 604 branches had been established.[4] In addition to the activities of the Gaelic League, the Gaelic Athletic Association (GAA) was founded in 1884 to promote specifically Irish sports. The Irish literary revival likewise aimed to promote an English–language literary movement that demonstrated particularly Irish characteristics: 'Yeats and Augusta Gregory, founders of the Irish Literary Theatre in May 1899, believed they could create a literature of world significance, written in English but essentially Irish – drawing on folk consciousness (and in Lady Gregory's case a constructed dialect), but transcending political localism.'[5]

According to Harry White, the cultural revival proved detrimental to Irish art music as the symbolism and ideology of Irishness weighed down on any prospective composers: 'The ultimate condition of music in Ireland would only become clear with its failure to function within the otherwise abundantly fertile terms of the Celtic Revival, except as a *symbol* of Irish cultural renaissance.'[6] However, the context of Irish harping was quite different to the musical space (both physically and ideologically) of composed art music at the turn of the century. I would argue that the very sentiment criticized by White may have spurred, or at the very least, maintained an interest in the Irish harp, even if that interest was born out of antiquarianism or indeed a romanticized notion of the instrument.

It is important to note that the harping activity at the beginning of the twentieth century was not necessarily a revival, but a continuation of an on-going musical practice, despite its very low-level impact. Ita Beausang makes several references to harping activity in the later nineteenth century.[7] Indeed, the harp became particularly evident at events associated with the commemoration of Thomas Moore. In 1869 John William Glover's daughters organized vocal and harp concerts: 'in an effort to bring our national instrument prominently forward hereafter, so that it may no longer be said that "The harp is silent in its native clime"'.[8] Further contemporaneous activities included the celebration of Moore's centenary in 1870:

> The celebration of the Moore Centenary in May 1879 was preceded by a three-day Irish Harp Revival in the Rotunda. The performers included a Swedish harpist, Adolf Sjoden, as well as a choir of pedal harps, a trio of ancient Irish wire-strung harps, a Welsh harper, 'one of the last surviving of the Celebrated Blind Irish Harpers' and celebrated Irish pipers.[9]

While this scant reference to harping does not indicate that the instrument was widely played at the time, it serves to prove that the harping tradition itself was still in existence at the end of the nineteenth century, even if only barely. Following from the 1879 'Irish Harp Revival' that clearly did not substantiate any significant increase in the numbers of harp players, the harp is mentioned again in 1884 when a concert for John O'Donnell featured 'Eileen Aroon' 'sung in Irish with harp accompaniment'.[10] In 1897, the lack of harpers' participation in the first Feis Ceoil was immediately addressed by the Gaelic League in Dublin: 'Recently the Gaelic League in Dublin got a consignment of Irish harps which were purchased by members, but of course it is too early to look for any successful results yet, though it leaves us not without hope that the Feis may witness the playing of a band of Irish harpers on the Irish harp.'[11] It is clear from this article that members of the Gaelic League had hoped, if not expected, that there would be some entries on the Irish harp and, in the absence of such, they decided to purchase harps to avoid this problem in the future.

The symbolism of the harp at the turn of the century weighed heavily after a century of antiquarian interest (see, for example, the work of Edward Bunting, George Petrie, Thomas Moore and others). Barra Boydell has effectively argued that the harp by the beginning of the nineteenth century had become the pre-eminent image of Irishness through its literary and musical expression. 'The Wild Irish Girl appeared a year before the first volume of Thomas Moore's Irish melodies which would popularize the harp as the symbol of Irish national identity through songs like 'That Harp that Once thro' Tara's Halls', 'The Origin of the Harp', 'The Minstrel Boy' and many others.'[12] Almost one hundred years later, the harp still carried the ideological and symbolic associations of Irishness. In a lecture given in 1898 by S. Shannon Millin to the Ulster Association, entitled 'The Irish harp, a lecture', he used the harp to demonstrate a very nationalist interpretation of Irish culture that perhaps had less to do with music than the title might suggest. Millin argued his case for the long-standing Gaelic civilization by quoting from Heccataeus, an ancient Egyptian historian who wrote about Ireland in 500 BC. Heccataeus described how the Irish worshipped Apollo and played their harps in honour of him. Millin used the harp to criticize contemporary English attitudes to Irish culture and civilization:

Think of it, ye classical scholars who sing the praises of Greece, that 500 years BC the Irish worshipped Apollo above all other gods. Think of it, ye poets and painters who place in the hands of Apollo a Grecian lyre, that the Irish harp was tuned in the praises of Apollo long before the Greeks had arrived at an advanced stage of musical refinement. Think of it, ye English politicians who taunt the Irish with being a barbarous people, that long before the ancient inhabitants of Britain had cast off the swaddling clothes of civilization the fame and erudition of Ireland had extended beyond the uttermost corners of Europe.[13]

Given the strong legacy of Moore, and the type of nostalgic language used in relation to the harp, in addition to a century of antiquarian interest in the Irish harp, it is not surprising that Millin used such polemical language in his lecture on the Irish harp. He concluded his lecture with reference to the Feis Ceoil as a possible 'saviour' of the harp and, indeed, music in Ireland:

> The movement known as the Feis Ceoil, will, if properly handled, have a tendency to restore to Ireland her former greatness in the art of song. The Irish, like the Babylonish captives, may be said to have hung their harps upon the willows. But the spirit of persecution which drove Handel from England to seek shelter on the Hibernian shore, has given way to a spirit of toleration, and the change must bring countless blessings in its train.[14]

At the start of the twentieth century, therefore, the Irish harp carried musical, symbolic and ideological implications. The harping tradition never actually died out, but was most certainly diminished from the mid-nineteenth century onwards.[15] In terms of harping today, the events of the early twentieth century had quite far-reaching effects in the second stage of the Irish harp revival (in the 1960s). The work of two central figures, Mother Attracta Coffey (M.A.C.) (died 1920) and her successor, Mother Alphonsus O'Connor (M.A.O'C.), both of Loreto Abbey, Rathfarnham in Dublin, provided a set of musical materials that would be drawn upon again in the 1960s and 1970s by the leaders of the art-music style of harping.[16] The publication of *Irish melodies transcribed and adapted for the Irish harp* by M.A.C. in 1902 is a critical piece of evidence in relation to what was being played on the Irish harp at the turn of the twentieth century.[17] The publication of this volume and the *Studies for Irish harp* by M.A.C. (which have been preserved only by the published work of Sheila Larchet Cuthbert) forms a second layer of linear development of harping in the twentieth century, starting with the work of M.A.C. Her most prominent pupil, M.A.O'C., was also influential in the harp world through her publication of *Irish airs* for harp.[18]

Close examination of the music of M.A.C. reveals much about the Irish harp in the early twentieth century. Analysis shows that it is stylistically identical to M.A.C.'s arrangement of Irish airs for concert harp and that her arrangements are situated within the canon of harp music published in the late nineteenth and early twentieth centuries. By drawing comparisons with the compositions of Welsh harpist, arranger and composer, John Thomas, and on the somewhat later work of M.A.O'C., it becomes evident that the Irish harp was treated from the perspective of the concert harp rather than from an indigenous folk-music, antiquarian or historical perspective. We can deduce therefore that players and arrangers viewed the harp as a living, viable instrument and did not approach the harp with revivalist intentions. On the other hand, the deep similarities between the music for concert and Irish harp by M.A.C., M.A.O'C. and Thomas show the concert harp repertoire of the late nineteenth century to be the primary influence for Irish harp style by the early twentieth century.

Sheila Larchet Cuthbert's work with the Irish harp in the 1960s and 1970s takes on further significance, given that she was one of M.A.O'C.'s students at Loreto Abbey, Rathfarnham. Larchet Cuthbert's inclusion of M.A.C.'s studies as progressive training aids to the novice harpist reincarnate the approach of M.A.C., and draw the Irish harp significantly closer to the style, repertoire and technique of the concert harp than did the singer-harpists of the 1950s. This link between Larchet Cuthbert and M.A.C. becomes cemented in the publication of the studies in Larchet Cuthbert's book and thus opens up a new branch of revival, linking the practices of Irish harping in the 1960s directly to the practices of the early 1900s as expressed through the music of M.A.C. and M.A.O'C.

In order to give appropriate consideration to the Irish harp revival in the mid–twentieth century, it is therefore essential that the early twentieth century is accurately addressed and not glossed over. Clearly, the publications of M.A.C. and the influence of her work demonstrate that there was some level of harping activity (in Dublin at least). Furthermore, this was a practical and physical usage of the harp, rather than antiquarian or otherwise. S.C. Lanier may have misjudged the extent to which the Irish harp was (not) in use at the time, by arguing that 'In the early years of the twentieth century, a revival of interest in the Irish harp tradition was stimulated by the work of Charlotte Milligan Fox (1864–1916).'[19] Milligan Fox's publication did not appear until 1911, nine years after M.A.C.'s *Irish melodies* for the Irish harp. It is therefore untrue to credit Milligan Fox completely for a renewed interest in the harp. While we do not know the exact numbers of harpers at the time, and it is most likely that the numbers were minimal, there were *some* Irish harpers at the time, for whom M.A.C. published her book of arrangements. Sheila Larchet Cuthbert described M.A.C. as follows:

> a very fine harpist, she was also well known outside the country. Now that at that time was really something, I'm talking about before the 1920s even. Her music, she did a lot of arrangements of Irish airs for Irish harp and concert harp. Concert harp that wouldn't have been so surprising, but Irish harp, very surprising at that time because practically nobody was playing it. It was almost, it was dying, if you like. But it never really died.[20]

Accounts of the Irish harp published in newspapers further attest to harping activity in Ireland. In 1903 the Lord Lieutenant ordered a harp from James McFall of Belfast, having heard harpist Florie Kerin play.

> Mr James McFall, Belfast, has received an order from the Lord Lientenant, for an Irish harp. His Excellency writes – 'Having heard the small Irish harp recently played in Dublin by Miss Florie Kerin, I was much pleased with the sweet and powerful tone of the beautiful instrument.' These harps are of Irish manufacture, and have been modelled on the ancient harps of the bards. They were the instruments used by the band of harpists from Loreto Abbey Rathfarnham, led by Miss Florie Kerin, which played at the recent Oireachtas. Miss Kerin is a Feis gold medallist and holder of the Oireachtas first prize for playing on the Irish harp.[21]

The reference to a 'band of harpists' in this article shows that Florie Kerin was not the only Irish harp player at that time. Another Florie is pictured in plate 1, in this instance, a Florie O'Connor with a McFall harp. This picture was taken by Rudolf Trebitsch of the Austrian Phono-grammarchiv on a collecting trip to Ireland in 1907. He also recorded three pieces by her, including 'The Dawning of the Day'.[22]

Newspaper articles provide detailed evidence of harping activity in the early twentieth century. In 1908, the excerpts from the adjudicator's reports of the Feis Ceoil were published in the *Freeman's Journal*. The adjudication of the harp was carried out by Mr Hans Wessely: 'There was some good playing on the Irish harp, an instrument with a romantic history, and one that should not be neglected by those desirous of fostering the love of native music in a country where national feeling runs so strong.'[23] An article entitled 'The Feis Ceoil, Harp Competitions' with the subtitle 'Loreto Abbey Scores', published following the harp competition in the Feis in 1909, gives quite a detailed description of the level of harping activity. The harp on this occasion was adjudicated by M. Achille Rivade of the Royal College of Music, London.

> IRISH HARP. Only three players on Irish harp put in an appearance. The test pieces were 'Studies for the Irish Harp, Nos. 1 and 4,' by M.A.C. whose high attainments as a harpist and musician are well known, and Nos. 1, 2, and 3, Book III, of 'Melodies for the Irish Harp,' by the same composer. M. Rivarde adjudicated in this class also, and decided as follows: 1st and gold medal – Miss Aggie Sherry, Foxford, Co. Mayo. 2nd and silver medal – Miss Kathleen O'Neill, Dominican Convent, Sion Hill, Blackrock.

> THE JOSEPH SEYMOUR PRIZE. This is an Irish harp, presented by Mr. Joseph Seymour, to be annually competed for, but to be won in three successive years before it can become the property of the candidate. The test pieces were two of the candidates own selection. The only competitor for this prize was Miss Aggie Sherry, who had taken the first prize in the Irish harp competition. She appeared on the platform with the intention of playing 'Annie Dear' and 'The Harp That Once', but M. Rivarde said her playing was so good in the previous competition that he was prepared to award the prize to her at once. Her playing was characterized by very good rhythm and remarkably nice tone.[24]

M.A.C. was a member of the community at Loreto, Rathfarnham. Therefore, there must also have been a harp teacher at Dominican College, Sion Hill (Blackrock, Dublin) at the same time. However, the low number of entrants to the Joseph Seymour prize shows that the Irish harp was still very much a minority instrument. One further mention of the Irish harp in the *Freeman's Journal* possibly refers to M.A.C.'s successor, M.A.O'C.

> A very enjoyable musical programme, under the direction of Mr John Roy, Librarian, Rathmines Public Library, was gone through. The special feature of the evening was the cordial reception given to Miss O'Connor, whose efforts on the Irish harp were so much appreciated that she had to respond with several encores ... and possibly unique feature of the programme was the dancing of an Irish reel to the music of the harp.[25]

This entry describes the Library Assistant's Association trip to Lexlip in July 1914. Interestingly, the harp player in question played a piece of dance music on the Irish harp. I would surmise that the playing of dance music on the Irish harp at the time was the exception rather than the rule as the published repertoire from this time does not include dance music.

The publications of M.A.C. and the above newspaper accounts all point to the existence of limited harping activity in the early twentieth century. My purpose in referencing this harping activity is to contextualize the publications that appeared at this time. This style and approach to Irish harping subsequently re-emerged in the 1960s as the art-music style of harping, led by Sheila Larchet Cuthbert and her contemporaries. This style can be characterized by the application of standard conventions of concert harping to the Irish harp, rather than the continuation of the style and techniques of Irish harping described by Bunting in his 1840 volume. M.A.C.'s Irish harp arrangements do not incorporate the techniques of the seventeenth-century harper-composers, such as the use of ornamentation or sparse accompaniment. Musically speaking, M.A.C.'s arrangements are stylistically identical to her arrangements for concert harp. This suggests that the conception of the Irish harp at the time was that its capabilities, while limited in range and chromatic possibilities, allowed for the playing of music that was contemporaneously popular on other instruments, such as concert harp and piano. There is no reason why this should not have been the case. Egan's portable harp, which was developed in the nineteenth century, and the subsequent 'neo-Irish' harp (to use Joan Rimmer's term) were in fact different instruments to those played by Turlough Carolan or Arthur O'Neill.

It is important to disentangle the commonly assumed notions about the Irish harp, such as that its legacy stems directly from the harper composers whose music Bunting notated. While this is partly true, the nineteenth century also forms part of the harp's history, a century which is commonly ignored in the context of the Irish harp. My labelling of the style in question as 'art-music' style relates to the complication that now exists in the twenty-first century, whereby at least two distinct style groups are evident. Here I seek to explore the development of the art-music style and demonstrate that its roots lie in the early twentieth century. The term 'art-music style' harping remains the most appropriate term as it describes not only the musical material but the process of arrangement, composition and performance at work in this branch of Irish harping.

M.A.C.'s *Irish melodies* (transcribed and adapted) for the Irish harp was published in 1902. There were at least three volumes published (see excerpt from the *Freeman's Journal* above) and these arrangements were set as the syllabus for the Feis Ceoil Irish harp competition. Book I contains the following twelve famous Irish melodies arranged specifically for the Irish harp:

1   Believe Me If All
2   She is Far from the Land
3   If Thou'lt Be Mine
4   Nothing In Life Can Sadden Us
5   I'd Mourn The Hopes That Leave Me
6   The Wedding of Ballyporeen
7   Kathleen O'Moore
8   Nay, Tell Me Not
9   Oh, Southern Breeze
10 The Time I've Lost In Wooing
11 Irish Love Song
12 Moll Roe

Unfortunately, Book I is the only extant copy available and therefore it must be viewed as representative of her approach to writing for the Irish harp. M.A.C. was well respected as a musician and an arranger. W.H. Grattan Flood mentions her in his *History of Irish music*: 'It is risky to mention persons still living, but the following names are sufficient to prove that Ireland can still boast of musical sons and daughters, inheritors of the traditions of past ages … Mrs. Milligan Fox … Sister

Attracta Coffey'.[26] Several notable points can be observed from the front cover of her 1902 publication. First, this volume is dedicated to Mother Mary Cecilia, St Mary's, Waterford (her *Irish melodies* for (concert) harp is dedicated to the Welsh composer and arranger, John Thomas). Perhaps Mother Mary Cecilia was also a harp enthusiast at the time. The layout and design of this book is quite similar in style to that of her *Irish melodies* for harp and to the later volume, *Irish airs* published by M.A.O'C. The front cover also features a harp, not the type of Irish harp that would have been played at the time but a version of the so-called 'Brian Ború' harp, which is held at Trinity College, Dublin. The difference here is in the end curve at the base of the bow, which does not feature on the Brian Ború harp. The florid design of the cover includes further imagery associated with Ireland in the form of shamrocks that sprout from the bottom right-hand corner of the page and surround the harp, reaching up to the title also (see plate 2).

'Believe Me If All' is the first piece presented in this book. The approach used by M.A.C. to the Irish harp was, in fact, identical to her approach to the concert harp. The melodic material remains in the right hand throughout this setting, with a left-hand harmonic accompaniment supporting the melody. The melody line is further harmonized by the use of chordal texture in the right hand, which is expanded at times to four voices, such as in bars two and ten. The arrangement of the melody is varied on the repeated sections of the melody; for instance, in bar one, broken octaves, forming single notes, are employed in the left hand, whereas on the repeat of this material in bar five, complete octaves are notated. The standard diatonic harmony is classical in style, with the use of harmonic conventions such as the cadence in bars fifteen to sixteen. A limited amount of chromatic harmony is used which provides colour and interest, such as the flattened seventh (flat I 6/4/2), in motion between I and IV6/3 in the bass line, bar thirteen. The notated dynamics are quite detailed which, as I will demonstrate over successive musical examples, is characteristic of the art music approach to Irish harping. Fifteen dynamic markings (including abbreviated dynamic notations, crescendo and diminuendo symbols) are used within this sixteen bar setting. This arrangement is not overly complex but does require a medium standard of proficiency to execute correctly. The trappings of the art-music style, such as dynamic markings, classical style harmony and the very use of a published score, are all evident here, as is the case with musical example 2, 'She is Far From the Land'.

Con espressione

Music Example 1: 'Believe Me If All', M.A.C.

The second arrangement published by M.A.C., 'She Is Far From the Land', is similarly a well-known air. Many of the same features evident in example 1 can also be observed here, such as chordal expansion of the melody in the right hand, classical style harmony, detailed use of dynamics and Italian tempo and expression markings. This piece requires quite a high level of technical proficiency from the Irish harpist. M.A.C. uses a secondary dominant in bar five (V6/3 of V, V of V, V). Almost all secondary dominants require blade changes on the Irish harp, and that is the case here. Further use of chromatic harmony is made in bar seven where a diminished chord I in second inversion (the G sharp can be enharmonically interpreted as A flat) demands that several blade changes be made. In order to prepare the two G sharps, they must be raised in the previous bar.[27] Chromatic harmony is a common device in the piano and, indeed, the concert harp repertory. It is unproblematic to add simultaneous accidentals when playing the concert harp due to the pedal mechanism. On the Irish harp this is, however, a different matter. If the pitch of a string needs to be altered, this must be done manually by the harp player for each individual string. This type of writing by M.A.C. demonstrates the underlying assumption of a perceived affinity between Irish and concert harp.

A further example of this concert harp style writing for Irish harp occurs in M.A.C.'s arrangement of 'Irish Love Song' (or 'Danny Boy' as it is commonly known). Again, all of the melodic material is in the right hand, except where the left hand echoes the melody (such as in bars eight and fifteen). Chordal texture is also used in the right hand, where three- and four-part voice leading can be observed. The chromatic harmony is denser here than in the other examples. In bar eleven, the following progression is used: vi, vii 6/3, vii 6/5/3, I 6/3, vii7 of V, V. Six separate blade changes are required of the harpist within a three bar period. This is quite challenging on the Irish harp.

Music Example 2: 'She Is Far From the Land', M.A.C

Music Example 3: 'Irish Love Song' (Excerpt), M.A.C.

M.A.C.'s arrangement of 'The Coulin' is helpful to examine by way of comparison her style of writing. This was published in her *Irish melodies* arranged for the harp, which was also published by the Vincent Music Company, London in 1902. In this instance harp most likely denotes concert harp (as Irish harp is given for specifically Irish harp publications. Also the keys used in M.A.C.'s volume are outside the normal key range associated with Irish harping publications). This volume contains six arrangements of popular Irish melodies for the harp:

1 My Gentle Harp
2 The Snowy Breasted Pearl
3 The Young Man's Dream
4 The Coulin
5 Lough Sheeling
6 A Cushla Machree

Visually and aurally stylistic affinities are evident to her arrangements for Irish harp. The harmonic arrangement here is less complex than in the two previous examples. She employs the same types of voice leading devices found elsewhere in her Irish harp arrangements, although this particular example contains more instances of suspensions than any example previously examined. It is interesting that she notates grace notes in this arrangement as this device is not utilized in her other arrangements. 'The Coulin' is set in the key of C flat major. This key is practically never used on the Irish harp, which is generally tuned in E flat. Therefore, some consideration was given to the nature of the instrument. Whereas harp fingering was intermittently notated in her publication for the Irish harp (such as in bars one to two of 'She is Far From the Land'), there is no fingering notated for any of the arrangements in this volume. The devices commonly employed for Irish harp by M.A.C. are also used in her work for concert harp: chordal expansion in the right hand; similar chord types and spacing; full and arpeggiated chords; the cadential 6/4; frequent use of seventh chords; detailed dynamics and performing instructions. 'The Coulin' exhibits all of these traits, as can be seen in example 4 below.

The front cover of M.A.C.'s *Irish melodies* for Harp is very similar in design to her volume for Irish harp. She dedicated this publication to harpist, composer and arranger John Thomas. Sheila Larchet Cuthbert commented on the relationship between the two harpists:

> She was also in communication, and this is important, with a very famous Welsh harp professor, John Thomas ... He was, in his time, a very eminent Welsh player, had won a great competition at Eisteddfod, he also was professor of harp in the Royal Academy of Music ... So he used to communicate with Mother Attracta and he sent her some of his music. Now he was doing very much the same thing. He was arranging very beautiful Welsh airs for concert harp and triple harp. She was doing this for Irish harp.[28]

John Thomas was a prolific arranger and composer for concert harp in the late nineteenth century. As Larchet correctly pointed out, both M.A.C. and Thomas were working on the same types of arrangements at the same time, and it seems that they were in contact. Not only is M.A.C.'s treatment of the Irish harp similar to her treatment of the concert harp, but her concert harp writing shows a clear affinity to that of her contemporaries. Thomas was a highly regarded composer and arranger, whose music for the harp is stylistically similar to M.A.C.'s. His arrangement of 'David of the White Rock', or 'Dafydd Y Garreg Wen', shows much similarity in terms of style and approach to the music of M.A.C. In the initial outlay of the main theme Thomas employs standard conventions such as maintaining the melody in the right hand, with chordal accompaniment in the left. The harmony is tonal and diatonic and follows standard conventions of voice leading. Texturally this is identical to the types of texture found in M.A.C.'s work. The treatment of the subsequent repeats of the melody in this arrangement shows that both Thomas and M.A.C. used the same types of harmonic language, textures, voice leading and expressive devices when writing for concert harp.

Music Example 4: 'The Coulin', M.A.C.

There are hundreds of examples of harp music from the mid- to late nineteenth century, from the work of Debussy and Tournier to Thomas, Naderman and many others. M.A.C.'s musical language for concert harp firmly situates her in the broader sphere of music written for

Musical Example 5 (i): 'David of the White Rock' (Excerpt), Thomas

concert harp at the turn of the century. The similarities in style and approach of M.A.C. and Thomas show two important features of her compositional style. First, if her writing for concert harp can be judged as part of the overall canon of late nineteenth- and early twentieth-century harp music (and as a harp arranger she was fully aware of the work of her contemporaries), then her music is representative of harp music at that time. Second, if it is determined that her concert and Irish harp writing belong to the same style grouping, then her music for the Irish harp falls into the category of art music, either composed or arranged for Irish harp.

Two further brief musical examples illustrate this point again. A musical device that was popular in the writing of John Thomas was the use of a double note in an arpeggiated texture:

Musical Example 5 (ii): 'David of the White Rock' (Excerpt), Thomas

A similar device is also used by M.A.C.'s successor, Mother Alphonsus O'Connor (M.A.O'C) in her *Irish airs* arranged for the harp. These arrangements are for concert harp, with only three melodies in the collection – 'Battle Hymn', 'Go Where Thy Glory Waits Thee', 'Avenging and Bright'.

'Go Where Thy Glory Waits Thee' carries many of the same conven-

Musical Example 6 (i): 'Go Where Thy Glory Waits Thee'
(Excerpt), M.A.O'C.

tions as the examples above. In example 6 (i), we can observe the same
texture-type that has been employed by both M.A.C. and Thomas in
their arrangements. M.A.O'C.'s use of chromaticism is also consistent
with that of the previous examples. In example 6 (i) above, the voice
leading in the bass shows the use of a descending chromatic scale
excerpt. M.A.O'C.'s arrangement includes two versions of the melody.
The first is harmonized in the type of texture laid out above. The second
version of the melody, from bars 16 to 30 (including a short coda), has
the melody line interspersed between rapid arpeggios.

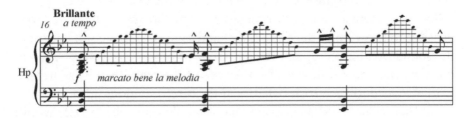

Musical Example 6 (ii): 'Go Where Thy Glory Waits Thee' (Excerpt), M.A.O'C.

Here we can observe her use of the double note device within an
arpeggiated texture, much in the same manner as Thomas. Her
arrangement style is similarly situated alongside that of M.A.C. and
Thomas. The impact of this stylistic orientation becomes immensely
important when one of M.A.O'C.'s most eminent students, Sheila
Larchet Cuthbert, takes up the task of publishing *The Irish harp book*,
under the auspices of Cairde na Cruite in the 1960s. The second stage of
revival, I will argue, is when the harp re-emerges as an art music
instrument, much in the same manner as it was perceived by M.A.C. and
M.A.O'C. in the early twentieth century. It is for this reason that the

work of these two arrangers takes on such significance for harping today.

The style of Irish harping described as 'art-music' style is therefore linked to the musical practices of the early twentieth century. This style was based on purely instrumental music, which is also a feature of the concert harp repertory. Despite the subsequent strong decline in harping before 1950, the re-emergence of a harping tradition associated with song in the 1950s provided fertile ground for the later promotion of the art-music style in the 1960s. The result of these cycles of decline and revival in Irish harping in the twentieth century is that the recent history of this instrument has remained unclear and undocumented to date. The lack of information has left the modern heritage of the harp unknown to contemporary harp players. Having assessed the key era of the early decades of the twentieth century, I will turn now to harping activities in the pre-revival period, up to 1950, when the association of the harp and song traditions was cemented.

Irish harping, 1920s–50s

Tom Maher's account of the harp in Ireland provides some interesting descriptions of harping events in the middle of the twentieth century. The following statement does not ring entirely true however: 'Indeed, it was possible to grow up in the 1920's [sic] and 1930's [sic] and not ever hear the sound of a harp despite the popularity of *Moore's melodies* wherein the harp was sainted. It was also the time of the great John McCormack who managed to keep Irish balladry at the forefront alongside opera and vocal Victoriana.'[29] Maher claims that the only time Irish people would hear a harp was in the films of the Marx brothers or by listening to a woman who used to play the harp in Duke Street, Dublin.[30] To accept these statements at face value ignores the work that was being done by harpists participating in the annual Feis Ceoil competitions, the Oireachtas and also those who played harp at the Celtic Congresses. It is true to state that harping from the 1920s to the 1950s was extremely limited in terms of numbers of harpists, but it still existed. Were it not for the work of these harpists, in particular the Ní Shéaghdha (also Ní Shé) sisters – Róisín, Máirín and Neassa – and nuns in convent schools, the harp revival of the 1950s could not have taken place in the same format or manner as it eventually did.

The *Irish Times* newspaper reported detailed notices about the entrants and results of the Feis Ceoil competitions. In 1922, 'the single entrant did not appear' for the Irish harp competition.[31] However, a gradual increase in interest in the harp over that decade can be observed. In 1925 only one entrant was listed for the Townshend Cup: 'For songs with Irish harp accompaniment there was only one entry – Miss Margaret Donoghue – who was awarded a Silver Cup, presented by Miss Carrie Townshend.'[32] This is the same Caroline Townshend mentioned in Sheila Larchet Cuthbert's *Irish harp book*.

> A very gifted musician both on the Piano and on the Irish Harp. For many years she lived at Glandore, Co. Cork. She was interested in everything Irish, the language, culture, music and taught the Irish Harp to anyone interested, especially to the local girls near her home. She always wore dresses with Celtic designs and large Celtic brooches. Later, when she came to live in Dublin, she was delighted to find herself teaching quite advanced musicians – Sanchia Pielou, the O'Shea sisters and many others. The late Mr Denis McCollough made a number of Harps at her request – the Brian Boru model.[33]

By 1927 there were eight entrants for the Caroline Townshend Cup. In the same year Townshend made a further effort to promote the Irish harp by reading a paper on the Irish harp at the Celtic Congress in July. At the same Congress, harpist Margaret O'Donoghue sang Irish airs to her own harp accompaniment. Margaret O'Donoghue subsequently won first prize in the Caroline Townshend Cup at the Feis Ceoil in 1929.

A newspaper article pictured O'Donoghue at her harp with her trophy in 1929.[34] The harp played by O'Donoghoe is the type that became known as the 'small Irish harp', or a Brian Ború harp. There are approximately thirty strings on the harp and each string is fitted with a semi-tone mechanism, making this a semi-chromatic harp. A significant difference between O'Donoghue's harp and the low-headed Irish harps of the thirteenth and fourteenth centuries on which this harp is modelled is that the latter types did not have any form of semi-tonal mechanism attached and were strung using wire strings (as was the norm before the nineteenth century). The decoration of the harp is quite florid and detailed with carvings on both the soundboard and fore pillar. O'Donogue's costume is also of interest. She wears a type of cape over her dress that has Celtic designs embroidered into it.[35] We can surmise from these limited accounts that there was in fact harping activity in Ireland in the 1920s. At this point it remains unclear exactly what the total repertoire of these harpists was. However, we do know that they were using the harp as accompaniment to singing. This marks quite a departure from the music of the first two decades of the twentieth century when the published arrangements and studies by M.A.C. were exclusively instrumental pieces.

Groups or 'bands' of harpists playing together seem to have been a popular form of musical expression for the Irish harp in the early twentieth century. The concert for Moore's centenary featured a trio of Irish harpers and Florie Kerin led a band of Irish harp players at Loreto Abbey, Rathfarnham. There are several photographs displayed in the Pearse Museum in Dublin that show groups of harpers. That museum also holds a McFall harp. In 1930 a new competition was inaugurated into the Feis Ceoil for such an ensemble: 'There is also noteworthy development on the instrumental side. In the competitions in the National Group section a welcome event should be the competition this year inaugurated for a group of Irish harps, numbering not less than three performers on the small Irish harp of the Brian Ború model'.[36] This article from the *Irish Times*, while ostensibly intended to announce the competitions, simultaneously serves to clarify a point of difference between Irish harps at the time. The 'small Irish harp' is the type played by Margaret O'Donoghue (see plate 3). This was occasionally referred to as a *cruit*. The 'Irish harp' denotes a floor-standing neo-Irish harp such as the McFall Irish harp. A further article from the same year also mentions the introduction of this competition for harp ensemble.

> There are many new competitions, and one prize, in particular – that offered by the Ladies Committee for the encouragement of the harp is particularly attractive. It does seem extraordinary that the harp, once the great Irish musical instrument has been allowed to fade in our midst, and at a moment, too, when in other countries it having been in vogue. The prize at this year's Feis will be for groups of harps, and while the entries may not fulfil all anticipations, it is a beginning which, no doubt, the schools and particularly the convents and colleges will appreciate for next season.[37]

According to Bluebird, the author of this article, the harp was in need of encouragement. Clearly if this were not the case then the competition would not have been instigated. The author also points to the convent schools as the most likely groups to benefit from this new competition. This is a further indication of the importance of the convent schools to the propagation and promotion of harping in Ireland in the twentieth century.

In 1932 two key names in relation to the Irish harp are mentioned in the *Irish Times*, Máirín Ní Shéaghdha and Treasa Ní Chormaic. Máirín and her sisters Róisín and Neassa were immensely influential from the 1930s onwards. Their contribution to harping was of the utmost importance to the survival of the harp through the 1930s and 1940s. They competed, performed and taught the Irish harp. Indeed, Máirín, or Mrs Ferriter as she was also known, was the teacher at the harp school at Dominican College, Sion Hill, whose students included Mary O'Hara. Treasa Ní Chormaic was described by Mercedes Bolger as:

'the real descendent of the old Harpers'. Her first harp was found in a bog and she was taught to play by her father. Later he obtained an Erard on which she mostly played her larger repertoire of traditional music. 'I don't think she had any further training but she was intensely musical, with a wonderful ear and excellent taste'. Mrs Bolger continues, 'Everything she played was arranged by herself ... On one occasion she played at the St Patrick's Day Concert at the Queen's Hall in London and literally brought the house down with her rendering of Brian Boru's March'.[38]

Both Ní Chormaic and Máirín Ní Shéaghdha were prize-winners at the Oireachtas competition in 1932. Ní Chormaic played the Irish harp while Ní Shéaghdha played the small Irish harp or *cruit*.[39] In the same year Ní Shéaghdha played at a concert for the Cumann Gaodhlach.[40] The arrival of Mr Briggs, harp maker, to Dublin in 1934 was cause for celebration. An *Irish Times* article strongly criticized the lack of availability of Irish-made Irish harps: 'clarsach making has been hampered in the Free State within the last two or three generations by the fact that there is not in this country a man who can make a clarsach. The only person in Ireland who has made an Irish harp in recent years is a Belfastman.'[41] The author then writes about the arrival that week in Dublin of Mr Briggs, the well-known Scottish harp maker. Briggs brought three harps with him to sell which were modelled on the Brian Ború harp, with a range of 31 strings.

> New hopes have been aroused, however, by the arrival in Dublin
> this week of a clarsach-maker who has been largely responsible for
> the clarsach revival in Scotland. He is Mr H.B. Briggs of Glasgow
> ...Yesterday an *Irish Times* reporter heard the clear, sweet notes of
> a clarsach played by Miss T. MacCormac, of Dublin. The
> impression was delightful as her fingers touched the strings in old
> Irish folk melodies. The tone strength was wonderfully varied, the
> quality excellent, and the lingering notes had an appeal that was as
> individual as it was pleasant.[42]

These clarsachs were significantly larger than the lap harps that had also
been popular at the time. They rested on the floor and could not possibly
be placed on the lap. They looked quite similar to the bow-pillared harps
that are in popular use today.

Throughout the remainder of the 1930s, harping activities were kept
alive primarily by the work of the Ní Shéaghdha sisters. They won
several titles at the Feis Ceoil both in the Caroline Townshend Cup and
in the competition for small Irish harp. They featured at various concert
performances and were also broadcast on the national radio station
2RN (founded in 1926). These broadcasts were advertised in national
newspapers. The Ní Shéaghdha sisters also participated regularly in the
Celtic Congresses held both in Ireland and in other Celtic countries.
Journalist Kitty Clive offered high praise of the music played by this
musical family:

> The number of young people who were at the Celtic Congress this
> year was due to the initiative of Professor O'Farrelly. Among these
> the three sisters, Mairin, Neassa and Roisin O'Shea [*sic*], created
> quite a surprise at the concerts and social functions. They willingly
> sang and played their harps together and so impressed all present
> and delighted them with their fresh young voices that they were
> much in request. Miss O'Shea is a graduate of the University
> College Dublin, and comes from an Irish speaking family in
> Dundrum. The three sisters, with their harps, are well known in
> Irish circles in Dublin, but Lord Semphill would like them to be
> known better across the water.[43]

The sisters clearly made a strong impression on their audiences. They
were noted for their singing to harp accompaniment, a discernible
change from harping at the start of the century. From the 1920s, but

particularly from the 1930s onwards, a shift towards song accompaniment became the primary use for the Irish harp. Maher's assertion that 'The line of traditional harp players was never broken' has relevance here. In the 1940s, further harping activity could be observed, not only in Dublin, but in Wexford and Cork also:

> During and after the years of World War 2 the Irish harp was saved from near extinction by the work of a few. Amongst the few were nuns and lay teachers in several convents. The principal ones in the Dublin area were Loreto Abbey, Rathfarnham, Dominican College, Sion Hill and the Dominican College, Eccles Street. The Royal Irish Academy of Music played its part as it so strongly pursues objectives today. The Irish harp was taught in the Cork School of Music. It had yet to regain true popularity.[44]

An interesting attempt by Mercedes Bolger in Wexford to revive the harp took place in 1940. She was aware of the Scottish Clarsach Society which had successfully revived the playing of the harp in Scotland and she announced her plans to do the same in Ireland, using the Feis Carman in Gorey as the vehicle through which this revival would happen.[45] The envisaged harp revival did not take place at that particular time but it is telling that there was sufficient interest in the harp for the mention of a revival to be taken seriously.

Accounts from the 1940s show more diverse activity in harp competitions. It appears that more players were active, and certainly more names were mentioned in the newspapers than in the previous decade. For example, in the 1930s, apart from the Ní Shéaghdha sisters, Leila Sheridan and Mary Carroll, are the only two names that appear in print in relation to the harp. In 1940 both E. De Reggie and Niall Breathnach are listed as prize-winners for the Dr Annie Patterson competition in the Feis Ceoil.[46] This is the only reference to a male harpist at the time. Lois Davidson and Mercedes Bolger are named in 1943,[47] as are Eibhlin Ní Cearbhaill, Dr Becker and Nuala Ní Shéaghdha.[48] In 1944 Blaithín Ní Annrachain is named and,[49] in 1948, the winner of the small Irish harp competition in the Feis was Geraldine Fennell with Eilish McCarrill taking first prize in the Townshend Cup.[50] This list proves that there were more numerous harpists in the 1940s competing in competitions, thus suggesting that there was more interest in the harp in this decade than had been the case in the 1930s.

A unique, first-hand account of a harp concert that took place in

1942 is presented in detail by Maher. His description offers an unparalleled insight into the reception of harp music at the time:

> At one concert in Collins Barracks, Dublin in 1942 five young ladies walked on carrying harps. The occasion which prompted an invitation to them to come was the one hundred and fiftieth anniversary of the Belfast Harp Festival. Before a packed gymnasium of soldiery in high spirits their appearance was stunning. Dressed in long white costumes with Celtic ornamentation they bowed, then busied themselves checking the note with each other for a few moments. Silence suddenly took over from banter and good humoured insults down amongst the audience. This was a rare sight – girls with harps no less. Every tune was greeted with rapturous applause and a few yells. Listening was concentrated. What made the occasion special was that not a soldier in the audience had ever seen an Irish harp, or indeed, heard one play. Yet twice a day they polished and cleaned between the strings of harps on the uniform buttons. The girls were the sisters Niamh, Roisin, Nessa and Mairin Ni Sheadha and the other Florence Fitzsimons. In years to come those sisters were to have a profound effect on the world of the Irish harp as players, teachers and workers in the cause.[51]

Although there clearly was harp playing in the 1940s it was not heard in many public fora, save for competitions and radio programmes. It would be a mistake to assume that participation of harp players in the Feis Ceoil meant widespread public dissemination. It was only after the harp revival in the early 1950s that the harp began to be heard regularly through the medium of radio and recordings. The harpists before the 1950s were not household names in the way that O'Hara and her contemporaries were.

It is inarguably evident that the Irish harp continued to survive throughout the first half of the twentieth century in Ireland. The music and song played by these harpists was a specifically Irish realization of both a musical and symbolic heritage, as demonstrated by their choice of repertoire, performance context and costume. This era from 1900 to 1950 can effectively be split into two phases, in which firstly the art-music style prospered and secondly, when musical style was orientated more towards song. The legacy of this period is of intrinsic importance to harping today: the publications, method and approach of M.A.C. re-emerged through Sheila Larchet Cuthbert in the second phase of the harp revival and served to form the basic methodological grounding for what is now known as the art-music style. The use of the harp for accompaniment to song became the only use for the harp in the initial harp revival, through which harp playing gained an unpredicted worldwide popularity. It is from the early twentieth century, however, that the teachers of the revival period came. Their preference for using the harp as accompaniment to voice had a direct effect on the style popularized in the harping revival of the 1950s. Therefore, the importance of these first fifty years is both in the realization of the contemporary history of the harp, and because this period holds the stylistic origins of the art music and revival styles.

CHAPTER 3

Revival

The 1950s in Ireland can be viewed as a starting point from which multiple changes in economic, social and cultural practices began to take place.[1] The economy in the early years of the decade was in difficulty, emigration was high and the rural landscape altered rapidly with large-scale migration to urban centres.[2] Cultural developments did however take place. Comhaltas Ceoltóirí Éireann and the Arts Council (both founded in 1951), and Gael Linn (founded in 1953), sought to promote Irish language and culture. Terence Brown comments on the positive interest in cultural development at this time: 'For the Gaelic revivalist, the 1950s also brought novelty of an encouraging kind ... By 1953 an American commentator could count "a minimum of sixteen major national organizations founded since 1940 for the promotion of particular aspects of the revival".'[3] In 1952, Fleischmann published his seminal book *Music in Ireland*.[4] It describes a musical life lacking in resources and organization. Both John F. Larchet and Donnchadh Ua Braoin, for example, point to the under-resourced state of music education. However, Larchet ends his article, 'Music in the secondary schools', on a positive note:

> At present it is obvious that a marked awakening of interest in good music, national as well as international, is taking place. Apart from the main contributory causes, such as broadcasting and the gramophone, this awakening may be traced at least in part to improved teaching in our secondary schools.[5]

Frederick May severely criticizes the lack of opportunities for Irish composers in Ireland at this time. In this scathing statement he also attacks contemporary music criticism:

> it is doubtful if any nation with such a wonderful storehouse of traditional music has made such a negligible contribution to art

music as we have … Maudlin sentiment and barren theorizing must be eschewed; musical criticism must be creative and not destructive, and one of the most destructive and useless types of criticism is that which starts out from an unwarrantable premise, such as that all good music must be demonstrably national in feeling.[6]

The employment opportunities for solo musicians were also very limited. Charles Lynch, in his opening paragraph describing the life of a concert pianist in Ireland, pointed out that it was rare that a pianist could expect to earn his/her entire living from performing.[7] Terry O'Connor further describes the dire state of affairs for solo performers: 'Apart from teaching, membership of our one professional orchestra – the Radio Éireann Orchestra – membership of the few café ensembles which still function, and, of course, of dance bands, there are no openings in Ireland for a string player comparable to those in England'.[8] This was the era when the revival of traditional music began. The results of this revival are evident in the thriving traditional music culture and industry today, both in Ireland and internationally.

Ideologies of nationalism and national identity were not as strong in the 1950s as in previous decades. However, the legacy of attempts to build an 'Irish Ireland' by the Free State and, subsequently, by the new Republic, left a residual tendency towards the expression of nationalism. National games were supported (through the Tailteann Games, for example), as was the Irish language, through compulsory Irish lessons in national schools.[9] Irish language-songs were taught in schools and it was still fashionable to sing songs with romanticized national sentiment (such as the repertoire popularized by harpists, for example). Terence Brown argues that: 'Ideologically the fires of economic nationalism and the quest for cultural self-sufficiency were waning, but as yet they had not been replaced by a coherent set of new values'.[10] However, state support for An Tostal festival demonstrates that a significant desire to promote Irish nationalism remained. Despite the revolutionary ideals and actions that resulted in the foundation of the Free State in 1922, a strongly conservative Ireland emerged in the first half of the twentieth century. Marie McCarthy asserts that: 'efforts to broaden the definition of Irish music and to move away from the polarization of native and colonial music cultures were marginalized as a narrow view of "Irish" music was enshrined in the cultural policy of the new nation state'.[11]

Musical expressions of nationalism were also linked to class distinctions, as formal music education was still conducted through second- and third-level education, both of which were private. Brown admits that artistic expression was often restricted by class based necessity:

> It would be wrong, it must be stressed, to make too much of these signs of a changing intellectual and cultural climate. For most people in Ireland in the postwar period, the amateur dramatic movement, which burgeoned in the 1950s in festivals and competitions, was their only point of contact with artistic activity of any kind. For many, literature, art, intellectual endeavour, or architectural innovation would have seemed luxurious irrelevancies set against the daily struggle for survival in years of economic despair.[12]

Furthermore, McCarthy explains that 'Music in second- and third-level institutions maintained the *status-quo* of teaching art music'.[13] At a time when traditional music was associated with rural areas, art music with urban centres and private secondary education, the teaching of art music reinforced notions of elitism associated with this type of music. Although the harpers of the 1950s revival sang and played Irish songs, their background as convent-educated ladies contributed to an association with an urban, middle-class identity.

The harp in the first half of the twentieth century was mostly the preserve of convent schools. Dominican College, Sion Hill became an important centre of harping from the 1950s onwards. Three of the best-known harpists from that era attended harp lessons while at Sion Hill, before embarking on careers as professional harpists. Mary O'Hara, Caitlín Watkins and Deirdre Ní Fhloinn commenced harp studies at the same time. The motivation for their choice of instrument was, however, extra-musical. Mary O'Hara commented on the series of events that led these three young harpists to the instrument:

> An annual pageant was performed by the school girls ... of ... Sion Hill ... During my last year at school the new pageant was about the life of Thomas Moore ... His verses are full of references to the harp as a symbol of Ireland. It was decided to bring in Máirín Ní Shéa to teach the harp for the occasion. Since I was known to have a good voice and had also been learning the piano

for eight years I was one of the three chosen to take lessons on the small knee harp. The other two were Déirdre Flynn (later Kelleher) and Kathleen Watkins ... Our new teacher worked hard with us and taught us enough so that we could accompany ourselves during the pageant. As things turned out she stayed on and we continued with lessons.[14]

She was chosen to learn the harp primarily because she could sing. Furthermore, O'Hara identifies the ability to 'accompany themselves' as an indicator of sufficient skill level. These two points actually characterize Irish harping of the 1950s and 1960s: first, harpists were viewed primarily as singers, indeed O'Hara described herself as 'first and foremost a singer'.[15] Second, the harp was mostly used to accompany singing and not for the performance of solo instrumental music. Despite the ensuing commercial success of these three harpists, the neo-Irish harp remained outside the mainstream of Irish traditional instrumental music. This exclusion was due to issues of commodification of the Irish harp; the use of neo-Irish harp style and technique instead of that of the traditional *cruit*; new performance contexts; and the use of harp exclusively as accompaniment to singing.

The particular sociocultural circumstances at any given moment impact the use-value of a commodity. The prevailing social circumstances and market requirements in Ireland in the 1950s had a particular use for the harpists of that time. In 1953 the Irish tourist board organized a festival to celebrate and promote Irishness, taking the image of the harp as their emblem. The following *Irish Independent* article from that year advises readers on how to embroider the *An Tostal* harp design:

> In Easter Week and the two following weeks of April when Ireland will be 'at home' to her friends from far and near, many readers will no doubt wish to show their fine needlework ... in making gifts and souvenirs for their friends as a reminder of 'An Tostal' when they are far away. One of the most suitable decorations is the National harp, the festival emblem.[16]

The author, Frances Burroughs, attaches particular importance to the symbol of the harp as a souvenir, making no reference to its identity as a musical instrument. Her attitude to the harp is perhaps indicative of the common perception of the harp in the early 1950s. It was primarily regarded as a potent symbol of Irish identity and less importantly as a musical instrument. The Irish Tourist Board flew the harpists O'Hara, Watkins and Ní Fhloinn to London to participate in the *An Tostal* festival there, with the aim of promoting Irish tourism. The harpists were given floor-length green and gold dresses for the performance.[17] *An Tostal's* selection of the costumes that the harpists wore is evidence that the latter group did not have complete artistic control over their performance. They subscribed to an enforced image conceived by the Tourist Board; an image that bolstered the Tourist Board's marketing campaign in London. The harp, therefore, in addition to the costumes and singing, in this context was used partly as a symbol of Ireland and Irishness and was consequently commodified by the Tourist Board. Thus began the popular association of the harp with singing 'colleens' in long dresses. The employment of singers and harpists transformed the use of the harp from symbolic to commodification. The harp's use-value was important as a representation of a very idealistic portrayal of Irishness. As I will discuss later, this association was unwelcome in the mainstream Irish instrumental tradition. The Irish Tourist Board was not, however, the only agency to commodify the image of the Irish harp. Guinness had, by the 1950s, a long association with the image of the harp; in 1862 Guinness first incorporated the harp into their brand and registered the harp as a trademark in 1867.[18] The harp used by Guinness was a version of the 'Brian Ború'/Trinity College harp. This model of harp has also been adopted by the government of Ireland as the national emblem.[19] When used by Guinness, this harp faces right as opposed to the left orientation of the government symbol. Harpists such as O'Hara and her contemporaries did not play this type of harp in the 1950s but a small lap harp. Essentially, these harps were like smaller versions of the neo-Irish harp. They were usually strung with gut strings, not metal, as the so-called Brian Ború harp would have been. Notwithstanding the differences in harp types, both were commodified and reproduced as a symbol of Ireland in the 1950s and 1960s.

Plate 5 shows a poster advertisement, launched by Guinness in 1958. The title is 'Girl Power' and the image was created by Victoria Davidson for the UK market.[20] Here the harp is still a version of the early-Irish harp but is now placed in context by the inclusion of the harpist. Both her hands are used to pluck the strings, one on either side of the harp. The caption 'Encore' suggests a concert setting for this performance (while also calling for another Guinness!). The stereotypical image of the young lady, complete with an elegant dress playing the harp, is utilized in this picture. Barra Boydell, in writing about the harp as a symbol, noted that the popularity of the harp in English noble circles in the seventeenth century resulted in more accurate depictions of the harp on coinage.[21] The image of a harpist playing a lap harp was, by 1958, becoming a common contemporary image (via publicity shots and album covers of Irish harpists) and, in light of this, we can observe more subtle details in this poster. At closer inspection, the curvaceous harpist here is not the demure convent-educated ambassador for Irishness. Her posture is quite provocative: closed eyes and one leg raised in a Cinderella-like pose on the footstool. The swing in her hair and dress suggest movement, which in turn implies a living tradition. The footstool has regal implications for this image, as does the overall dress of the harpist, thus reflecting the contemporary association of the harp with formal and prestigious performance settings. The use of colour in this picture is significant, combining regal red with gold and the Guinness-brown bottle. The bottle top, harpist's hair and the legs of the footstool, all gold in colour, give symmetry to the poster and suggest opulence. The harpist's red dress which is 1950s in style complements the red, possibly velvet, covering of the footstool. The traditional 'Irish' green only appears as the colour of the harpist's shoes. This image serves to poke fun at the traditional image of the harpist as an Irish colleen. The harpist is frivolous as opposed to reserved; daring as opposed to quietly demure.

By comparison, the cover image of Mary O'Hara's 1973 album, *Mary O'Hara's Ireland*, bears striking similarities to the 1958 Guinness poster at first glance.[22] The image of O'Hara is representative of the common image portrayed by harpists of the time. O'Hara's posture is straight and aristocratic, with her right hand placed on the strings and her left resting carefully, in a ladylike manner on her leg. However, the provocative daring of the Guinness harpist cannot be detected in this restrained and respectable image. The 'Irish' green is strongly visible as the background colour on the original album cover. The proportion of the picture taken up by O'Hara's harp is quite large and therefore re-asserts the 'Irishness' of the image. O'Hara projects the embodiment of the convent-educated young Irish woman.

Plate 6 shows a cartooon that was used as a press ad for the UK market in 1970. The man is holding a harp, some shamrock and a blackthorn stick. He also has shamrock in his hat. The young girl, complete with a bow in her hair, asks him 'How do I know you're Irish?' In order to prove that he is Irish the caption reads 'Give him a Guinness!' Perhaps in this instance the girl did not recognize the legendary symbols of Irishness, but was satisfied by the invocation of Guinness. The man in this cartoon is far less refined than the harpist of the first image. His hair is unkempt and he appears clumsy beside the delicacy of the young girl. The harpist's confidence is not reflected here, as the man is forced to prove his nationality. This advertisement was most likely aimed at Irish expatriates living in the UK as the symbolism could have been easily interpreted by a viewer with knowledge of Irish stereotypes and, in turn, this interpretation leads to humour. This picture owes much to the type of cartoon and caricature that was common in English magazines, such as *Punch*, *Judy* and *Fun*, in the nineteenth century, in which the Irish 'Pat' or 'Paddy' was portrayed with physical similarities to an ape, as Perry Curtis describes: 'this truly "dangerous" creature looked like a cross between monstrous ape and primitive man owing to his high and hairy upper lip or muzzle, concave nose, low facial angle and sharp teeth.'[23] Guinness is conveyed as the ultimate credential of Irishness, even more so than the harp, blackthorn stick or shamrock. Nevertheless, the importance of this picture is that it shows the strength of the harp as a symbol and stereotype of Irishness.

The use of the harp as a symbol of Ireland in itself is not problematic. However, the association of the harp with shamrocks and colleens presents a problem if the harp is to be accepted as part of the mainstream instrumental tradition. This type of association denigrates the integrity of the musical instrument and overly emphasizes its 'Irishness'. Mary O'Hara described one such instance of 'stage Irishness' that occurred while performing on the *Ed Sullivan Show* in New York on St Patrick's Day in 1957:

> To my horror I saw them carrying on two giant cut-out shamrocks and placing them at the back of the stage. I was dumbfounded when I was asked to sit with my harp in one of them ... There's nothing wrong with the shamrock as such, but when it is perennially associated with leprechauns, shillelaghs, green beer and Delaney's donkey's, I feel it is prostituting the true image of our beautiful country and of its ancient culture. It smacks of stage-Irishism.[24]

O' Hara's recognition in this instance of 'stage Irishness' is almost ironic as she is often cited as its main propagator. Although musically speaking, her harping (and that of her contemporaries) is quite stylistically similar to harping today, the notion of 'stage-Irishness' and commercialism still lingers in relation to these harpists. In a radio interview, Laoise Kelly commented on the images that the harp often evokes in the public mindset: 'I grew up always hearing ... "Give us a tune, Mary", if I was getting into the Dublin taxi or "O'Hara, give us a song" or something like that'.[25] This anecdotal recollection evidences the strength of association between the harp and singing in popular culture and of Mary O'Hara's widespread popularity as a singer and harpist. The commodification of the Irish harp was widespread during these decades (Bord Fáilte initiated the use of the harp as a symbol of tourism). While Guinness had long associations with the national emblem, it was not until the 1950s that they began to depict the harp as an actual 'musical' instrument. Up to this point, its usage was purely abstract and symbolic in form. However, with the 1958 advertisement, the harp was depicted as a functional musical instrument. The change from harp as symbol to harp as instrument is important as these uses of the harp immediately show the harp as a living instrument. The commodification of the harp as musical instrument therefore promoted the harp and this new brand of 'stage Irishness' on an international level. An interesting point to note is that the commodification of the harp in this way was facilitated by the musical-visual tastes of audiences and the suitability of the harpist as a symbol to express the social qualities of 'Irishness' at the time. The national emblem, for example, presented the harp abstractly without a harpist. This poses no problems for musicians as firstly, no music is being suggested and secondly, the emblem uses the early-Irish and not the neo-Irish harp. Timothy D. Taylor acknowledges the impact of social factors on the commodification of music:

> it is not productive to speak simply of music as a commodity in general; one can only speak of particular ways and circumstances in which music becomes a commodity, and specific historical nodes in the complex history of the commodification of music in a particular culture ... it is essential to view the commodity not simply as a social form that can be understood in and of itself, but a social form that must be understood historically and dialectically.[26]

The Irish harp was commodified with such success in this era due to the particular historical circumstances I have outlined thus far. The successful commodification of the harp image served also to alienate the harp from the mainstream of tradition, as popular opinion viewed the harp as inauthentic and a vehicle for stage Irishness.[27] The 'Irish harp' of the 1950s and 1960s was a slightly smaller version of today's neo-Irish harp, although similar in structure.[28] The average number of strings was 30 to 34. Due to their small size, these harps were often placed on a small stool to raise the height of the instrument; alternatively, the player might sit on a low stool.

Harpists customarily sat with both legs to the left side of the harp, rather resting the harp in between the knees, as is the norm today for both concert and Irish harp. This may have strengthened the strong feminine association with the harp. Sitting to the side of the harp slightly restricts the movement of the right hand, one cannot stretch it as far in this position as when sitting with the harp in between two legs. The harp is more balanced when placed in the latter position and therefore rests less on the performer. Ideally, the harpist should not bear the weight of the instrument on his/her shoulder as this can cause posture difficulties. The harp should be balanced, rather, on its own centre of gravity, allowing the player maximum flexibility when playing.

In the context of the Irish harp in mid-twentieth-century Ireland, the feminine association with the harp was strong and has its roots in the nineteenth century. After the decline of the itinerant harpers and, later, the harp schools, the harp became a drawing-room instrument. Music by the likes of Thomas Moore popularized the harp in the drawing-room setting through publications aimed at music making in the home. In the nineteenth and twentieth centuries in Ireland the Irish harp was taught in convent schools, often by nuns, thus, the common forum for harp teaching was in an all-female environment to female students. In light of this it is unsurprising that this gender association was propagated. Moreover, the particular flavour of gender association with the Irish harp was quite conservative. The type of Irish harpist that emerged in the 1950s was promoted as a young 'colleen' in a long, feminine and conservative dress as an ideal symbol of Irishness. An interesting parallel exists with the rise of women's gamelan *beleganjur* in Bali. Michael B. Bakan comments that

> cultural symbols such as women's *beleganjur* ostensibly designed to project images and reflect values of women's empowerment in modern Indonesia, are in actuality used to reinforce stereotypes, or

sociocultural myths that reinforce the stability and durability of male-dominated structures of power whose legitimacy depends on widespread public assumptions of women's marginality.[29]

The cultural symbol that was the Irish harpist in these decades did not challenge the established status quo of gender issues in Ireland or in the Irish diaspora, as these harpists projected a specifically feminine harp technique. The issue of class divide and an urban/rural dichotomy was also present. The harp was associated with middle-class convent secondary schools in a time when all secondary education was private. Traditional music was not normally associated with the urban middle class in the 1950s (until after the folk music revival in the US, UK and Ireland). These tensions further contributed to the musical isolation of the harp from traditional music during this era.

Despite the physical posture adopted by these harpists, they continued to use the standard concert-harp hand technique for playing. Irish harpists have long employed an identical technique to concert harp players; the thumbs point upwards, the fingers point down and each finger returns to the palm of the hand after sounding a note. Today, this is not the only technique used as players of the 'traditional' style use a looser technique. 'Art-music style' can be used to describe the former technique and 'traditional-music style' to describe the latter.[30] Today, both concert harp and Irish harp players rest the harp at the top of the right shoulder; harpists playing these smaller harps generally rested the harp far lower on their shoulder. The string tension was generally lower than on more modern harps and consequently the tone quality was not as full as modern harps. Maintenance of tuning was occasionally an issue with some low-tensioned harps.

The early-Irish harp in its original format (*cruit*) was smaller than the neo-Irish harp and rested on the ground or on the feet of the harper. The technique used for playing the *cruit* was quite different, given that harpers used their fingernails to pluck the strings up until the end of the eighteenth century.[31] The harp rested on the harper's left shoulder instead of the right. However, with the development of the concert harp in Europe and the neo-Irish harp in Ireland, harpists began to lean the harp on their right shoulder. As harps began to expand in size, they required placement on the floor instead of on the knee. For example, the thirty-five string large low-headed Otway harp, dating to the seventeenth century, was far too large and robust for placing on the knee, as was also the case with the

Dalway harp, which dates back to 1621.[32] Indeed the 'quintessential' Irish harp, the Trinity College or Brian Ború harp, dates back to the thirteenth century. This harp was vastly smaller in comparison to the size of harps that harpers such as Turlough O'Carolan used in the seventeenth and eighteenth century. Some critics of the neo-Irish harp in the 1950s and 1960s viewed the technique of the early-Irish harp as somehow more authentic than that of the neo-Irish harp. Seán Ó Riada, for example, negated the possibility of including the neo-Irish harp in the 'ideal' band as it did not represent the traditional method of playing. Furthermore, he wrote: 'To revive the true harping tradition was impossible: instead, a style of harping was developed which was based mainly on Welsh harping, quite different from the Irish style. The only thing traditional about present-day harping is the instrument itself.'[33]

The visible growth and development of the Irish harp throughout the past seven centuries along with the gradual change in technique from left to right shoulder and from fingernails to fingertips shows that the tradition has continued to develop and change. The 'traditional' music canon of the twentieth century largely dates from the seventeenth century onwards.[34] At what point, therefore, can the 'authentic' Irish harp be named? What are the criteria that rule out the neo-Irish harp as authentic? Colin Graham argues that authenticity in the Irish case is a 'layered' authenticity: 'its repeated forms of self-sustenance and validation give it a layered authenticity'.[35] This concept that a text or artefact (such as the Irish harp) is rendered authentic by recurring validation and self-referencing may shed some light on the rejection of the neo-Irish harp in the twentieth century. The 'historical' harp tradition (which had drasti-cally declined by the end of the eighteenth century) was 'authentic' because it was a self-replicating and self-referencing tradition. The harpers' oral repertoire encompassed newly composed tunes as well as older harp music. The music evolved constantly, to the extent that by 1792, Arthur O'Neill criticized Turlough O'Carolan's music as being too modern.[36] The neo-Irish harp tradition, on the other hand, was merely in its primary stage of development in the 1950s. As it was not yet estab-lished, it may therefore have been viewed as an inauthentic and tokenistic enterprise.

Seán Ó Riada expressed his dissatisfaction with this new style of harping: 'it is a pity we do not try to reconstruct a style closer to the traditional style, instead of propagating an invented style which has nothing to do with the tradition'.[37] Furthermore, Breandán Breathnach also criticized the harp as being 'non-traditional' and directed his attack at the newly founded Comhaltas Ceoltóirí Éireann: 'A lack of discernment in distinguishing the genuine from the spurious is evident in the activities directed towards the public; the running of competitions for harp ... for instance, can hardly be squared with its professed aims of promoting traditional music.'[38] However, if the harp tradition gamut is accepted as one continuous tradition, incorporating new elements and experiencing episodes of both growth and decline, then the neo-Irish harpists of the 1950s contribute to that overall long, authentic tradition. While the individual harpers of this era may have propagated a somewhat stylized version of traditional music, they added to both the canon of harp music and the Irish harp tradition. Their musical isolation from mainstream traditional music lasted only until the 1980s, by which time the neo-Irish harp had been played in a stylistically coherent manner for thirty years and thus was considered, 'authentic'. Ó Riada's assertion that harping at that time 'had nothing to do with the tradition' does not ring true when the music of this era is examined.

The Irish harp found new popularity during the 1950s and 1960s and consequently emerged in new performance contexts. After *An Tostal*'s use of the harp, many more performance opportunities emerged for harpists. Radio and television became important fora for harp performance as did concerts. The relatively cheap availability of records helped to disseminate harp music to a wider audience than previously possible and air travel facilitated long-distance travel for tours. In Ireland, Radio Éireann provided a popular forum for artists to perform. Mary O'Hara first performed on radio in 1953 as part of Radio Éireann's 'Children at the Mike' program. She performed on a regular basis for both Radio Éireann and for Gael Linn.[39] O'Hara achieved particular success through the medium of television; she performed on both the 'Garry Moore Show' and the 'Ed Sullivan Show' in the United States. However, her television performances often reinforced the 'stage Irishness' image, as the earlier citation regarding the 'Ed Sullivan Show' demonstrated. O'Hara, Ní Fhloinn and Watkins all recorded solo records which proved to be very popular. Their radio and television appearances reinforced the popular appeal of their version of traditional music. The popularity of their music can be judged by the number of recordings produced by these harpists. By 1960, Caitlín Watkins and Deirdre Ní Fhloinn had recorded two albums each and Mary O'Hara had released three.

In addition to recorded music, the harp was often played in concert settings, not only by these three harpists but by many of their contemporaries also. Sr Carmel Warde of Dominican College, Sion Hill described the demand for harpists at that time:

> Looking back over the 1950s and 1960s I recall very happy busy days preparing for Jury's Cabaret, Ballsbridge, Dublin 4. A troupe of Sion Hill Harpists, maybe twenty girls in all would entertain the guests for two hours. Christmastime was another highlight for our Harp School … Before the Summer holidays we awaited invitations from Bunratty Castle, Co. Limerick, Killarney Hotels and the Hilton Hotel, London for our harpist to entertain guests for a week or two. The invitations always came.[40]

This description highlights the demand for harpists during these decades. Harpists played in a concert setting, spatially distanced from the audience by the stage, costumes and set lists. The Gael Linn Cabaret was typical of the type of performances that took place. The now female-dominated tradition (due to its association with convent schools) in this context was vastly different to the tradition at the end of the eighteenth century. However, the sociocultural conditions of eighteenth-century patronage and composition had also changed. The patrons in the 1950s and 1960s were the concert goers and music purchasers. The harpists of that era, responded therefore to the changing social conditions. Indeed, traditional musicians in general moved towards the concert hall. Ó Riada's renowned recording with Ceoltóirí Chualann, *Ó Riada sa Gaeity*, is a further example of this.[41] At this concert in 1969 all of the performers wore black-tie, thus importing the customs of art music into a traditional music context. Nevertheless, traditional music in general was at that time (and still is) available in other performance settings. The céilí and informal session (in private homes or elsewhere) provided an intimate musician/audience setting. Harpists did not, however, participate in the communal or group performance of Irish music. Harping was very much a solo tradition of singing to harp accompaniment. There are two exceptions to this: the aforementioned harp groups, such as the Sion Hill Harpists, and the 'variety show' or cabaret.

Despite the clear evidence of ensemble harp playing, the Irish harp still maintained a difficult position. Just as it was not integrated into mainstream traditional music, neither was it integrated into the Western art music tradition as this role had long been fulfilled by the concert harp. The limitations in terms of chromaticism, range and volume render the concert harp the obvious choice in a Western art music setting. Mary O'Hara describes her experiences of both accompaniment and art music in her autobiography:

> I don't envy people who have to accompany others. The first and last time that I got involved in that sort of team work I made a right haims of it. Sometime in 1955 John Reidy (Seán Ó Riada) asked me if I would accompany the Radio Éireann Singers who were singing a piece of his on a programme in which I was also singing a solo. In John's contemporary composition I was required to count seventeen-and-a-half bars of silence before coming in with a vigorous discord ... when the live performance was in progress I slipped up somewhere in my figures and from that first inaccurate entry to the bitter end I didn't know whether I was coming or going. Exacerbation and resignation vied for supremacy on John's poor distraught face as he conducted his esoteric work to the end. In my philistine way I wondered if my mistakes sounded that much different from what the composer originally intended.[42]

The performance contexts of the neo-Irish harp slightly inhibited the possibility of participation in the mixed-instrument ensemble of Irish traditional music. The harpists' high concentration of concert perform-ances further strengthened the divide between mainstream traditional music and the harping tradition in the 1950s and 1960s.

The use of the harp as accompaniment to singing has been a function of the Irish harp throughout its history. Colette Moloney argues that the harpers at the Belfast Harp Festival used the harp for accompaniment to song and for instrumental pieces:

> The fact that the organizers had planned to have an Irish scholar present to transcribe song texts adds weight to the argument that some harpers also sang or recited. It would seem likely, from Bunting's notations, that when the harpers sang a melody they also played an accompanied version of the tune on the harp.[43]

The most notable feature concerning the harp during the 1950s was its almost exclusive use for accompaniment to singing. Due to the immutable association of harp and voice during these decades, the music of the harp was rarely heard in isolation. Any conclusions that people drew regarding the harp were coloured by the accompanying song style. I propose that it was directly because of this linkage that the harp music of these decades has been disregarded.

This transcription is of Deirdre Ní Fhloinn's version of the traditional song 'Do Cuirfinn-se Féin Mo Leanbh a Chodladh' as recorded on her 1958 album, *Irish traditional songs*.[44] It is possible that Ní Fhloinn learned this version from her harp teacher at Sion Hill, Máirín Ferriter (née Ní Shéaghdha),[45] as Ní Shéaghdha's grand-nephew Cormac De Barra, who also studied with Mrs Ferriter, sings a very similar version on his album, *Barcó*. De Barra acknowledges the influences that both his grandmother Róisín and his grand-aunt Máirín had on his singing.[46] On the sleeve notes to De Barra's recording he cites Máire (Máirín) as his source for this song.[47]

The issue of making value-judgments regarding the quality of a singer's style is complex and difficult. A coherent definition of 'traditional' style in singing is highly problematic. The range and breadth of styles and techniques evident in traditional singing preclude the possibility of a standard definition. Furthermore, the bilingual aspect of traditional singing further negates an all-encompassing general definition. Some commentators have offered broad terms by which singing may possibly be judged, while recognizing the impossibility of pinpointing an exact definition. The late Frank Harte (1933–2005) also recognized the difficulty in addressing style in traditional singing: 'I mentioned there the word "style" … now that's the word that makes all the difference, that's the word that's hard to explain. It's hard to find the dots on the paper to explain exactly what you mean by a singer's "style"'.[48] More specifically, John Moulden cites ornamentation as an important marker of traditional style. He also mentions tempo, stops and vocal quality as important stylistic elements.[49] Julie Henigan describes performance technique as consisting of 'tone quality, vocal registration, ornamentation, rhythmic variation and phrasing'.[50] The song by Deirdre Ní Fhloinn is notated here in standard staff notation. There are many inherent difficulties with this notation.[51] The melody as transcribed can only be an inaccurate version of her song as the considerable freedom she affords the melody is impossible to notate. Ní Fhloinn's personal singing style is similar to that of many of her contemporaries. While she does employ a very free rhythm she does not use the

Musical Example 7: 'Do Chuirfinn-se Féin', Deirdre Ní Fhloinn
(transcription by Helen Lawlor)

essential traditional processes of ornamentation and variation in her singing. Her vocal quality is clear and makes some use of vibrato and glissando. Ní Fhloinn's singing could not be considered *sean-nós* due to the lack of variation and ornamentation in her singing, despite the fact that the song is in Irish; the language of a song does not dictate its style. Ní Fhloinn's style could be described as falling under the umbrella title of 'traditional'. Her harping is stylistically similar to that of her 'traditional' forbearers, her contemporaries and 'traditional' style harping today. Therefore, it was the impenetrable association of harp as accompaniment to song that thwarted recognition of the positive developments in harping during these decades.

Musical example 8 is my transcription of 'Is Ar Éireann Ní nEosphainn Cé hÍ' played by Mary O'Hara on her album *Irish Traditional Folk Songs*.[52] O'Hara plays one full verse and chorus of the song on the harp before the voice enters. This is one of the few songs in the recorded repertoire with such an extended harp introduction.

In between phrases one and two, the harp interjects with a short neighbour note motif in the treble before the song phrase continues (bar

Musical Example 8: 'Is Ar Éireann Ní nEosphainn Cé hÍ',
Mary O'Hara (transcription by Helen Lawlor)

2). O'Hara uses this motif repeatedly throughout the song. She adds harmony notes to the melody as an alternative method of variation. In the left-hand accompaniment she employs octaves (blocked and broken), arpeggios, triads and inversions. The harmony is diatonic, except for one instance in bar 12 whereby she harmonizes the melody with an applied vii6/3 moving to V7. This gives a falling chromatic line in the accompaniment of C - D natural - Db. Interestingly, O'Hara uses ornamentation in the melody line, in the form of the roll in bar 12 leading up to the note B, in addition to the aforementioned neighbour note motif. O'Hara's use of chords in the treble is a further example of ornamentation. In the second and third rounds of this tune O'Hara varies both the right- and left-hand lines. Thus, in this excerpt the harpist displays two of the most crucial features of traditional music: variation and ornamentation. The absence of singing in the introduction allows the listener to assess the solo harp style without the dominating presence of the voice. O' Hara's harping in this instance is stylistically similar to 'traditional' style harping today. This style, established from the 1980s onwards, is now fully integrated into mainstream traditional instrumental music and accepted by traditional musicians as representative of 'traditional' harping.

In the interest of comparison I will now briefly discuss 'Scott's Lamentation' from the Bunting collection.[53] This is one of only ten tunes from the Bunting manuscripts and the three printed volumes that has a notated bass.[54] This version was transcribed by Bunting from the playing of Denis Hempson. Bunting cites the composition date for 'Scott's Lamentation' as 1599. Notwithstanding the well-documented criticisms of Bunting's work,[55] we can extract some useful information from this score. Hempson was the only harpist at the Belfast Harp Festival of 1792 who still played with his fingernails.[56] Bunting's comments inform the reader that Hempson played in a style that could be considered 'old' or traditional in 1792:

> Denis A Hampsy or Hempson, with whom the Editor of this collection was many years ago struck as a model of the old Irish school, was born shortly after Carolan, in the year 1695 ... The pieces which he delighted to perform were unmixed with modern refinements, which he seemed studiously to avoid; confining himself chiefly to the most antiquated of those strains which have long survived the memory of their composers, and even a knowledge of the ages that produced them.[57]

Furthermore, Hempson used ornamentation in his playing, as Bunting discusses:

> The intricacy and peculiarity of his playing often amazed the Editor, who could not avoid perceiving it in vestiges of a noble system of practice, that had existed for many centuries ... In fact, Hempson's Staccato and Legato passages, double slurs, shakes, turns, graces &c. &c., comprised as great a range of execution as has ever been devised by the most modern improvers.[58]

In the 1840 volume Bunting included a detailed description of the types of ornamentation used by the harpers.[59] These ornaments can be summarized as follows: selections of single grace notes, running scalic figures, trills or shakes, left- and right-hand chords.[60] The types of bass devices used by Hempson (single notes, octaves, thirds, fourths and arpeggiation) are also used by O'Hara. While such a brief comparison does not necessarily render O'Hara's version 'traditional', it serves to demonstrate that her approach is stylistically similar to the notated version of Hempson's.

Musical example 9 is my transcription from Gráinne Hambly's recording of 'Eleanor Plunkett'.[61] Hambly, O'Hara and Hempson all use the same types of accompanimental devices, such as rolled chords, treble chords and arpeggiation. Given that the harp was used primarily as an accompanimental instrument in the 1950s and 1960s it is justifiable to use this aspect as a means of comparison. While Hambly may not have

Musical Example 9: 'Eleanor Plunkett', Gráinne Hambly

consciously attempted to recreate a similar accompanimental style to O'Hara's or Hempson's, the common usage of similar devices by modern harpists serves to consolidate a style that is now considered 'traditional'. At the risk of forcing a retrospective 'dialogue' between the likes of Hambly and previous generations of harpists it remains interesting to note that many similarities do exist.

Musical example 10 is a partial transcription (by the author) of 'Binn Luisín Aerach a'Bhrogha' as sung by Seán Ó Sé and accompanied by Seán Ó Riada and Ceoltóirí Chualann. On the cover of the Ó Riada sa Gaiety CD, Ó Riada is cited as the composer of the original music and melody.[62] Nevertheless, this and 'Is Ar Éireann Ní nEosphainn Cé hÍ' use the same melody. Ó Riada's harpsichord accompaniment is similar in both style and function to O'Hara's accompaniment of the same melody. One of the most interesting features of this accompaniment is the interjections between phrases. In bar five, Ó Riada employs a neighbour-note motif/long roll that fulfils the same musical function as O'Hara's, notwithstanding that Ó Riada's version is slightly more florid. Ó Riada has considerably more freedom in approach to his accompaniment than did O'Hara, as Éamonn de Buitléar provides a chordal accompaniment on accordion for part of the song. The types of chordal devices used by O'Hara are again heard here. The harmony is mainly diatonic with two exceptions. In bar six Ó Riada progresses from chord I to an applied vii7 chord, to V. In bar 12, the second chord functions as an applied vii7 to IV. Interestingly, both O'Hara and Ó Riada used chromatic chords in the same phrase. Therefore, in musical terms, these two versions are similar in their harmony, accompanimental devices and melodic interjections. The 'invented tradition' of harping in the 1950s is actually very similar in this instance to Ó Riada's 1969 accompaniment and, as I have shown, to today's harping.

When musical features and analysis are taken into account it becomes clear that the dichotomy between traditional music and the Irish harp in the 1950s and 1960s was not due to musical reasons. As I have outlined, the commodification of the harp served to alienate the instrument from the mainstream tradition. The harp had been relatively silent during the first half of the twentieth century and thus the musical style that emerged in the 1950s was alien to the notion of 'traditional' harping. The gut strung neo-Irish harps may have been viewed as in some way less authentic than the prototype early-Irish harp. In performance, the harp was often seen in formal settings that were removed from the

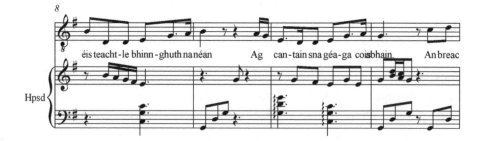

Musical Example 10: 'Binn Luisín Aerach a'Bhrogha',
'Ó Riada sa Gaeity' (transcription by Helen Lawlor)

mainstream tradition. Finally, the strong association of the harp with the voice undoubtedly clouded harp reception at this time. Musical analysis shows that Ní Fhloinn, O'Hara, Hempson, Hambly and Ó Riada all use similar accompanimental styles. The harp music of the 1950s and 1960s, while unfortunately disregarded by many in its day, holds an important position in the tradition of Irish harping. The harp music of this era has much to offer musicians and scholars alike and deserves, as I have demonstrated, a more positive approach with a full consideration of the prevailing sociocultural conditions. One central value of this music is that it brought new popularity and audiences to the Irish harp on a global scale. Subsequent developments in harping would most likely not have taken the same format were it not for the harpists of the 1950s. Their performances and broadcasts brought the harp into the public mindset as a living musical instrument, albeit primarily as accompaniment to song.

CHAPTER 4

Art music and the Irish harp

The Irish harp revival of the 1950s popularized a very distinct type of harping, that is, harp as accompaniment to song. Despite the steady decline in popularity of singing to harp accompaniment over the past twenty years, the importance of the 1950s revival was in the very act of popularizing the harp once more. The harp was brought into the sphere of public consciousness, thus facilitating a transformation of the newly revived tradition in the following decade. In her article 'Music revivals: towards a general theory', Tamara Livingston offers a model by which music revivals may be analyzed.[1] She notes that often, music revivals take on new directions after the initial revival has occurred.

> Some music revivals may exist as distinct movements only for a few years while others ... may survive the good part of a century ... I would suggest that when there is no longer an overriding concern for 'authenticity' ... revivals break down into different styles. In such cases revivals may stimulate new innovative styles and thus cease to exist primarily as a revivalist genre. On the other hand, revivalist strains of a genre, distinguished by the term 'traditional', may exist alongside new styles generated by, or merging with, revivalist genres.[2]

It is useful to consider the harping activity of the 1960s, specifically the consolidation of art-music style harping from the theoretical perspective of Livingston's music revival. The 1950s activity stimulated a 'new innovative style' in the 1960s, which could not have been considered were it not for the foundations laid down in the 1950s whereby the harp was once again popularized. The song and harp combination witnessed in the 1950s gradually declined, but still maintained a presence, while the popularity of playing published arrangements of song airs and purely instrumental pieces rose. Livingston's model serves well as an overarching theoretical model from which to view these developments in the tradition, while Bart Feintuch's analysis of the Northumbrian piping revival offers a more nuanced reflection on a particular revival. Feintuch's analysis is also very helpful as an aid to understanding the processes of change that occurred in the 1960s. Feintuch insists that revivals often result in musical change rather than musical resurrection.

> The term *revival* implies resuscitation, reactivation, and rekindling, and many revivalist musicians assert that they're bolstering a declining musical tradition. But rather than encourage continuity, musical revivals recast the music – and culture – they refer to. They are actually musical transformations, a kind of reinvention.[3]

This is certainly true of harping from the 1960s. The revived tradition subsequently became a transformed tradition. The methods for this transformation, as outlined by Feintuch, includes the publication of standard music books to allow for musical standardization and the dissemination of a core repertory.[4] Similarly, the art-music style of Irish harping is built upon the dissemination of such a repertory. Feintuch further clarifies his interpretation of revivals in the following statement:

> Musical revivals ... create their own canons of repertoire, of style, of authenticity. This is a sort of creative editing, a paring away of those characteristics and features deemed inappropriate and a reorganization of what is left ... Although the piping revivalists make constant reference to 'the piping tradition', what they have actually done is create their own historically conditioned and socially maintained 'artistic paradigm', a transformation of the music – and culture – they think they have revived.[5]

The new repertory 'created' in Irish harping was a combination of old and new compositions, arranged and newly composed for harp. The act of publishing arrangements at once changed the nature of the harping tradition as it existed at the end of the 1950s and revived a turn-of-the-century practice of publishing Irish harp arrangements, a move away from oral- to literacy-based learning. From the 1960s an 'artistic paradigm' of harping was evident in Ireland, which was, in fact, a transformation of the previous strand of Irish harping. The harp revival follows the stages or characteristics of Livingston's model and is reminiscent of the processes described by Feintuch. The results of the harp revival in Ireland included a wider dissemination of harp music through publications and concerts and a broadening of the interest base through teaching activities. The opening up of the tradition to a wide range of audiences is characteristic of revivals in general and indicative of the revivalist intentions of key participants.

Art-music style harping today remains a popular strand of Irish harping, although none of the three strands (art, traditional or early-Irish harping) are necessarily mutually exclusive. The posture changed from sitting beside the harp to resting the harp in between the knees, as is customary in concert harp playing. The art-music style is characterized by a literacy-based transmission and a unique repertoire. The art-music repertoire is fundamental to this style but, interestingly, for the harp it encompasses both new music for harp and music of the harper-composers. Essentially, it draws on art-music practices in terms of transmission and repertoire. This style of harping operates within the same systems as other art-music instruments as it is taught through music institutions (including the DIT Conservatory of Music and Drama and the Royal Irish Academy of Music) and often students take the relevant grade examinations associated with these institutions. The main annual competition is the Feis Ceoil and syllabi for both this and the grade examination show a clear differentiation from the repertoire types associated with traditional-music style.

Cairde na Cruite, 'Friends of the Harp'

The key event in the consolidation and development of the art-music style of Irish harping was the foundation of Cairde na Cruite in 1961, as this was the first concerted attempt to provide direction for harping in Ireland in the twentieth century. Moreover, the foundation of this society was spurred on not only by harpists, but also by cultural enthusiasts, some of whom desired to spread a love of the Irish language through song. The active harp teachers in the late 1950s and early 1960s had a very mixed musical orientation. Sheila Larchet Cuthbert was an important arranger of music for the Irish harp and was trained as a concert harpist by Tina Bonifacio in Liverpool. She was principal harpist with the Radio Éireann Symphony Orchestra. Larchet Cuthbert (as outlined in chapter 2) first began Irish harp with Mother Alphonsus O'Connor in Loreto Abbey, Rathfarnham. She was fully immersed in the literacy based approach to harping and entirely familiar with the international concert harp repertory. Sisters Máirín and Róisín Ní Shéaghdha, the former of whom was teacher to Mary O'Hara, taught traditional songs orally with harp accompaniment at Sion Hill. They were both renowned Irish scholars and had a strong interest in Irish culture. Another figure of importance was Caroline Townshend, who arranged Irish song airs for harp. She was teacher to Mercedes Bolger of Gorey. Mercedes Garvey (Mercedes Bolger's daughter) spoke about Caroline Townshend in an interview:

> A great lady, who lived first in Cork and she was one of what you would call the ascendancy ... She came up to Dublin and started teaching the Irish harp. And my mother heard about her and used to drive up to Dublin, now this is from Gorey. She used to drive up, round about once a week and learn the harp from her. And Carrie Townshend was pretty old at the time and practically blind. And my mother said she used to put her in front of her (she was in Fitzwilliam Square or one of those houses, with big windows), and she used to put her in front of the window so she could see what way her hands were working, you know, with the light of the window.[6]

It is evident, therefore, that among the founding members of Cairde na Cruite were harpists steeped in both the oral- and literacy-based methods of harp playing, some of whom sang to harp accompaniment and others who played exclusively instrumental pieces on the Irish harp. This variety of stylistic orientations is important as it shows that apart from the popularity of the harp as accompaniment instrument, there is little evidence to indicate that a single harp style or approach existed at this time.

The interest held by these harpists in Irish culture met with further encouragement from Cearbhall Ó Dálaigh, a Supreme Court judge, in 1961. He was an ardent member of the Irish political party Fianna Fáil, which was then led by Eamon de Valera.[7] The following excerpt from an interview with Sheila Larchet Cuthbert details the foundation of Cairde na Cruite, the organization that effectively organized and consolidated the harping tradition in Ireland, producing influential publications and instituting teaching methods. These publications in particular served to realign the Irish harp from accompaniment to Irish song into the world of instrumental Western art music.

> Cairde na Cruite, that was founded by not harpists at all, they, the harpists, didn't have the idea ... the idea came from three people: the former president of Ireland, Cearbhaill Ó Dálaigh, Fionnán MacColuim, a great Irish scholar and Colm Ó Lochlainn, an Irish singer of songs ... and, of course, the other very important figure, Eibhlín Ní Chathailriabaigh ... Cearbhaill Ó Dálaigh, being the type of man he was, was at the time Chief Justice and he invited us all to the Four Courts ... And his idea was ... to restore the Irish harp to its former glory, to teach ... and to publish music.[8]

Indeed, while the society's aims have evolved over time, the central focus initially was to promote the harp and to publish harp music. Today, Cairde na Cruite is still involved in the promotion of the harp and the publication of harp music; it aims to integrate the harp into mainstream Irish traditional music, to facilitate the provision of teachers and to introduce 'a wider audience base to the ancient courtly harping tradition through information giving, recording and performance of the music'.[9] From the outset, Cairde na Cruite attempted to promote the harp in public by organizing concerts to showcase harp music, an activity in which they still regularly engage. The following newspaper clipping gives an interesting review of their second concert:

Irish Harp Recital
Founded a short time ago with the object of restoring the Irish harp to a place of honour, and to make more widely known and appreciate what survives of the heritage of the Irish harp, Cairde na Cruite (Friends of the Harp) presented their second concert in the Royal Hibernian Hotel, Dawson street, Dublin last night.

A very interesting seventeen item programme included new arrangements of Irish airs for the harp, for voice and harp, and for violin and harp.

An outstanding item early on was 'Romansaiocht I gcoir bhedlin agus clairsigh' especially composed for the occasion by Eamonn O Gallchobhair and played by Maire Keegan (violin) and Mercedes Bolger (harp). Miss Bolger was also heard to excellent effect in 'Blind Mary' (by Mercedes McGrath) and 'Rondeau' by the French composer, Jean Phillipe Rameau.

Grainne Ni Eigertaigh sang to her own harp accompaniment and Joan Burke was among those who played the small harp.

The second half of the programme was mainly devoted to Welsh, Breton, Scotch and Irish harp music, played by Mairin Ni She, Roisin Ni She, Aoife Ni Chiosain, Mairead Ni Chiosan, and Nancy Calthorpe.

R.A.B.[10]

The author, R.A.B., hints at the repertoire types that were later cemented by Cairde na Cruite's activities and publications: instrumental airs, song airs and harp as an ensemble instrument. The first piece mentioned, 'Romansaiocht', composed by Ó Gallchobhair, falls into the category of composed art music for Irish harp. 'Blind Mary' is one of many examples of traditional Irish airs arranged for harp. This was played by Mercedes Bolger, one of the founding members of Cairde na Cruite.[11] She also played a 'Rondeau', presumably transcribed for Irish harp, which is again a clear example of the art-music repertory. Gráinne Yeats' use of the harp for accompaniment to song represents another strand in the complex variety of styles played on the Irish harp. The small harp was also present, while other Celtic music was incorporated into the programme. A second article, published by the 'Irish Times', gives a less than favourable review of the same event:

Cairde na Cruite Gives Concert

Cairde na Cruite (the Friends of the Harp) held their second public concert on Friday at the Hibernian Hotel, Dublin. Like the first, this clashed with a concert by the Radio Eireann Symphony Orchestra: let us hope that more care will be exercised next time.

It was clear that the young society is advancing. The evening contained more than half-a-dozen works or arrangements done specially for the occasion, and there was on the whole rather a higher general standard among the dozen performers than before. The society must still make up its mind about its ideals of professionalism or amateurishness.

Indicative of the latter were a later start; far too long a concert; a programme sheet with far too many inaccuracies; and the invitation to Prionnsias O Ceallaigh to act as compère. Even Mr. O Cealaigh's expert charm could not disguise the parochial or variety nature of a compère, apart from his not having been told of the programme's inaccuracies.

Since the harp still is in process of revival, and since we are unlikely to want to hear the sort of noise the old harpers made (with fingernails on brass strings), inevitably there will be a good deal of stylistic variety and experiment.

But the society should determine that at their public meetings, only a really professional standard of technique should be permitted. Thus, in each half, there was certainly one item well below the required standard, though most of the great [sic] was really well played and sung. And I am delighted to report far fewer lapses of tuning than before.

One interesting experiment was the story of the 'Children of Lir' sung by Aoife ni Chiosain, accompanied at the harp by Mairin ni She, and danced by Mairead ni Chiosain. Whether simple classical ballet is a desirable medium is still in doubt since the platform arrangements were hardly adequate but the idea is worth pursuing.

On the other hand, the undoubtedly folky quality of Roisin ni She's voice helped to make the Breton 'Eun Alarch' very impressive.

Mercedes Bolger's usual complete expertist and professionalism are a great pleasure, especially in Mercedes McGrath's arrangements of 'Blind Mary', and in a Rameau Rondeau, a useful extension of the instrument's sphere.

Another useful sphere is in the lute song, of which Gráinne ní Eigeartaigh gave us Robert Johnson's 'Full Fathom Five' (composer for the première of 'The Tempest'), and 'Callino Costure Me'. If Gráinne ní Eigeartaigh took the latter strangely slowly, she also gave a characteristically professional performance.

Eamonn O Gallchobáir's Romance for Violin and Harp (played by Máire Keegan and Mercedes Bolger) showed the matching timbre of the two instruments – even if D major is not the best key for the harp. Joseph Groocock's accompaniments of two Carolan's tunes showed a nice blend of characteristic harp music, and the 18th-century manner, while T.C. Kelly's arrangements were graceful, if inclined to encourage buzzing.

Next time, perhaps, we might have fewer performers per concert and really high standards throughout.

C.A.[12]

The overriding impression given by the author of this article is that he did not particularly favour the harp and, aside from complaints regarding the general organization of the event, C.A. actually praised the music when it was mentioned. What this article does serve to illustrate is that the task faced by Cairde na Cruite, in attempting to revive the art-music style of harping and to move away from the more populist approach of the singer/harpists in the 1950s, was a difficult one. The public perception of the music and the role of the harp was quite different to that held by Mercedes Bolger, Sheila Larchet Cuthbert and others. They were attempting to present the harp on a par with other instruments by playing solo art-music repertoire (such as the Rameau piece) on the Irish harp. Singing to harp accompaniment still held a place in this concert, and indeed in the general activities of Cairde na Cruite, but this was no longer the prime focus of harping activities. The event served to attract much media attention nonetheless. The following excerpt is by Mary MacGoris, *Irish Independent* music critic:

> It was rather like the twelve days of Christmas at the Hibernian Hotel with eight harpists harping in various styles and groupings at the Harp Concert given by the society formed last year and known as Cairde na Cruite.
>
> The programme was divided into two sections – the first with an emphasis on art music with an Irish bias, the second mainly presenting Celtic folksong ... One of the aims of the society we were told by the compere Proinnsias O Cheallaigh, is to encourage composition for the harp, and in addition to various arrangements, mostly by the harpists themselves, offered two original pieces.[13]

MacGoris' comments are insightful, as she points out the division evident in styles: 'art' and 'folk'. Proinnsias O Cheallaigh's announcement that new compositions were sought further illustrates the society's early intentions for the harp. These intentions were initially brought to fruition with the work of Sheila Larchet Cuthbert in 1975.

The strong emphasis on music publishing in the early days of Cairde na Cruite is directly linked to art-music practices. The concept of having definitive versions of both treble and bass arrangements is central to concert harping and, from the 1960s onwards, was imported into Irish harping. Transmission up to this point had remained substantially oral-based, although publications by Edward Bunting among others from the nineteenth century onwards had already introduced a literate element to harping. In the following interview excerpt, Mercedes Garvey suggests that one of the defining differences between those who used the harp for song accompaniment and those who pursued the 'art-music' style was their approach to the music, that is, whether their approach was oral or literacy based.

> they did it by ear. She did it by her head ... Well, you see I think the people, it was the same kind of music because it was Irish music and possibly they got the tunes from the books, you know [Bunting], but they were by ear really, I would say.[14]

Garvey points to an inherent difficulty in trying to pinpoint the various styles at work in Irish harping. Almost all of the music is 'Irish', whether the repertoire is newly composed, arranged or adapted. The differences arise then in stylistic approaches to music rather than solely in repertoire. In another interview, Sheila Larchet Cuthbert commented further on the perceived difficulty of oral transmission, thus explaining why Cairde na Cruite placed such a strong importance on the act of publishing music: 'I think teaching without music, that's a wonderful way of carrying things on but it, in the end, restricts.'[15] The initial direction taken by Cairde na Cruite was therefore a literacy-based approach and the society purposefully set about producing resources for teaching (although the society today adopts both a literate and an aural approach in its annual festival workshops). Sheila Larchet Cuthbert was selected to compile and edit a book under the auspices of Cairde na Cruite. She explained that the need for such a volume arose from the lack of suitable teaching material. This is a valid point and one that reinforces my assertion that the methodology used in harp teaching from the 1960s onwards became increasingly literacy based.

> So all of us who were teaching, all of us: Mercedes and myself, and Gráinne Yeats coming in. We all arranged music for the students. But the good ones would come in and say 'well I've done that, what will I do this week?' And you weren't in the position to say 'go down to McCullough Pigott's and get'. There was nothing. So the most important thing of all was to publish. And without Cairde na Cruite, that couldn't have been done. Because, what that succeeded in doing was focusing all the activities into one particular thing.[16]

The Irish harp book

The Irish harp book, edited and arranged by Sheila Larchet Cuthbert, was Cairde na Cruite's first publication. This volume became highly influential in harping circles and contains some seminal works that helped to define and shape the 'art-music' style of Irish harp playing. Larchet Cuthbert gives detailed instructions throughout the book on finger placement and harp technique. There are twenty-seven studies, all of which are taken from Mother Attracta Coffey's *Irish harp tutor* and *Twenty-seven studies*.[17] The incorporation of these studies into Larchet Cuthbert's book is important in terms of asserting a stylistic lineage. Larchet Cuthbert consistently draws upon these studies, utilizing between one and three in each chapter of the book. She therefore identifies the stylistic orientation of this volume with the work of Mother Attracta Coffey, the earliest twentieth-century exponent of the art-music style of Irish harping. M.A.C.'s work involved solo harp arrangements of well-known Irish airs, using the melodic and harmonic techniques popular in art music.[18]

An examination of the repertoire types included in this book is beneficial in order to show the emphasis placed on certain musical practices by Cairde na Cruite and the book's author, Larchet Cuthbert.[19] The following series of graphs show an analysis of the specific repertoire types included in Cuthbert's volume. Out of 55 pieces in the book, 25 were solo harp arrangements or newly composed pieces; 14 were for voice and harp, and just 7 for harp ensemble. Figure 1 below illustrates this division.[20]

This division is indicative of the stylistic direction that was taken by Cairde na Cruite at the outset. The author of the book was aware of the rich variety of harp-music sources available:

> And I was introducing the neo-Irish harp and its possibilities and all of that. So, the three sources: the great treasury of music that we have that is perhaps nearly considered to be almost the greatest in the world, the treasury from, of course, the Bunting manuscripts. The second then, those who were playing the harp at the time, and arranging. That's why they're all there, why you'll find them all there. The Ní Shés, everyone who was teaching and playing ... My third thing was we can't keep looking back all the time. We've got to look forward. So I wrote to all the composer colleagues, who of course I know for a long time through the orchestra and every-

thing and I was astounded at the response. I wrote to them, telling them, I did out, all illustrated for them, the possibilities for the harp. The keys it could play in, the thirteen keys that were available, and asking them to write something for either solo harp, original piece; an arrangement of something for harp; or for more than one harp, even multiple harps, whatever they liked. Every single one, people unlikely, Professor Boydell, Gerard Victory. They all became, I think they were challenged by it! But they all wrote back to say yes they would.[21]

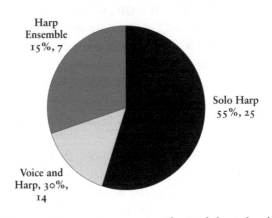

Figure 1: Repertoire types in *The Irish harp book*

Within the collection of solo harp pieces, the vast majority are arranged airs. These airs include newly composed arrangements such as 'An Cóitín Dearg' by Aloys Fleischmann and 'Carolan's Concerto' by Sheila Larchet Cuthbert.[22]

There is no contribution in the book from Seán Ó Riada, and despite his criticisms of the harp, Larchet Cuthbert clearly stated that it was merely circumstantial difficulties that resulted in this omission:

So, the only one missing is, and sadly conspicuous by his absence, Seán Ó Riada, and you wonder why? Seán was an extraordinary person. Seán, I'd heard him play in the Abbey Theatre, the most beautiful version of 'Sliabh na mBan'. So I wrote to him and said 'Seán, I'd be so honoured if you'd send us, if you've no objection, this beautiful arrangement'. 'Sheila, you'll have it by' whatever it is. Well, time passed, and I met him one day, actually in Wicklow Street, and he pulled me into the entrance to a shop, it was a fashion shop! He said, 'Sheila I know, "Sliabh na mBan"'. I said, 'Seán, we cannot go with this book without you. And it's nearly going to print now.' 'You'll have it next week'. Well. And, of course, after that he became so ill. So that's really regrettable because he was such an obvious person. I'm just telling you there was no other possible reason why he was not there.[23]

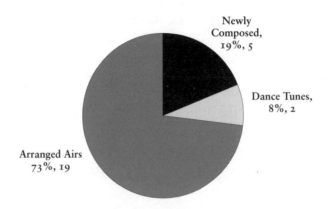

Figure 2: Repertoire types – solo harp pieces

The very small percentage of arranged dance tunes fits with the overall approach of the art-music style. The newly composed pieces were in response to requests by Larchet Cuthbert to prominent contemporary composers. It is these pieces, perhaps, more than any other repertoire type that necessitate the application of the term art-music style. They were newly composed for the instrument, following contemporary writing styles of twentieth-century art-music practices. The following statement from Charles Acton reveals the common assumptions held by people about the harp, and shows Acton's realization of the harp's possibilities: 'This ... should provide a real incentive for young harp players to find out the instrument is more than just a ladylike accompaniment for arrangements of traditional tunes.'[24]

'Three Pieces for the Irish Harp' by Gerard Victory is a case in point. The first movement of this work is forty-seven bars long and is in ternary form (the middle contrasting section occupies only ten bars of the piece). The style of writing here is unequivocally modern and is a far cry from arranged airs for the harp. While the piece has a broad tonal centre of C, it is ostensibly atonal. The triad of C is arpeggiated across bars one to four, but the presence of a D sharp and B flat prevent the establishment of either a C major or minor tonality. Other techniques that point to Victory's modernist writing can be observed in musical example 11 below. The ostinato pattern presented in bars one to six recurs in various guises throughout the piece and is one of the unifying factors between sections A and A[1]. The only section of the piece that avoids ostinato entirely is section B (bars 20–30). Victory employs a highly articulated form of writing for the harp; a style that fits well with contemporary writing. Within the first eight bars, three different techniques of attack are employed: *tenuto* (bar 2), *staccato* (bar 3), *marcato* (bars 3–6). These first eight bars could be interpreted as a form of sentence: the statement occurs in bars 1–2; complimentary repetition in bars 3–4, elaboration in 5–6 and liquidation in 7–8. While such formal structures do not always occur in modern pieces, the principal melodic content of both sections 1 and 3 (A and A[1]) is contained within these first eight bars, and a definite ternary form is identifiable in the movement as a whole, thus allowing for the possibility of a defined formal structure within the opening section.

Musical Example 11: Gerard Victory, bars 1–8

Victory decidedly moves away from a fully melody-dominated approach to harp music in this piece. Unlike arrangements of song airs by other composers in Larchet Cuthbert's volume, the melody is not all-pervasive in this piece. Melodic fragmentation is frequently used by Victory and rhythmic interest often takes precedence over the melody, such as in musical example 12 below.

Musical Example 12: Victory, bars 9–10

The tonal centre of C is reinforced here (bars 9–10) with a steady quaver pedal in the bass clef. This results in an augmented 2nd clash with the D sharp in the treble clef.

Section B (musical example 13) is the first section that is in a different metre. This entire ten–bar section is in triple metre and gives the feel of a waltz. Three note clusters (A, B flat and C) provide rhythmic accompaniment in the treble clef, featuring the characteristic detailed articulation present throughout the piece. The melodic material here is related to that of bars 9 and 10, but is now subjected to intervallic expansion. Victory uses quite a syncopated rhythm for the melodic material, as can be observed in the musical example below. In bar 11 (section A), the composer utilized three short *glissandi* of one crotchet beat and with a

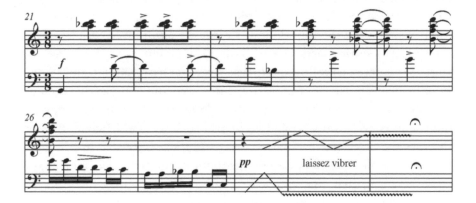

Musical Example 13: Victory, bars 21–30 (Section B)

range of approximately one octave. This technique is further expanded from bars twenty-eight to thirty, both in intervallic and temporal dimensions. These prolonged *glissandi* suspend the rhythmic development of section B, with a combination of harmonic, melodic and textural effects taking priority.

Bars thirty-one to forty-seven are a return to a variation of section A, with four changes of time signature taking place. The piece ends with a temporally expanded version of bars one to six, resting on C". From my analysis of this piece, it is clear that the work in question can be classified as a piece of art music for the Irish harp. The existence of such a repertory and its promotion by Cairde na Cruite (through publications and concerts) validates my claim that from the 1960s onwards the dominant style in Irish harping was the art-music style of harping. The effects and influence of this style were so pervasive that even the previously oral transmission of song became literacy based. Two fundamental differences in musical style can be observed here between art-music harping and what came both before and after: first, arrangements were written down, published and therefore definitive. Second, the existence of this repertoire resulted in a shift to literate transmission.

The demarcation of style on the harp is not a simplistic matter, however. Despite approaches of orality or literacy, the repertoire remained shared in some ways. Those harpists who had learned music orally and those who studied harping through literate means continued to work for the promotion of the harp simultaneously, under the umbrella of Cairde na Cruite. This is not surprising, given the history, repertoire and heritage that is shared by all practitioners of the Irish harp. An interesting point raised by both Sheila Larchet Cuthbert and Mercedes Garvey in fieldwork interviews was that the people who initially suggested the founding of Cairde na Cruite were not harpists, but cultural enthusiasts. Cearbhaill Ó Dálaigh was described by Mercedes Garvey as follows: 'He was a terrific Irish scholar and I don't think he was a musician, but terribly interested and completely taken up with things Irish and the music and the language. Mainly the language and the music.'[25] In his book *The British folk revival*, Michael Broken observes the links between nationalism and the folk revival in Britain in the 1930s. Folk song was viewed throughout the revival as a means of expressing a British identity. Broken quotes Ralph Vaughan Williams: 'The art of music ... is the expression of the soul of a nation, and by a nation I mean ... any community of people who are spiritually bound together by language, environment, history and common ideals, and above all, a continuity with the past.'[26] This perspective has relevance here as Irish language songs with harp accompaniment continued to be identified with a specifically Irish identity in the 1960s. Irish-language songs dominate in *The Irish harp book* (as illustrated in figure 3 below). Moreover, Cairde na Cruite actively incorporated the Irish language into their publications and activities.[27]

The inclusion of songs with harp accompaniment in *The Irish harp book* was reflective of common practice of the time. Although I am attempting to classify the complex and diverse stylistic practices of Irish harping in a written, academic format, the practices of singing to harp accompaniment and the development of the art-music style co-existed for some time. There was never a clear-cut divide as to when harping as accompaniment to song began to decline in popularity and harping as a solo expression of art music took precedence. Nevertheless, from the early 1960s onwards and particularly from when Irish harp music began to be published regularly, both solo harping and song to harp accompaniment became literate rather than oral practices. Whereas the harpists of the 1940s and 1950s composed their harp arrangements to songs orally, with the advent of Cairde na Cruite, song accompaniments were published, alongside solo harp pieces. The literate transmission of harp music was not a new phenomenon, music had been published for the Irish harp as far back as 1902.[28] The crux of the difference between pre- and post-Cairde na Cruite was that in addition to the growing propensity for solo art music on the Irish harp, all music on the instrument was taught, composed and arranged in a manner that required music literacy skills. The shift in emphasis from the oral to the

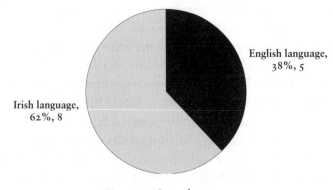

Figure 3: Song languages

literate served to further align the Irish harp with art music, rather than Irish traditional music.

Nancy Calthorpe

Nancy Calthorpe (1914–98) was an important figure in Irish harping from the 1950s onwards. Her publications combine solo harp pieces and song with harp accompaniment and she was a prolific arranger of music for the harp. In 2007 I was given access to Calthorpe's collection of manuscripts and notebooks by Úna McSweeney, for which I am very grateful. This collection consists of 105 pieces of music, 13 copybooks, 2 photographs and several letters. The copybooks proved immensely significant. While they were not personal diaries, they contain Calthorpe's study notes which she made continuously throughout her life. She was a very diligent and dedicated scholar who carried out in-depth research into her arrangements. The collection of music comprised copies of works by other authors, as well as original, incomplete, and fair copies of her own arrangements. It is, however, from the notebook collection that I garnered the most interesting information, given that over seventy-three of her arrangements were published and remain in the pedagogical repertoire.

Nancy Calthorpe was born on 17 January 1914 in India, as her father was an army officer and stationed there. In 1915 her father died and shortly afterwards Nancy and her mother returned to Ireland. Calthorpe's maternal family were musicians; her grandmother was organist at Ballybricken church in Co. Waterford. Calthorpe commenced her own musical training in Waterford under Professor Begas (a Dutch organist), with whom she studied voice.[29] Calthorpe subsequently qualified as a teacher of voice and piano and began teaching in the Ursuline Covent in Sligo; she also taught at Loreto Abbey Rathfarnham and at Dominican College, Sion Hill. In 1952 she began teaching in the Municipal School of Music (now the DIT Conservatory of Music and Drama). Evelyn Hearns described how Nancy came to begin the harp: 'It was while teaching in Sion Hill that she first encountered Máirín Ní Shéaghdha, a well-respected Irish harpist and teacher. Nancy took harp lessons from Máirín and developed a great interest in Irish music. She had a deep affection for the instrument and had to struggle to pay for her own harp'.[30] Despite what can be assumed to have been an oral introduction to the harp, Calthorpe's approach remained literacy-based. In 1985 Calthorpe was made head of the singing department in the College of Music. She designed and subsequently introduced the first diploma course for the teaching of the Irish harp in 1988.[31] She published six volumes of harp music and a further volume was published posthumously by Waltons in 2000.[32] Calthorpe was a well-respected performer and arranger for the harp and was given the freedom of the city of New Orleans for her contribution to Irish culture (see plate 7).[33]

The copybook collection given to me yielded some very interesting information about Calthorpe as an arranger and a scholar. Her early manuscript copies read like those of any undergraduate music student: harmony and counterpoint exercises, examples of vocal ranges and notes on form. These copies show her early musical training to be exclusively Western art-oriented. Nevertheless, Calthorpe had a strong interest in Irish culture, as did many of her contemporaries. One of her copybooks, entitled 'The Story of the Irish Harp', opens with the following quote from Thomas Davis (see plate 8):

> Music is the first faculty of the Irish; and scarcely anything has such power for good over them. The use of this faculty and this power publicly and constantly to keep up their spirits, refine their tastes, warm their courage, increase their union and renew their zeal is the duty of every patriot.

Calthorpe's arrangements for the Irish harp are her lasting legacy to the instrument. One song air in particular, 'Eileen Aroon', appears to have been a very important piece for Calthorpe. She has four different entries in her notes about this tune, the first of which is fifteen pages long, noted from volume 1 of *Stories of famous songs* by S.J. Adair Fitz-Gerald, published in 1901. A further source for this tune came from a 1930 publication, *Panpipes*, which was a supplement of *Music and Youth*. 'Eileen Aroon', which means Eileen, my darling, was composed by harper Carrol O'Grady (also known as Cearbhall Ó Dálaigh) in the late seventeenth century.[34] The song tells the story of Eileen and the harper; they were in love with one another, but she was due to marry another man. Just before the wedding ceremony the harper, in disguise, played this tune for Eileen at which point she recognized him and they eloped. Calthorpe's 1977 arrangement of this piece is for solo harp.

Calthorpe's arrangement is a classic example of an art-music style arrangement of a traditional Irish tune. The first four bars are an intro-duction based on the last phrase of the melody. Immediately, the original structure of the melody is altered to suit an instrumental arrangement. The harmony used is standard tonal harmony, with mainly tonic, sub-dominant and dominant chords. An important element that defines the art-music style of arranging is the use of art-music devices such as fragmentation, strict rhythm, *alberti* bass, pianistic textures, chromatic harmony and the division of the main tune between treble and bass. Calthorpe's arrangement displays many of these elements; for example, the melody in bar twenty-one is an octave higher than in its original appearance and a very clear pianistic texture is used here. In bar twenty-four, the melody passes from treble to bass and then moves back to the treble in bar twenty-nine. The Italian performing directions and published arrangement remove this from the oral repertoire and bring it into the realm of art music. While certain un-conventional voice leading patterns can be observed (such as consecutive 5ths in bars three and five), the use of these does not diminish the piece's identity as a composed arrangement of an Irish air. My application of the definition art-music style to this piece is based on an analysis of the processes involved in its arrangement and transmission in addition to the immanent musical features of the piece. Calthorpe taught harmony in the College of Music and from her notebooks, it is quite clear that she understood the conventions of classical voice leading. My hypothesis in this case is that the consecutive 5ths were intentional, perhaps to convey the ancient genesis of the tune. Furthermore, she committed this arrangement to publication and must, therefore, have been satisfied with it. Despite any peculiarities of voice leading, it remains a composed arrangement of an Irish air that references the style and techniques (as outlined above) of art music. This manuscript version written in Calthorpe's hand is shown in plate 9.

Calthorpe was also well known for her arrangements for voice and harp.[35] Her arrangement of the well-known Irish air 'Eanach Dhún' both demonstrates her style of writing for song and gives an insight into her approach to arranging. The following note by Calthorpe was written in one of her copybooks containing notes on some of the songs she had arranged.[36]

The Tradgedy [*sic*] of 'Anach Cuain' took place September 4th 1828, when 31 men and women set out for a fair in Galway in a not very seaworthy boat. A little way from the shore a sheep put his foot through the boat. A woman put her scarf into the hole to try to keep the water out, not successful, a man put his Banín through the hole when panic broke out and all jumped into the water and were drowned, except for one woman who threw out a bag of wool on which she lay till she was saved. Eighteen bodies (some say 19) were recovered and laid out at Muckross. A commemorative plaque in the village of Anneghdown bears the names of the victims as follows

Bridget Farragher, Mary Costelloe, Judith Ryan, Bridget Hughes, Mary Newell, Winifred Jordan, Mary Flynn, Bridget Cunley, Catherine Malloy, Mary Carr, Michael Farragher, Michael Cahill, John Cosgrove, John Concannon, Thomas Burke, Patrick Foran[?], John Forde and Timothy Goaley

It is said that one year after the great tradgedy [sic] (some say 10 years), Rafftery the blind poet composed his now well known poem in which he speaks of 'a whole boat load swept away on a lovely day without wind, or rain. The great wonder of the crowd to see the victims stretched out on their backs. The wailing and lamenting of terrified people tearing their hair out and claiming their dead. Young boys for whom the autumn of life had not yet begun being carried to the church and waked in their wedding suits, "Oh God of Glory, what a Great Sorrow"'.

In June 1982 I had tea in the home of Mr Farragher of Annaghdown (Father of a Sister of Mercy in Galway) who told me his Great Grandfather was a victim of the tradgedy [sic] and said the old people seldom spoke about it. He pointed out to me the spot where the corpses were laid. (Almost outside his own door) After my visit I felt a strong desire to set Rafftery's beautiful poem to the equally beautiful old Irish air for voice and Irish harp. To which I humbly hope I have done some justice and paid my tribute to the memory of the 'Great Sorrow' of Annaghdown.

Nancy Calthorpe

Calthorpe was keenly aware of the emotional and historical context attached to the song.[37] Her arrangement of 'Eanach Dhún' is similar in style to her setting of other Irish song airs. The important point to remember in this analysis is that while the harp arrangement itself may be more simplified than in solo harp pieces, the role of the harp here is as accompaniment. Similarly, it is difficult to play complex harp accompaniments to song. Therefore, harp accompaniments such as this give the necessary space in terms of rhythm and texture for the song melody to be clear. Calthorpe's version of 'Eanach Dhún' is set in the key of D (dorian mode) and opens with an instrumental introduction motivically linked to the final phrase of the tune (see plates 10–12). Within the introduction, Calthorpe uses harp *glissandi* and a motivic treatment of the melody. The complexity of the harp line is significantly pared down on the introduction of the song air. The range of harmonic exploration is limited to the standard range of diatonic chords. In terms of rhythm, Calthorpe employs some syncopation in the harp line, but never uses detailed figuration. She briefly explores the idea of canon between treble and bass clef in the interlude between verses one and two of the song (bar twenty-one). The harp accompaniment in the second verse is quite similar to that of verse one, with some textural differences, such as rolled chords where they were initially played *secco*. The arrangement ends with an instrumental coda, which is a variation of the introduction but now heard one octave higher and in slight variation.

Calthorpe's treatment of this song is indicative of the general approach used in the art-music style. The arrangement is composed, set, published and therefore definitive. This practice is directly linked to the general processes and practices of art music as a whole and does not reflect common practice in Irish traditional music or Irish traditional song.

There is ample evidence to show that Cairde na Cruite succeeded in furthering the initial revival of the harp and that they fostered an interest in harping in general. There was a significant rise in publications for the Irish harp after the publication of *The Irish harp book*. Oifig an tSoláthair was instrumental in producing a series of pieces for the Irish harp. Ruth Mervyn and Oilibhéar Ó hEidhin both published harp music in this series; the former for solo harp and the latter for voice with harp accompaniment. Ruth Mervyn had previously contributed an arrangement of 'An Fhallaingín Mhuimhneach' to *The Irish harp book* and also arranged music for 'The Irish Harp Duo' (Mercedes Garvey and Gráinne Yeats). Musical example 14 is one of Mervyn's own compositions. The piece is in ternary form, the second A being a variation of the first. The writing here is quite Romantic in tone and figuration with regular use of seventh chords and suspensions. Mervyn's use of an arpeggiated accompaniment over the left-hand melody is reminiscent of the

Musical Example 14: 'Inis Caol'. Bars 1–20, Ruth Mervyn, *Ceol don chruit* (Dublin: Oifig an tSoláthair, n.d.)

style of writing of John Thomas and Mother Alphonsus O'Connor.[38] 'Inis Caol' cannot be described as a piece of Irish traditional music as the structure, melody line, and type do not fit into any of the established criteria of traditional Irish music. It is still an 'Irish' piece as the composer is Irish and it uses an Irish-language title. Essentially, it is a piece of art music (as opposed to traditional), composed for an Irish instrument in the art-music style.

There are many more examples of such pieces, particularly those by Éamonn Ó Gallchobhair and T.C. Kelly.[39] Even the many song-air arrangements and song accompaniments by Nancy Calthorpe, Ruth Mervyn, Mercedes McGrath, Brian Boydell, Gráinne Yeats (and many other arrangers and composers) belong to the style designation 'art music'. The composed, arranged and published music falls into this category not least because of its method of transmission. When the published score acts as a definitive version then the piece may be judged to belong to the 'art-music' style of Irish harping. This musical practice flourished as the harp became incorporated into grade syllabi in the RIAM and the DIT Conservatory of Music and Drama. This style remains widespread today; it was not until the 1980s that there even existed another method of playing solo music on the harp.

An Chúirt Chruitireachta

One of the key methods through which Cairde na Cruite succeeded in promoting the harp (in addition to their publication activities) was by teaching. The Royal Irish Academy of Music in Dublin had established harp lessons in 1888 under the tutelage of Priscilla Frost.[40] In 1957, the Municipal School of Music (now the DIT Conservatory of Music and Drama) introduced harp lessons, with Sheila Larchet Cuthbert as the first teacher.[41] As demonstrated in chapter 2, the Irish harp had long occupied a place in the Feis Ceoil. Among the aims of Cairde na Cruite from its outset were to teach and to promote the harp. These aims were further achieved by running annual summer schools for the harp. The annual harp summer school now held at An Grianán in Termonfeckin, Co. Louth has evolved into an international harp festival of repute that attracts performers and participants from all over the world and has become a staple event in the annual harping calendar. An Chúirt Chruitireachta was first established as an annual summer school in 1985; however, other summer schools had been run by Cairde na Cruite in advance of this.

Harpists' Course.
A resident course for harpists and other interested people, organized by the Harp Society, Cairde na Cruite will be held in the Downshire House Hotel, Blessington, Co. Wicklow, from October 29th to 31st. The director of the course will be Sancia Peilou (Mrs. Norman Massey) of the BBC Scottish Orchestra, and it is being subsidized by the Carnegie Trust.[42]

This notice in the *Irish Times* was for the third such course, therefore the first was probably in 1969. The Irish harpists were not alone in this activity; Phia Berghout and Maria Kortinska ran a harp summer school in Holland.[43] The establishment of a regular summer school for Irish harping was an important turning point in the development and promotion of the harp. Since 1985 An Chúirt Chruitireachta (A Court of Harpers) has been held in the same place every year. There were twenty-five harp students at the first course which was run by Mercedes Garvey and Gráinne Yeats.[44] Mercedes described to me in an interview the difficulty of teaching without adequate resources in the first year:

> Gráinne and I ran it and there was no music. So Gráinne and I wrote out arrangements and things. This [*My gentle harp*] wasn't published. I mean, I had all my mother's arrangements. And I used some of those. And Gráinne got Michael Yeats' sister to loan a thing for photocopying. And we copied these yards of music and that was what was used at that first thing.[45]

It is evident that initially a very literate-based approach to the transmission was used at that time by the teachers. An article published in the *Irish Independent* in 1989 reveals much about the early activities at the harp school.[46] In the early years of the summer school, harp accompaniment to song was taught. At the 2008 summer school Gráinne Yeats remarked that she was delighted to see a resident singer at the harp school, as the singing element had gradually gone out of An Chúirt Chruitireachta.[47] Interestingly, a male harpist was chosen for the 1989 newspaper article photo, despite the fact that all of the organizers of that festival were female and that the Irish harp remains a predominantly female instrument.

> The heavenly sound of harps took over An Grianán in Termon-feckin, Co. Louth yesterday at the start of the 4th Annual Irish

Harp Summer School which continues for the week. It brings together all of the various artists who are involved in preserving the tradition of the Irish national instrument from players to singers to dancers and harp makers. The residential summer school organized by Cairde na Cruite includes daily classes in harp technique, singing to harp accompaniment, session playing with other instruments, ensemble playing, traditional ornamentation, whistle playing, traditional singing and Irish dancing. Along with Irish harpists from 10 years upwards there are also students of the harp from the UK, the Continent, and the US. And after classes, nightly recitals which are open to the public are given by many distinguished players. The Summer School organized by Helen Davies is again directed by Gráinne Yeats with Mairéad Hurley, Liaison Officer, and has a total of six teachers participating – Sheila Larchet Cuthbert, Mercedes Bolger, Máire Ní Chathasaigh, Aine Ní Dhuill, Elizabeth Hannon and Aibhlín McCrann.[48]

Since the foundation of the summer school it has grown immensely. There were over sixty harp students in attendance in 2008, with ten harp teachers (nine Irish harp, one concert harp) and one singing teacher.[49] I was struck by the diversity of styles that were promoted during the harp week. A marked plurality of both the oral and literate approaches could be observed on the course, which reflects the present aims of the society.

The role and rationale of Cairde na Cruite have developed over the past forty years. Initially, it was founded to 'revive' the harp and to foster a love for the Irish harp and for Irish music. The key personnel were aware of its intentions and it was a focused and dedicated movement, as the following excerpt from an interview with Mercedes Garvey shows:

HL: When Cairde was being founded, did you think of it as a revival or just as a promotion of the harp?

MG: Oh, it would be a revival of course. Yes, it was because it was there from centuries past and it was a revival. And a sort of a building up really.[50]

Cairde na Cruite has succeeded in its aims to promote the harp; the sheer volume of harpists now playing is testament to this. Its publications have provided a body of repertoire suitable for solo instrumental playing on the Irish harp, harp accompaniment to song and harp in ensemble.[51] The diversity in approach to harping today within Cairde na Cruite shows a move away from strict adherence to the art-music style of playing. Nonetheless, this style of harping is still very strong, regardless of the activities of Cairde na Cruite. The direction initially taken by that organization led to the development and consolidation of the art-music style of playing, but the organization and the style are not inextricably linked. It was useful, however, to trace the development of that style through the early activities of Cairde na Cruite, who initially focused on a literacy-based approach to harping.

The art-music style of harping remains a central force in Irish harping today, existing alongside the other two major strands of Irish harping (traditional-music style and early-Irish harping). There is nothing to prevent a single harper straddling all three styles and it is quite common for harpers today to combine study of both art-music and traditional-music styles. In art-music style harping there remains a focus on the literate transmission and a composed/arranged art-music repertoire. New works continue to be composed for the Irish harp.[52] The only harping organization for the (neo) Irish harp is Cairde na Cruite, the organization that effectively led the revival and consolidation of the art-music style of Irish harping in the 1960s. The roots of this style lie in the early twentieth century but were revived by the key revivalists from the 1960s onwards through their publication activities, style, approach and transmission methods. The song tradition which saturated Irish harping in the 1950s continued, but gradually lost momentum as solo Irish harping gained popularity. The new compositions and arrangements for Irish harp that appeared from the 1960s onwards provided a body of published repertoire for the Irish harp that facilitated the change from oral to literate transmission. The key factor in art-music style harping is that transmission (even of song accompaniments) became literacy based. The Irish harp was incorporated into the pre-existing grade-exam system and, ultimately, could be identified as an art-music instrument. Cairde na Cruite, while initially central in the development of the art-music style, does not actually represent this single style strand. Today, its position is one of plurality, whereby all styles of Irish harping are fostered. The literate element of Irish harping served, however, to isolate the harp from the mainstream of Irish traditional music until the 1980s when the next phase of the harp revival or transformation emerged.

CHAPTER 5

Style and context: traditional Irish harping

The third phase of the harp revival began in the early 1980s, during which harp players began to play the Irish traditional dance music repertoire on the harp, following the oral methods of transmission used in traditional music. They similarly made a break in terms of style, technique and approach from both the song and art styles that had gone before. Bruno Nettl cites the introduction of new technology as a potential cause of musical change and the following description by Janet Harbison displays clearly how the introduction of a new type of Irish harp helped to precipitate changes in the tradition.[1]

> In 1968 or 1969, the dramatic visit of the three Japanese gentlemen to our harp room in Sion Hill, and a short time later the resulting first generation of Aoyama harps to arrive in McCullagh Pigott's [sic] music shop, was an event to prove of great significance. These were the first harps of real quality and tone to allow for greater effect and enjoyment in playing instrumental music. They differed in style from our existing harps in that they were a generally heavier, more strongly constructed instrument, with a string span of four-and-a-half octaves ... The new instruments were strung with nylon rather than gut with a consequently brighter ... sound ... I was happy to exploit all the new instrumental possibilities, accompany or arrange for my friends and indulge in the vast dance music repertoire which all my traditional musician friends outside school were playing nightly.[2]

This new model of Irish harp certainly had an impact on the tradition. The sound was significantly louder and the increased tension, combined with standardized string spacing, facilitated the playing of dance tunes at speed. Ensemble playing is a key characteristic of traditional-style playing, as highlighted by Harbison. In this context the harp is played with other traditional instruments, as either melody or accompaniment.

Harbison describes the introduction of the Aoyama harps as occurring in 1968 or 1969, however, the first main blossoming of the traditional-music style of harp playing began in the 1980s. Harper Máire Ní Chathasaigh similarly discussed her motivation for adapting dance music to the harp:

> When I was in my early teens, I'd already been playing the whistle and the fiddle and lots of different things. I grew up playing both traditional and classical music, side by side. But what I wanted to do is play traditional music on the harp. I wanted to play dance music on the harp, which hadn't been done before ... There were hardly any teachers outside of Dublin. There was nobody decent at all outside Dublin, actually. The harp had become very much an urban instrument. It had become completely disassociated with the oral tradition, with people who played music in the countryside. The people who played dance music and slow airs, who were part of the oral tradition, learned the music orally.[3]

The type of harping pioneered by Ní Chathasaigh and Harbison represented a watershed in the history of the Irish harp. The dance repertoire associated with the oral instrumental tradition of piping, fiddle playing and other melodic instruments had never before been applied to Irish harping, which, as Ní Chathasaigh elucidated, was considered part of an urban rather than rural tradition. Philip Bohlman argues that the historic divisions between rural and urban in folk music are blurred in modernity: 'Urbanization topples one of the most sacred tenets of folk music theory: the distinction between rural and urban.'[4] The development of traditional style harping brought the harp into a new musical context, and integrated it into the 'rural' Irish music tradition. Historically, in Gaelic, and subsequently in Anglo-Irish, Ireland, the harper was a musician of high social prestige, who practised a solo art form, and whose only ensemble playing was at most accompaniment to song or courtly poetry. Dance music was associated with the peasant class and fell far beneath the harpers' social status. More significant than the application of a new repertoire in the 1980s was the revival of an oral transmission for Irish harping. Art-music style harping had fostered literate methods of transmission, while the 1980s transformation demanded an oral approach in order to integrate with the mainstream Irish instrumental tradition. This approach impacted technique also, as the classical technique of art-music style subsided in order to allow more fluent playing of improvized ornamentation and variation. Ní Chathasaigh's seminal 1985 album *The new strung harp* gave substance and credibility to this new style of Irish harping.[5] On this album, five tracks consist of tunes from the dance tune repertoire played at speed using a 'traditional' style. Carolan pieces and songs comprise the remainder of the album. Ní Chathasaigh arranged all of these pieces herself for the recording: none were arrangements composed by other harpists or composers, as had become the norm in many art-music style harp performances.

This new approach of playing the dance tune repertory by adapting ornamentation from other melody instruments allowed young musicians to engage with the mainstream instrumental tradition from which they had previously been excluded. Noted harper Michael Rooney commented in an interview that:

> I started off on the whistle and the fiddle … and concertina before I started the harp and as a result I was learning 'trad' and I was young enough so that when I started learning the harp … It is hard to play traditional music on the harp and what … I just assumed that you could. And I think that if you go in with that sort of notion then it takes the sort of difficulty or the whole psychological element out of it, so, yes, it had a huge impact, because every tune I was learning on the other instruments I was transferring onto the harp.[6]

Similarly, Kathleen Loughnane described her interaction with traditional music and musicians:

> So we were picking up ideas like everybody and essentially after that in terms of teaching, I can say the traditional musicians of the country. The singers have been my teachers, mainly, in terms of style. [...] It's the kind of unbroken continuous oral tradition that I've been very much in touch with since I was, [...] twelve.[7]

The results of such changes in the tradition have had pervasive effects. There now exists a vibrant tradition of traditional style harp in which the harp is used for the purpose of playing traditional dance music, without any recourse to music notation or composed arrangements. This last stage of revival was in fact a transformation with the result that the harp was integrated into a tradition of which it had never previously been a part. However, the term revival can be applied to the learning style and approach which now encompasses both oral and literate methods.

Style

The concept of style in Irish traditional music has been subject to much debate in the academic literature. The main issues focus on the determining features of style in relation to musical materials, expression and sometimes repertoire. Moreover, notions of individual, regional and musical style remain central to the discourse of Irish traditional music in the 'lived' experience of musical interactions at sessions and concerts, through online media such as listserves and fora and informal discussion among practitioners. Niall Keegan elaborates on this point:

> The use of the words of regional style both affirms the 'traditionality' of the performance and thus performer and also that of speech performer. The use of such terminology places the performance both geographically and diachronically in the context of a local social continuum … Speech about regional style is important in that it creates a sense of place, identity and tradition amongst many musicians.[8]

Given the relatively static nature of the repertoire of Irish traditional music, considering that the majority of the repertoire is 'traditional' rather than newly composed, it is therefore unsurprising that style occupies such a central place in the musical, academic and interpretive discourse of Irish music. When discussing developments in Irish harping from the 1980s onwards, a contextualization of style will demonstrate that this branch of harping stylistically adheres to the principles of mainstream Irish traditional music.

Keegan's article 'The verbal context of style in traditional Irish music',[9] outlines five parameters or 'conceptual units' of style in Irish music:

1   The style which is the Irish musical tradition.
2   The style associated with a particular instrument.
3   The style of any one of the musical 'dialects' which are char-
    acterized by different levels of predominance of certain tech-
    niques, methods and repertoire.
4   The style of an individual musician.
5   The style of an individual performance.[10]

The first of these ideas conceptualizes Irish music in relation to a broader
context of European or Celtic music. Its style and repertoire are
identified as Irish because they are differentiated from any other musical
culture. Mark Slobin's idea of micromusics provides a useful framework
here in terms of the relationship between interculture and superculture.[11]
While Keegan uses his first category to define what Irish music *is* or *is
not*, the argument is also applicable to Irish harping. Traditional-style
harping is 'traditional' because it adheres to the same musical principles
(oral tradition,[12] recognized repertoire, use of characteristic ornamentation, variation, phrasing, rhythm and approach) as Irish traditional
music. Harping in this style can be defined by what it is not; that is, it is
not newly composed or arranged art music that may or may not draw on
Irish repertoire for the basis of its musical materials. Additionally, it
follows the aesthetics and stylistic conventions associated with Irish
traditional music rather than those of 'art', 'classical', 'Western' or any
other type of harping. From this perspective, Irish traditional music is
taken as the superculture, and traditional-style harping is an interculture. The superculture, according to Slobin, 'provides a set of
standardized styles, repertoires, and performance practices that anyone
can recognize, if not like a common coin of the musical national
currency that we all carry around every day.'[13] In this case Irish traditional music is the stanardized set of styles, repertoires and performance
practices. The unique position of traditional style harping is as a distinct
entity or interculture to Irish traditional music.

Keegan's second formulation, 'The style associated with a particular
instrument', refers to possibilities or constrictions due to instrument
construction. For example, the low D cran on the pipes is generally cited
as a musical response to the physical demands of the instrument where the
standard long roll is impossible due to the absence of a lower auxiliary
note on the chanter. The particular physical characteristics of the harp
demand that attention be given to both the treble- (right) and bass- (left-)

hand styles. The construction of melodic style through ornamentation, emphasis, phrasing and variation is determined in traditional-style harping through the right hand while harmonic style is expressed through the left hand. Regional styles as they are commonly thought of in relation to other traditional instruments do not exist in the same sense in Irish harping but Keegan's fourth category, 'The style of an individual musician', is relevant to discernible styles in this tradition. The influence that harpists such as Janet Harbison and Michael Rooney have had can be observed in the style of younger harp players who imitate the chordal progressions and ornamentation devices employed by these harpists to great effect. Furthermore, to date the most widely absorbed changes in the tradition have often been as a direct result of the actions (or style) of an individual. Keegan's fifth formulation, 'The style of an individual performance', has special relevance to musical context. The context of performances associated with traditional-style harping are the performance contexts of Irish traditional music: sessions, music groups, concert performances, recitals, recordings and festival performances. Keegan's attempt to categorize the ways in which notions of style are formulated in the Irish music tradition are applicable to the conceptions of style relating to traditional-style harping. This theoretically helps to confirm the place of the harp within the mainstream Irish tradition.[14]

A second, standard source on style in Irish music is Lawrence E. McCullough's, 'Style in traditional Irish music'.[15] McCullough focuses in more detail on constructions of style based on the musical materials of Irish traditional music:

> The term 'style', as used by traditional Irish musicians, denotes the composite form of the distinctive features that identify an individual's musical performance. The elements of style can be translated into four main variables: ornamentation, variation in melodic and rhythmic patterns, phrasing, and articulation. These variables can be viewed as stylistic universals for this idiom in that their occurrence or non-occurrence characterizes every perform-ance and serves as the basic evaluative standards by which an individual's performance is judged by other musicians.[16]

Once again, the constitutive features of style as outlined by McCullough both theoretically and in relation to specific fiddle musical examples can easily be appropriated for analysis of harp style. While some harpists

compose new works for Irish harp, the majority of their musical expression is the interpretation of the dance tune, airs and harper-composer repertory. Therefore, stylistic affinities and differences manifest themselves in each player's manipulation of McCullough's 'variables'. A further aspect, unique to harping (and piano playing), is the use of the left-hand accompaniment which adds another layer of style to harp playing.

A third attempt at defining not only style but Irish music can be found in a publication by the Irish Traditional Music Archive (ITMA) entitled 'What is Irish traditional music?'. The following excerpt is quite extensive but it serves to justify my rationale that the harp is now situated (in its 'traditional' guise) within traditional Irish music as a subculture of both 'Irish' music and harping.

- It is music of a living popular tradition ... this does not form a static repertory ...
- Being oral music, it is in a greater state of fluidity than notation-based music ...
- It is European music. In structure, rhythmic pattern, pitch arrangement, thematic content of songs ...
- The bulk of it comes from the past, and is of some antiquity ...
- It is passed from one performer to another, or handed down from one generation to the next, more by example than by formal teaching ...
- Repertories and styles have originally evolved in given regions and localities, but natural processes of diffusion and especially the modern communications media have spread them more widely ...
- It is music of rural more than urban origins, a reflection of earlier population distribution ... Much traditional music is now performed and commercially produced in urban areas ...
- Solo performance, in which subtleties of style can best be heard, is at the heart of the tradition, but group performance is common ...
- harmonic accompaniment, when possible on an instrument, is generally of a simple kind ...
- The bulk of the instrumental music played is fast isometric dance music – jigs, reels and hornpipes for the most part;

1 Florie O'Connor

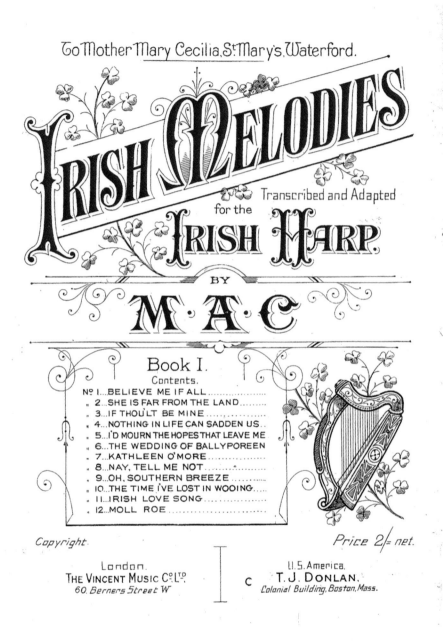

To Mother Mary Cecilia, St Mary's, Waterford.

IRISH MELODIES

Transcribed and Adapted
for the
IRISH HARP.

BY

M·A·C

Book I.

Contents.

Copyright.

Price 2/= net.

London.
THE VINCENT MUSIC Cº LTD.
60. Berners Street W

C

U.S. America.
T. J. DONLAN.
Colonial Building, Boston, Mass.

2 Front cover of Mother Attracta Coffey, *Irish melodies
transcribed and adapted for the Irish harp* (London, 1902)

3 Miss Margaret
O'Donoghue, *Irish Times*,
4 May 1929, p. 10

4 *Irish Times*, 6 May 1934, p. 4

5 Guinness
advertisement: 'Girl
Power'

6 Guinness advertisement from 1970s

7 Nancy Calthorpe New Orleans poster

"Music is the first faculty of the Irish; and scarcely anything has such power for good over them. The use of this faculty and this power publicly and constantly to keep up their spirits, refine their tastes, warm their courage, increase their union and renew their zeal is the duty of every patriot"
Thomas Davis

8 Thomas Davis quote by Nancy Calthorpe

9 Manuscript in Nancy Calthorpe's hand of 'Eileen Aroon'

10 Manuscript in Nancy Calthorpe's hand of 'Eanach Dhún'

11 Manuscript in Nancy Calthorpe's hand of 'Eanach Dhún'

12 Manuscript in Nancy Calthorpe's hand of 'Eanach Dhún'

13 Liadán performing at An Cúirt Cruitearachta, 2008

14 Replica of Lamont harp

15 Lamont harp facsimile (detail)

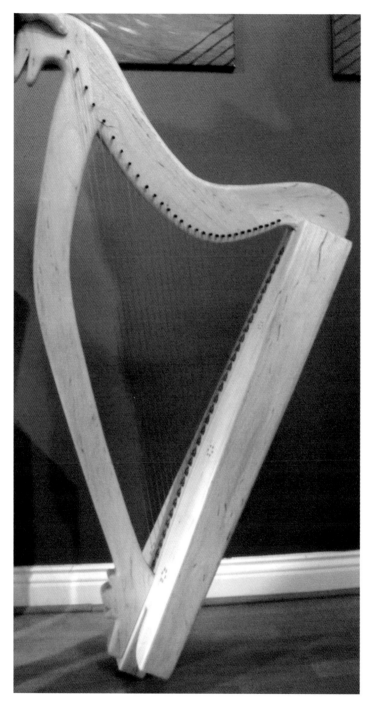

16 Facsimile of the Downhill harp

17 Egan harp (1821) at Birr Castle

18 Detail of ditals on Egan harp

19 CCÉ concert tour promotional picture

20 Water feature at Ritz-Carlton hotel, Powerscourt

21 Water feature (detail)

22 Irish harp symbol at Casalattico Irish Fest 2009

23 Samuel Beckett Bridge, Dublin

> slower listening pieces composed for an instrument or adapted
> from song airs form only a small proportion.[17]

Each of the ten points above can be used as a frame of reference for
understanding the nature of traditional harping. The harp represents the
fluidity of the tradition through its history and present state. In
traditional-style harping, the favoured transmission method is generally
oral transmission and the repertoire follows mainstream traditional
repertoire. The harp has one of the oldest living repertoires of all traditional instruments. Points six and seven affirm the interaction of history
with modernity and post-modern experiences of music that is constantly
negotiated by all traditional musicians. The variety of performance
contexts outlined in the ITMA article are similarly available to harp
players, while point nine brings harmonic accompaniment into the realm
of Irish traditional music. All of these aspects of 'what traditional Irish
music is' apply to traditional-style harping. In terms of construction
definitions, Irish harping can be said to have a branch of harping that
follows the stylistic parameters of traditional music in terms of musical
materials, repertoire, transmission and performance contexts. The
following musical examples clearly demonstrate how harp players have
transferred the conventions of traditional music to the Irish harp in order
to consolidate this aspect of the tradition. Harpists from the 1980s
onwards transformed the harping tradition through their application of
this music and approach to the Irish harp and therefore this style represents a further development in the Irish harp revival.

Musical Examples

Irish harping is characterized from *c.*1980 onwards by the playing of
Irish traditional music on the Irish harp – traditional-style harping. Five
key stylists, Máire Ní Chathasaigh, Janet Harbison, Kathleen
Loughnane, Michael Rooney and Gráinne Hambly (among others) have
published arrangements of their traditional tunes and written about their
understanding of the harping tradition. The following excerpts categori-
cally demonstrate that all of these harp players are working from within
the style and aesthetic of Irish traditional music. It is this aesthetic that
fundamentally underpins their musical explorations and boundaries, as
each player acknowledges the established tradition from the very outset.
Five key themes are identifiable throughout their writings. These themes,

namely transmission, ornamentation, variation, rhythm and harmonic accompaniment are also essential to general analyses and discussions of style, such as McCullough's, Keegan's and the ITMA's above. In relation to transmission Michael Rooney notes 'traditional Irish music is an oral tradition, one that is passed on from generation to generation'.[18] Similarly, Gráinne Hambly argues that: 'I learned the harp "by ear" and now teach using this method ... This is the traditional way of learning Irish music ... I believe that ideally harpers should learn by ear and work out their own arrangements, personal to themselves'.[19] The emphasis placed by these harpers on the traditional method of transmission highlights the importance of intrapersonal oral transmission. The topic of ornamentation likewise receives significant attention. Here Hambly's introduction is the most detailed and comprehensive wherein she provides important stylistic guidelines, directing readers to well-regarded sources on Irish music (Breathnach, Ó Canainn and Vallely) with regard to reading further about ornamentation in this idiom.[20] Furthermore, she acknowledges the now-common practice of borrowing ornamentation from other instruments:

> It is possible to achieve an effect similar to a roll on other instru-
> ments by repeating the same string ... The closest to this on
> another instrument would be the bow triplet used by fiddle
> players, an ornament now also being imitated on other instru-
> ments ... This ornament, which is particularly associated with the
> Northern style of fiddling, is sometimes referred to as a 'treble'.[21]

Michael Rooney links ornamentation with the creative process in traditional music:

> The musical ideas presented here such as ornamentation, variation
> and accompaniment only apply to one 'round' of the tune. I try to
> vary each round of the tune for my own sake and for the listener's
> enjoyment. Adding subtle ornaments and variations to the melody
> and accompaniment on the 'spur of the moment' is exciting and it
> is this creativity which gives the Irish musician his/her own musical
> style.[22]

As does Kathleen Loughnane: 'There is nothing sacrosanct or final about the written arrangements and it is only by listening to traditional musicians, especially the solo player, that a sense of style and ornamentation is acquired.'[23] This element of individual interpretation is one of the parameters by which style in Irish music (in general) is judged. Máire Ní Chathasaigh's cautionary tone also firmly establishes the importance of style and artistry in harp playing:

> It is important to point out that ornamentation is an essential feature of traditional Irish music. The music must *on no account* be simplified and stripped of decoration in order to make it technically easier to play: the soulless hybrid which results from such a simplification is not artistically valid. Finally, no amount of detailed technical direction from me will make the music come alive on the page. An extensive programme of listening to solo recordings of traditional musicians of a high calibre is most strongly to be recommended ... Recordings by uilleann pipers are perhaps most instructive of all: I suggest listening to anything by Willie Clancy, Séamus Ennis, Liam Ó Flynn or Tommy Reck, all of whom are performers of great subtlety and artistry.[24]

Personal creativity and the use of variation occupies a central role in the introductions of Hambly and Loughnane. Hambly argues that 'it is up to each individual performer to translate this basic outline into a musical performance. This is done by adding ornamentation, variations and putting their own "spin" on the tune'.[25] Similarly, Loughnane advises that 'repeated sections may be varied with extra ornaments or improvised variations ... Ornamentation is an essential feature of traditional music playing – there is an infinity of ways to ornament and vary a tune.'[26] The notion of a 'traditional' rhythm is also explained by Ní Chathasaigh, who gives detailed descriptions of the characteristic rhythms associated with polkas, slides, double jigs, slip jigs, hornpipes and reels in her introduction. Gráinne Hambly concisely argues that 'double jigs are notated in groups of even eighth-notes, but are never actually played this way. In performance the first note of each group of 3 should be accented and lengthened slightly to give the tune its characteristic lilt or swing.'[27] Finally, the application of harmonic accompaniment is the subject of discussion by Rooney and Hambly; Rooney explains that 'the use of seconds, thirds, fourths, fifths, sixths, sevenths, octaves, ninths, tenths and suspended elevenths resolving to tenths are all common features of my chordal accompaniment.'[28] Hambly describes the process of harmonic accompaniment as follows:

Performers should try to experiment with their own ornamentation and bass, as this is what Irish music is all about –
spontaneous musical expression within a given melodic and
rhythmic framework ... When approaching arranging, there are
three important features of Irish music to bear in mind. Firstly, this
music is primarily melodic in nature and nothing in the
arrangement or interpretation should distract from this. Many
Irish tunes are modal ... It is important not to superimpose
classical notions of harmonic 'correctness' on such tunes ...
Finally, this was originally music for dancing ... I prefer to avoid
full chords, sticking mainly to drones (octaves, 5ths or open 'bass'
chords i.e. without the 3rd) combined with occasional 3rds or
single notes.[29]

Both Hambly and Rooney acknowledge their personal preferences for
accompanimental and harmonic devices in arrangement. The issues that
permeate these introductions clearly demonstrate that these books are
conceived as existing within the mainstream Irish instrumental tradition,
with an understanding of the harp as simply another traditional
instrument. The theoretical discourse of style as it applies to traditional
music in general is replicated here in relation to the harp. While historically the Irish harp may not have been used for playing instrumental
dance music, it is absolutely evident that these harp players encounter
the same stylistic experience as do players of any other melodic
instrument and that the notion and title 'traditional' harp has become
synonymous with this particular playing style that has emerged in Irish
harping. Moreover, the following four musical examples show that the
treatment of the musical material, the melody, is subject to the very
processes that categorize traditional music, such as personal interpretation, ornamentation and variation.

In her arrangement of the double jig 'The Queen of the Rushes'
(musical example 15), Ní Chathasaigh notates ornamentation throughout (including detailed instructions on fingering). The open octaves
allow for more detail in the melody line without cluttering the overall
sound. As notated, the most prevalent ornaments are grace notes,
passing notes and added repeated notes. The repeated tones, such as in
bar two and evident throughout, give this version a rhythmic drive that
is quite characteristic of her playing. On her album *The new strung harp*
she also uses triplets and trebles in the first round of the tune. In the

Musical Example 15: 'The Queen of the Rushes', Máire
Ní Chathasaigh, *The Irish harper volume 1*, p. 23

second round she varies the written arrangement by increasing the
frequency and complexity of ornamentation, such as adding trebles to
the B in bar one as well as some changes to the melody, such as extending
the interval from a descending 3rd to an octave leap (B–B$_{I}$) in bar nine.
The syncopation in the accompaniment in part three of the tune adds
interest without obscuring the melody.

Gráinne Hambly includes two versions of the popular hornpipe 'The
Tailor's Twist' in her collection. She immediately asserts the continuity of
the tradition by citing both James Morrison (whose version was
recorded in 1935) and Noel Hill, two iconic players in the tradition. By
citing these she is demonstrating that the source for her music comes
from within mainstream Irish traditional music.

> This hornpipe was recorded by the well-known Sligo fiddle player
> James Morrison in 1935. I learned the tune from the concertina
> player Noel Hill, and this was one of the first tunes I arranged
> myself for the harp. Although it is written in even rhythm, it
> should be played more like triplet rhythm, with emphasis of each
> pair of eighth-notes.[30]

The left-hand accompaniment of the second version is more complex
than the first, with syncopation and arpeggiated chords where originally
there were sustained octaves. Hambly includes less in the way of
prescribed ornamentation than Ní Chathasaigh, having given a detailed
argument regarding individuality in her introduction. However, she does
highlight the conventional rhythmic emphasis usually associated with
hornpipes in the Irish tradition.

Musical Example 16: 'The Tailor's Twist', Version 1, Gráinne
Hambly, *Traditional Irish music arranged for harp*, p. 16

Musical Example 17: 'The Tailor's Twist', Version 2, Gráinne
Hambly, *Traditional Irish music arranged for harp*, p. 16

'The Wild Geese' is a standard tune in the traditional harp players'
repertoire. Nevertheless, Kathleen Loughnane gives it a unique
treatment here. Her notation of the air is extremely detailed by
comparison to the previous two musical examples, setting out the air
with detailed melodic ornamentation and technical devices (such as
harmonics) in the left hand. Loughnane's arrangement shows a clear
affinity to the *sean nós* style of singing as the original air is subjected to
frequent and elaborate ornamentation. Unlike arrangements of airs in
the art-music style, Loughnane maintains the melody in the right hand
throughout, or, in the singing register. The rhythm of the air when played
is free rather than in strict 3/4 time, but the notation of airs requires
some indication of meter.

Musical Example 18: 'The Wild Geese', Kathleen
Loughnane, *Affairs of the harp*, p. 12

Michael Rooney's collection of tunes differs from the previous three
in that it is a collection of original pieces composed by Rooney in the
traditional idiom. Irish traditional music is a living tradition, and new
pieces become integrated into the 'traditional' repertoire over time. It is
impossible to predict whether a particular tune will or will not become

integrated, given that such integration only occurs by regular performance of the tunes by the Irish music community.[31] Rooney composed the slip-jig 'Land's End' in 2004 while touring in the United States. 'Land's End' was a house where Rooney and his wife stayed in Montauk, Long Island. The important issue here is that Rooney has approached his composition from within the established melodic, rhythmic and harmonic framework of Irish traditional music. The first part of the tune essentially outlines the tonic and dominant triads. The second part is also based on an elaboration through melody of these chords, with brief instances of subdominant and sub-mediant. The tonal language used throughout is standard European or Western harmony, which is also the tonal language of many tunes in the Irish repertoire. Where Rooney's personal harmonic style comes to the fore is in his left-hand accompaniment. His chord choices extend the tonality of the tune, which could also be harmonized with very basic, diatonic chords should one wish to do so. However, Rooney seems to strive to create a slightly dissonant accompaniment in this instance, drawing on upper dissonances of diatonic chords. He utilizes a VII7 chord in bar two as a substitute for five and in bar seven harmonizes the crotchet F' with chord iv, giving a iv7 effect. In bar eight he employs a 4–3 suspension over the bass A, a device which he acknowledged a preference for in his introduction. The chordal pattern outlined in musical example 19 is maintained for the second part of the tune. The accompanimental style in this instance is consistent with Rooney's personal style of playing.

With regard to musical style, it is the case that the harpists I have discussed above, as representative of the broader harping tradition since

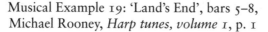

Musical Example 19: 'Land's End', bars 5–8,
Michael Rooney, *Harp tunes, volume 1*, p. 1

the 1980s, all approach the repertoire, both ideologically and stylistically, from within the musical, technical and educational parameters of Irish traditional music. The assertions they make in relation to the traditional process, prove true when their music is examined. This development in Irish harping can justifiably be described as a transformation of the tradition. Art-music style continues to exist and thrive, while the traditional style has developed as a distinctive branch concurrently. The popularity of this style is witnessed most visibly in the main fora for the development of this style: summer schools and competitions. The harp has now reached equivalent levels of competition entry at the CCÉ Fleadh Cheoil na hÉireann, so that the age categories – under-12, 12–15 and 15–18 – generally have fourteen competitors per category. This is the maximum number of competitors in any All-Ireland Fleadh.[32] Success at this competition offers prestige to the winners as it is a well-established and respected competition. The number of festivals catering for harp students is also increasing: the annual Willie Clancy Summer School added harp to its schedule in 2008 and now has four harp classes. Twenty-two out of twenty-nine summer schools and festivals cater for harp students and competitors annually (See Appendix 3). All of this serves to show that this branch of Irish harping has become established within Irish traditional music. Furthermore, the context in which this harping occurs is identical to the context and experience of other traditional musicians.

Context and experience of traditional harping

John Tomlinson, in his book *Globalization and culture*, argues that 'Globalization disturbs the way we conceptualize "culture". For culture has long had connotations tying it to the idea of fixed locality.'[33] While he rarely pinpoints any particular culture or subculture, Tomlinson's arguments have relevance to the discourse of culture in general, and to Irish music (which includes traditional-style harping) in particular. He uses the term 'deterritorialization' to describe a fundamental impact of globalization on the (post-) modern condition in which experience is not fixed to place:

> This experience [of deterritorialization] is fundamental to the way we live our daily lives in modern societies: it touches nearly all aspects of our mundane practices, it has become 'naturalized' and

taken for granted in the routine flow of experience and yet it is a complex and ambivalent cultural condition. It is important to stress this ambivalence and therefore to distinguish the condition of deterritorialization from the claim that global modernity, in its massifying, centralizing moment, is destructive of real localities.[34]

The concept of deterritorialization is applicable to the experience of traditional-style harping in the twenty-first century. The locations where this music is experienced are varied and far-reaching, as the music is not fixed to certain locales or landscapes. This is the same experience as occurs in the globalized performance of Irish traditional music. Hammy Hamilton commented in relation to the Irish music community that:

> I think the major value of these [technologies is] that because the Irish music world is very sort of spread out, you know. There aren't really that many people involved in it, but these days they're spread over a very large area. And, I think, it enables a very sort of disparate community of players and people involved in Irish music to be in contact with each other.[35]

Hamilton further acknowledged that 'just about everybody who is a professional, or even a semi-professional musician would rely on playing outside Ireland for the major part of their income.'[36] Irish harpers are not excluded from this condition. The Irish diaspora, particularly in the US, provides an important audience for Irish traditional music. Some of the biggest music festivals, such as the Milwaukee Irish Fest, take place in the US. Philip Bohlman notes in a similar manner to Tomlinson that:

> The music of diaspora at once describes the conditions of being displaced from a homeland, and it inscribes the history and geography that connect a displaced culture to that homeland, or at the very least to a place claimed as home. The music of diaspora is about places of being and places of becoming, of connecting the present with its absence of place to the past and the future, where place can be imagined as real.[37]

The touring schedule of prominent harp players shows that their audience are indeed global but that the music played by these musicians realizes the expectations of such audiences: that the music they encounter will be traditional Irish music, the music commonly associated with the 'homeland'. Merely performing to audiences throughout the world does not imply that the music is 'traditional', but rather the schedule of workshops, summer schools and Irish traditional festivals proves that traditional-style harpers experience their music promotion and audience interaction the same way that other instrumentalists do. The overwhelming majority of gigs, concerts and workshops take place in Ireland, the UK, Western Europe and the eastern United States, areas that represent the main centres of the Irish diaspora throughout the world. Where gigs have taken place outside of these routes, they have usually been at international harping events, such as events in Brazil, Paraguay and Italy. Despite Australia's continued popularity as a location for the Irish diaspora there is little evidence that harpists have included it in their touring schedule. Perhaps this is due to the often prohibitive expense of air travel to Australia from Ireland, given that the primary aim of tours is often a commercial one. The audiences for Irish harping appear to be located in the areas where there is a connection to the 'homeland' (Ireland).

The locations for Irish harping complement the map of 'Europe's Celtic fringe' used in Philip Bohlman's *World music, a very short introduction,* with harping activies adding a further area, the east-coast United States. In addition to belonging to the tradition that is Irish traditional music, traditional-style harping may also be conceived of as belonging to the broader Celtic music fringe. James Porter notes that the locations for Celtic music follow historical emigration patterns:

> the huge movement of populations from Ireland, Scotland and Wales in the eighteenth and nineteenth centuries have given rise to a contiguous New World cultural pattern of music-making which displays, nevertheless, two important differences from that of the Old: first, the language element is almost totally absent ... second, the local character of the idiom, even when the music stands on its own without a verbal text, has been shifted towards more homogenous aesthetic concepts.[38]

Furthermore, he argues that:

> Celtic musics, whatever the definition applied to them, have never existed in isolation, and searching for a 'pure' musical Celticity is

an unrealistic pursuit. Present-day, 'pan-Celtic' conflations are a different matter. They are of recent origin, and are part of a worldwide trend in many different kinds of musical activity over the last few decades.[39]

The participation of today's harpers in such Celtic events as the Festival Interceltique in Lorient, Brittany, and the Pan-Cetlic harp competitions follows from earlier harp players' participation in Celtic congresses and interaction with other Celtic traditions, such as the Ní Shéaghdha sisters' regular participation in these congresses and Mary O'Hara's sustained engagement with Hebridean folk song. However, participation in the Celtic music network of festivals and concerts does not negate a musician's Irish musical identity, rather: '"Celtic", unlike "Breton", "Gaelic" or "Welsh", is a third-order ethnic label based on a language group (cf. Germanic, Romaic, Slavic) rather than on a specific primary region (e.g., Munster Gaelic). Thus a layered notion of identity emerges, that individuals display variously depending on context'.[40] I agree with Porter's identification of a 'layered' identity, and using this interpretation, an Irish harpist can be described as being a 'harper' within 'Irish traditional music', which may or may not fall into the category 'Celtic'. Of all of the so-called 'Celtic' instruments, the harp offers particular associations of romanticism. This in itself is a common trope in the myth of Celticism: 'Romanticism is not primarily a creative process, but a re-evaluative process ... Romanticism is a re-evaluation, in the centre, of peripheral features.'[41] Furthermore, Bohlman pinpoints the harp as the most commonly employed musical realization of 'Celtic' identity.[42] He also refers to the layered identity at play: 'Musicians acquire credibility as Celtic by emphasizing authenticity, on one hand, and by consciously recontextualizing authenticity through revivals, on the other.'[43] That is, by emphasizing the very *Irishness*, and *traditionalness* of their music, Irish harp players can avail of the potential Celtic markets. This is done not through a hybridization of their music, but by situating it firmly in mainstream Irish traditional music, a ready-made cultural currency.

A further aspect of the development of traditional-style harping is that the harp has, at times, been integrated into music groups as both melody and accompaniment instrument. The most notable instance of this is harpist Derek Bell who performed with the Chieftains from 1974 until his death in 2002. Bell's virtuosic solo playing (which owes much in terms of technique to the concert harp) helped to substantially raise the profile of the Irish harp by the very merit of its visibility. For example, the Chieftains' album *Celtic Harp* was awarded a Grammy. This international recognition of their work, and their collaboration with traditional-style harper Janet Harbison helped to substantiate the harp's claim as a viable traditional instrument. All-female band Liadán also include harp as the centrepiece of their traditional band. In plate 13, the harp is playing in an ensemble with two fiddles, piano accordion, flute and whistle. This group have achieved considerable success to date, thus furthering the aural and visual presence of the harp in an ensemble format.

To conclude this chapter I would like to draw once more on Mark Slobin's 'Micromusics of the West, subcultural sounds' as a framework for viewing the current harp scene. The purpose of this chapter was to define and analyze traditional-style harping as it has developed over the past thirty years and as it exists today. The musical places and spaces occupied by this strand of the tradition are shared with mainstream Irish traditional music, but are, in ways, also shared by other branches of the Irish harping tradition, such as the art and song styles. Slobin's terms (superculture, interculture and subculture) can be applied as the basis for demonstrating complex layers of interdependency. Irish traditional music in this instance is the superculture wherein the instrumental and song traditions become secondary layers of intercultures. Traditional-style harping is a subculture of traditional instrumental music, but also has links to the song tradition through the 1950s revival. Likewise, the art-music style of Irish harping is a subculture of art music, instrumental (traditional) music and the song tradition. The wire strung/early-Irish harp revival is linked to Irish harping, the harper-composer repertoire and Irish traditional music (which in turn is at times 'Celtic' music). What this chapter demonstrates is that traditional-style harping occupies a complex role within 'harping' and 'traditional' music. However, it is through the experience of style and context that the harp can be interpreted as operating within one or other musical system. Furthermore, while some harpers may specialize in a particular style, this does not prevent them from experiencing an alternate type of harp music.

CHAPTER 6

The early-Irish harp in its modern context

This chapter explores the revival of the early-Irish harp as it presently exists in Ireland. The early-Irish harp (also known as *cruit, crott*, or 'wire-strung') is the principal term used to describe replicas or facsimiles of the pre-nineteenth-century lever harps (or neo-Irish harp). However, confusion regarding terminology persists, as Simon Chadwick explains:

> Terminology in this field is complex and ambiguous. I use 'early Irish harp' to refer to the historical instrument of sturdy shape and with metal wire strings. Especially in the 17th century, it was known in Britain and on the Continent as the 'Irish Harp'. Since it was indigenous to the Highlands of Scotland as well as Ireland, a more inclusive modern terminology is 'Gaelic harp' or, to avoid offending present-day Gaels who prefer the Victorian revival instrument, 'early-Gaelic harp'. Its name in Gaelic is *cláirseach* (Irish) or *clàrsach* (Scots).[1]

The revival has a particularly historical ethos and is situated largely within the 'Early-music' movement, in its broadest terms. Research has been undertaken into the early-Irish harp tradition by Colette Moloney,[2] Joan Rimmer,[3] Ann Heymann[4] and Gráinne Yeats.[5] The most detailed and important source on instrument construction, *The Irish and Highland harps*, was published by Robert Bruce Armstrong in 1904.[6] The revival of harp performance began in the 1970s with the work of Gráinne Yeats. Several other key performers have also been active, including Derek Bell, Paul Dooley, Ann Heymann and Siobhán Armstrong. The revival has links to other such revivals, such as the Gaelic harp (*clàrsach*) revival in Scotland through collaborations with Scottish harpers such as Bill Taylor.[7] This chapter will focus on instrument type and style, the role of revivalists, and transmission.

Instrument type and style

The early-Irish harps (which are sometimes referred to as wire-strung) that are played today are replicas (facsimile or otherwise) of historical Irish harps, such as the Brian Ború/Trinity College harp, the Dalway harp or the Lamont harp.[8] Potentially any extant harp could be reproduced in facsimile and played. Except on very rare occasions, the original harps are not played. The facsimile harps are based on a small number of extant Irish harps which, according to Simon Chadwick, number sixteen complete harps and two sets of fragments.[9] These include: the 'Queen Mary Harp' (National Museum of Scotland), the 'Lamont' (National Museum of Scotland), the 'Trinity College' (Trinity College, Dublin) (dating up to the fifteenth century); the 'Otway' (Trinity College, Dublin) and 'Balinderry' (National Museum of Ireland) from the sixteenth century; the 'Cloyne' fragments (National Museum of Ireland); the 'Kildare' (National Museum of Ireland), 1672; the 'Downhill' (Guinness Storehouse Museum) 1702; and the 'Bunworth' harps (Museum of Fine Arts, Boston), 1734.[10]

Siobhán Armstrong describes the importance of playing facsimile instruments:

> After that [buying facsimile of Trinity College harp] I realized … that is an important part of this work that we do as historical musicologists and instrument players, is that you should really be working hard, if you're interested, to try and have the most accurate facsimile you can have and that's a never ending search, because you can never build the perfect facsimile. There's too many parameters. It can never be quite perfect enough, but you should strive. And so this was pretty good, but it's not perfect, there are lots of things that are not right compared to the original. That now, as we look more and more at the original in Trinity, we can see; oh, this and that and the other and string spacing and idiosyncrasies here, there and everywhere.[11]

The Historical Harp Society of Ireland (HHSI) has made substantial progress in promoting the early-Irish harp by commissioning a number of facsimiles from harp maker David Kortier. During my tuition with Siobhán Armstrong as part of my doctoral research I was fortunate to be given the opportunity to rent two different facsimiles. The first of these was a replica of the seventeenth-century Lamont harp, which falls into the large low-headed Irish harp category (see plates 14 and 15).

This is a thirty-two string harp, strung with metal strings with a range of C to f". Following the historical method, two adjacent strings are tuned to the note G below middle C. These are known as '*na comhluighe*' and they are said to represent the divide between male and female on the harp.[12] There is no F in the lowest octave. The harp measures 97cm in length and is constructed with a mortise and tenon join at the top of the soundbox. The soundbox is made from willow, the neck and pillar are made from cherry wood. As is evident from plate 14, the facsimile has no carvings or designs. The soundbox is designed to be similar to the original one-piece soundboxes of these instruments. There are no holes at the back of the soundbox to change strings; this must be done through the front. As the detail in plate 15 shows, there are no levers or semi-tone mechanisms on this harp, as would be the case on a neo-Irish harp.

The second harp I was given access to was a facsimile of the Downhill harp (see plate 16). The Downhill harp was played by harper Denis Hempson. This is a large high-headed Irish harp. The Downhill facsimile is a thirty string harp, again with metal strings and a range of C to d". The tuning is identical to the Lamont in that *na comhluighe* (two adjacent G strings) are used and the F in the lowest octave is omitted. The harp measures 130cm in length. Mortise and tenon joints are used on the soundbox in this harp also.

There are no feet/balancing mechanisms on these harps, so they must be placed horizontally when not in use. Historically, they were played resting on the left shoulder, with the left hand for the treble and right hand for the bass. This is the opposite to the playing technique of the neo-Irish or concert harp. Ann Heymann was one of the first harpers to adopt this historical technique: 'I decided I better approach it the correct way so I started with playing with the left hand high, the right hand low; I couldn't figure out really any big reason why, why that would be not good; I thought it might make a difference.'[13]

The work of key harpers, such as Armstrong, Heymann and others such as Bill Taylor in Scotland, has resulted in a wider availability of early-Irish harps. The HHSI offers a rental scheme so that students can rent a harp before ordering their own. This serves a dual function: first it gives the novice harper immediate access to a harp and second it affords students the opportunity to try several types of harps before ordering one. Important makers include Paul Dooley (harper and harp maker, Co. Clare), David Kortier (Minnesota) and Davy Patton (Co. Roscommon).

Bodhrán maker Séamus O'Kane (Co. Derry) recently collaborated with harp maker Michael Billinge (Co. Cork) to make a replica of the Downhill harp for a TG4 documentary *Banríon an Cheoil* (Queen of Music).[14] Paul Dooley makes exclusively early-Irish harps, modelled on his own experiments during the 1980s to build a harp for himself to play. These are based on fifteenth-century harps. David Kortier makes early-Irish, neo-Irish (or lever harps) and electric harps.[15] His work has become quite prominent as he collaborates with the HHSI to produce facsimiles of extant early-Irish harps. Davy Patton is a sculptor and instrument maker. He constructs his harps as facsimiles of extant Irish harps using Irish willow. Colm O'Meachair (Co. Dublin) is an Irish harp maker who occasionally makes wire-strung harps.[16] These makers are responding to the increased demand for such instruments, particularly over the past eight years, since the inauguration of the Summer School of early-Irish Harp.

The playing style of the early-Irish harp is also quite different to that of the neo-Irish harp. Strings are plucked with the nails, rather than with the fleshy part of the finger tips. The hand is also in more of a 'C' shape with the fingers facing the strings. Thumbs can either be above or below the index finger. The sound produced by nail-plucked metal strings is vastly different to the sound of the neo-Irish harp. It has a much stronger and brighter tone, which rings out clearly. This in turn affects playing style and technique due to the sustained resonance of the metal strings. Damping must be regularly employed in both treble and bass hands in order to keep the harmonic resonances consonant. However, damping can also be used to create and dissipate dissonances where desired:

> So the idea of three [notes] in a row, you've got, dissonance. You have all these choices just when playing a melody line and so there is harmony, you've got dissonance, you have a tonal in dissonance against it resolving in, so it's really a linear aspect … When playing three notes in a row … I take out the middle note.[17]

Revivalists

The revival of the early-Irish harp occurred after the revival of the (neo-) Irish harp, which began in the 1950s. The early-Irish harp revival, therefore, did not coincide with either the folk music revival (in America and England in the 1950s and 1960s) or the early music movement led by Arnold Dolmetsch in the 1920s.

> While other early instrument traditions, such as harpsichord and lute, were revived during the early and mid-20th century, the early Irish harp remained neglected, and it was the 19th-century Romantic replacement that was revived instead. When interest did begin in historical reconstructions of early Irish harps, their so-called 'Celtic' provenance gave them second-class status alongside the more familiar classical instruments. What work was done happened in isolation; the instrument was rediscovered a number of times, for example, by Arnold Dolmetsch, Gráinne Yeats and Derek Bell.[18]

The revival occurred in Ireland, Scotland and Brittany. While in the Irish case, the harp revival had really only gathered momentum from the 1950s, the harp revival in Scotland preceded this by over fifty years. In c.1892 the Duke of Argyll asked a bagpipe maker in Edinburgh to make three *clàrsachs*. Six more were subsequently made by Robert Buchanan. These harps were modelled on the Queen Mary harp (dating to the fifteenth century), with some minor alterations. While the Feis Ceoil was instigating competitions in Ireland at the end of the nineteenth century, An Comunn Gàidhealach started a competition for *clàrsach* in 1892, which lasted up to 1909. In 1914 Miss Patuffa Kennedy Fraser emerged as a central figure in the harp revival. She played the 'Celtic' harp, made by George Morley in London, and sang Hebridean song to her own harp accompaniment. In the 1920s the Royal Celtic Society instituted more prizes for competitions and in 1931 Comunn na Clàrsaich (The Clarsach Society) was founded under the presidency of Mrs Campbell of Airds.[19] This society is still in existence today and organizes the annual Edinburgh International Harp Festival.[20] The revival gathered significant momentum in the 1970s with the emergence of performers such as Alison Kinnaird. Her 1978 recording *The harp key, crann nan teud*, while using gut-strung harp, drew almost exclusively on historical Scottish repertoire.[21] She subsequently began to play and record on wire-strung harp.[22] Other key harpers who specialize in Scottish repertoire include Bill Taylor and Karen Marshalsay. The 'revival' of the Breton harp can largely be attributed to Alan Stivell, who was born Alan Cochevelou and later took the stage name Stivell. He first played the

Breton harp in public in 1953, this harp being a replica of the Trinity College harp, built by his father, Jord Cochevelou.[23] His first album, *Telenn Geliek, harpe celtique*, was released in 1964 and was followed in 1972 with *Renaissance de la harp celtique*.[24] Stivell has continued to perform and record on harp and other Breton and Celtic instruments. Other Breton performers include the group An Triskell, featuring Pol and Herve Queffeleant.[25]

In Ireland, Gráinne Yeats was one of the first musicians to play a replica of a wire-strung harp. Around 1970, Yeats obtained a replica of the seventeenth-century Sirr harp from harp maker, Jay Witcher. At that time it was impossible to buy an early-Irish harp in Ireland. Yeats describes how she procured an early-Irish harp and describes Jay Witcher's role in the revival of harp construction:

> You couldn't get them, they weren't made. Nobody was playing wire-strung harps then. I went to America on one of my regular tours there, and I landed in a place classed Alamoso ... in Colorado. After that concert I was talking to a man from the college and he said, 'By the way, we have an Irish harp.' I expected it to be one of those Clarke harps. They're gut-strung and very small like an Irish harp, but an American-style Irish harp. He brought it out and it was a Jay Witcher. Well, Jay Witcher is the best harp maker of that kind in the world ... He began to make replicas of well-known harps, so when I saw this I was enthralled. I wrote to him and asked him to make me a harp, which he did ... I asked for the 17th-century style SIRR harp, and he made it for me. He's been making harps for me ever since, and we have become close friends. He revived the making of wire-strung harps. In addition, I revived the playing of them. So, between the two of us, we were proud of having re-started that.[26]

Yeats proceeded to revive the practice of playing the early-Irish harp, basing her interpretation on detailed study of the extant manuscript sources and playing using the traditional damping technique. She published several articles in the music journal *Ceol* on the historical harp tradition, and her 1980 book *Féile na gCruitirí* helped to raise awareness of the harping tradition.[27] Her 1992 double CD, *The Belfast Harp Festival*, remains of crucial importance as it brought the historical reper-toire to life using a historically appropriate instrument.[28] On one of the

CDs Yeats, playing the early-Irish harp, recorded music that Edward Bunting collected at the 1792 Belfast Harp Festival. The other CD contains a selection of Carolan's music, also performed by Yeats on early-Irish and neo-Irish harps.

Paul Dooley plays and makes early-Irish harps. His harp is modelled on the Trinity College harp, although he has added four extra strings in the bass register.[29] Dooley plays using the fingernail technique, but rests the harp on the right shoulder rather than the left (as did harpers up to the early nineteenth century). His approach to harp repertoire is unique as he combines historical repertoire (including music of the harper composers), traditional Irish dance music and Welsh music (as illustrated in the Robert Ap Huw manuscript).[30] Dooley's emphasis on traditional Irish dance music is unusual in comparison with other early-Irish harp performers, who mostly specialize in historical repertoire. For example, the majority of the tunes on his 1996 recording *Rip the calico* are from the dance tune repertory rather than that of historical harper-composers.[31] While Dooley's more recent recordings demonstrate more emphasis on historical repertoire, in performance he still combines dance and historical music.[32]

Ann Heymann is widely recognized as one of the individuals who has spear-headed the revival of early-Irish harp playing. She published the first tutor book for the early-Irish harp, *Secrets of the Gaelic harp*, and her first solo recording, *Queen of harps*, was a seminal development in the revival of the early-Irish harp.[33]

> Since the 1970s, Ann Heymann, who plays only the early Irish harp, has been the most important exponent in the field, and continues to lead new research and discoveries ... She is also responsible for most of the important new developments in the revival, including the study of key source texts, the interpretation of historical techniques and the development of working string regimes for replica instruments.[34]

Heymann's entry into the music of the early-Irish harp was through a revivalist route. She was influenced by bands such as Ceoltóirí Chualann and Planxty. She first began by playing harp with céilí bands in America:

> So I was working back in time really from traditional aesthetic, trying to find the earlier music of the harp and I actually started playing okay with a céilí band with whistle and brought the harp

into that, but played in Irish bars in the States, and that would be five nights a week, accompanying ballads and rebel songs and playing some dance tunes and Carolan, always with the intent of going back earlier.[35]

Heymann also plays on facsimile harps now, and at a workshop in Dundalk IT had facsimiles of the Trinity College and Dalway harps. Heymann readily acknowledges the importance of harp makers in facilitating her interpretation of early-Irish harp music.

> But the instrument itself has been absolutely essential to the development of my approach and playing techniques. The very existence of Jay Witcher's historical Gaelic harp copies in the early 1970s allowed me to begin my work, and all of my efforts since then have been aimed at most effectively transmitting musical messages contained within the instrument – freeing the instrument's voice, as it were.[36]

She travels to Ireland annually to teach at the HHSI harp summer school, with occasional performances in Ireland also. The main part of her work is US-based where she participates in a very active wire-strung harp scene.[37]

Siobhán Armstrong had a slightly different route into early-Irish harping. Her entry was through the early-music movement, in which she remains active. Armstrong initially studied neo-Irish and concert harp in Dublin with Nancy Calthorpe and Mercedes Garvey respectively.

> I started playing all kinds of other early harps first and early-Irish harp was the last historical harp that I started to play … I was doing a musicology degree at Trinity so while I was at Trinity I was more interested in Renaissance and Baroque music than anything else … I was trying to play things like Handel on my neo-Irish harp and my left hand would be buzzing changing all these semitone levers. So I knew the kind of music I wanted to play but I didn't quite have the harp on which I wanted to play it … in my final year at college, Andrew Lawrence-King, the early harper, came to one of the early music festivals … in Dublin … and played a concert where he played Spanish baroque harp and Italian baroque harp. I was entranced.[38]

On the completion of her studies at Trinity, Armstrong moved to Germany where she began lessons over the course of a year with Andrew Lawrence-King on early wire-strung harps. She gradually moved to the early-Irish harp and has focused particularly on this over the past ten years. The transfer to early-Irish harp was relatively easy for Armstrong:

> It was a hop, skip and a jump for me anyway because I already played with historical techniques, meaning that my fingers were sort of perpendicular to the strings rather than, fingers down, thumbs up ... I already had nails because I played Spanish baroque harp with nails and I was playing my *Arpa doppia* with nails, so I didn't even need to grow nails ... I could already do it, I just needed an early-Irish harp in front of me.[39]

Armstrong has made a very significant contribution to the revival of the early-Irish harp in Ireland as she is Chair and founder-member of the HHSI and course director of the annual summer school. She teaches in Waterford on a weekly basis, Dublin, Cork and Galway on a monthly basis, thus promoting further the early-Irish harp. Her recorded output is quite varied, ranging from solo early-Irish harp recordings, to collaborations with *sean nós* singers and early music ensembles.[40]

Transmission

In order to gain some insight and understanding into the early-Irish harp scene I studied with Siobhán Armstrong over the course of 2009. These lessons gave me an invaluable insight into the transmission methods and ethos of the wire-strung harp scene and Armstrong's involvement with it. The music collections of Edward Bunting are a primary source of teaching material, as harpers try to remain as close as possible to the historic tradition. The first tune I learned was 'Mailí Bhán', this being one of the first tunes that harpers in the seventeenth century learned.[41] Ann Heymann also made mention of this tune in her workshop:

> Well I'll start with ... the first hand position, this is from Edward Bunting's notebook; he publishes this in his 1809 book. But he got it from Denis O'Hampsey and this is one of the early tunes that student harpers were taught and it's kind of neat because the first tune is 'Fair Molly', 'Mailí Bhán' [plays segment of the tune]. Now it's interesting because that tune has the same hand position as, or

can have the same hand position as for 'Burns March', which was
the fourth tune taught [plays segment of the tune]. And also the
same position as 'The Butterfly', which was another one of the
early pieces [plays segment of the tune] ... Bunting says, that the
first piece, 'Fair Molly' ... 'fixed the student harpers troubled
hand'.[42]

This quote from Heymann shows the level of detail and scholarship with
which she (and others) engage with the early manuscript sources in order
to ascertain the most correct information. During my first lesson with
Armstrong, we worked from a handout with the notation, text and
supplementary information about 'Mailí Bhán'. The first system (above
the score) showed the set fingering patterns for both bass and treble
hands. There was no need to write fingering in on the score for this tune
as the harper places all of the fingers on the designated strings, as per the
directions, and then this position covers the full range of the tune. The
melodic material is partially shared between the treble and bass hands;
for example, the D in the melody line is played by the bass hand. A very
simplistic G-drone accompaniment is used in the bass here. This was
Armstrong's own arrangement of the accompaniment and as it is used
for the first lesson, it is understandably simple. Armstrong took this
particular version from Bunting's manuscript number 12; the words and
translation are from Dónal Ó Sullivan's 'Bunting Collection'. This was
quite an accessible air for the novice early-Irish harper as it provides the
student with an opportunity to play 'authentic' music for the harp using
the historical hand position mentioned by Heymann.

Several tunes of this type were completed in the lessons, including
arrangements by Armstrong of 'The Kerry Polka', 'Tallis's Canon', 'Aon,
Dó, Trí', 'Cill Chais', and 'Thugamar Féin an Samhraidh Linn'. All of
these were fixed-fingered tunes, progressively increasing in melodic
complexity and thus requiring more informed damping choices. New
techniques, such as the 'rest-stroke' (which is when the thumb plucks
one string and then 'rests' on the adjacent lower string as a damping
mechanism), were also introduced. Initially, Armstrong combines oral
and literate techniques, before moving towards manuscript-based
research with her more advanced students:

The most effective approach to teaching is whatever the best way
is for a student to take the information on board ... If I'm teaching

early-Irish harp, I tend to teach things by ear during the lesson and give them the music at the end of the lesson … and then work through the music at the very end of the lesson so that they can take it away and know that if they forget what they've learnt they can check it out on paper. Now if somebody can't read music at all, but they're interested, then you very, very slowly start them off doing that so that in the fullness of time they'll at least have a working knowledge of written music. With people who read music, then I still like to teach lots of repertoire without looking at the page because compared with say neo-Irish music, there's so much information that you need to … play a piece of early-Irish harp music because of the damping. So it's not just a matter of which finger plays which string but which finger is damping which string while another finger plays another string. This is an awful lot of information and it's difficult enough to pick up when you're showing somebody but it's infinitely … easier to sort it out by showing someone than to indicate it on a page. That's where the complexity really sets in.[43]

Armstrong included some Scottish repertoire in the classes. It is well documented by Bunting and others that Irish harpers travelled throughout Scotland and England in the sixteenth, seventeenth and eighteenth centuries, and it is probable, therefore, that they encountered the music of their Scottish and English contemporaries. An interesting piece learned was her arrangement of 'Wo Betyd Thy', taken from the Straloch Manuscript.[44] The melodic material of this arrangement is again divided between the treble and bass hands. Underneath the bass hand, the fingerings are notated. In this piece fingers in brackets related to fingers that rest on strings rather than play them. This gives the playing fingers more balance and strength. The technique of placing several fingers on adjacent sides of the melody/bass note also facilitates

(2)
3
(4)

Figure 4: Example of fingering notation of 'Wo betyd thy waerie bodie'

damping. The harper can then place sets of fingers on consecutive strings in order to damp and play at the same time.

Towards the final stages of my tuition, Armstrong moved to a more complex and detailed process. Instead of simply presenting me with arrangements that she had already completed, she showed me copies of Bunting's original manuscripts (or other collectors). The next step was to transcribe the notation from the manuscript source onto regular manuscript paper, leaving a staff for the bass accompaniment. The reasons that these needed to be transcribed are two-fold. First, the keys that Bunting notated some melodies in are not keys in which one can easily play on the wire-strung harp without re-tuning the entire instrument. Second, some of the manuscripts have several options for playing a tune. After transcribing and arranging a complementary bass for the tune, the fingering patterns for treble and bass hands must be worked out to accommodate damping. The final stage of preparation is then to incorporate ornamentation. This is done through consultation with Bunting's 1840 volume in which he published a detailed table of the types of ornaments used by eighteenth-century harpers, with the Irish terminology.

The early-Irish harp revival is consistently gaining momentum and rising in popularity, attracting new players to the instrument; however, the revival remains in its infancy. A 2010 television programme broadcast by TG4 and funded by the Northern Ireland Screen Irish Language Broadcast Fund (ILBF) shows that there is support for this music and its promotion. This programme documented the making of a facsimile Downhill harp by Séamus O'Kane and Michael Billinge and followed harper Nollaig Brolly's investigations into the early-Irish harp. The programme culminated with a commemorative concert of Dennis O'Hampsey's airs in Derry at which well-known harpers, including Nollaig Brolly, Laoise Kelly, Paul Dooley (Ireland), Alan Stivell and Myrdhin (Brittany), Alison Kinnaird and Bill Taylor (Scotland), and Ann Heymann (USA), played.[45] A further indication of the growing popularity of the instrument is the growing number of students attending the annual HHSI summer schools. In 2009, twenty-five students in total attended this festival. Moreover, there are facsimile harps available for rent and purchase, and an increasing number of recordings and year-round opportunities for tuition in Ireland. Clearly, the neo-Irish and early-Irish harp traditions have much in common, but, as yet, they are mainly operating in different performance contexts (the former is situated both in art music and traditional music, the latter in early music), with a different ethos evident in the two spheres. The revival, while strong, is still relatively small in scale, although it appears that it will continue to grow in strength.

CHAPTER 7

Transmission and Irish harping

Transmission in Irish music is a complex topic as it brings to light issues of style, context, musical meaning, educational settings and the place of Irish music in modern Ireland and among the diaspora. The harp tradition creates further complications as the two styles of harping, traditional and art-music style, reflect considerably different teaching methodologies. This chapter, ultimately, emphasizes the performative nature of effective transmission. Two different approaches exist in Irish transmission; the first, art-music style, largely follows the conservatory tradition; and the second, traditional-music style, is embedded in the practices of traditional Irish music. The social, cultural and musical aspects of conservatory transmission practices have been accurately described by Henry Kingsbury in his book *Music, talent & performance*.[1] Kingsbury keenly observes the musical considerations of artistic expression of the score in performance: 'taking meaning in this ... sense – the sense of music "meaning" as perceived feeling in performance – meaningful music making is of utmost importance to everyone in the conservatory'.[2] He also emphasizes the importance of personal interpretation, even when faced with the 'authenticity' of the score. His analysis is applicable to the art-music style of harping tradition, and his processes of interpretation and expression of musical meaning also apply to art-music style harping. Even though scores exist they must be musically interpreted, as with all art-music style performances.

This chapter will focus on traditional-music style transmission, drawing parallels with traditional music in general. While many harpers learn harping in a formal class-based setting, it is impossible to generalize as to the experience of all harpers. Therefore, a full consideration of transmission in the Irish context cannot be achieved without first examining the other common methods used by Irish music practitioners to experience and presumably, therefore, transmit Irish music. The many methods of Irish music transmission include: the master/student approach, transmission through methods of secondary orality (such as with music recordings) and the use of text-based resources. These methodologies can also occur via the medium of the internet (in addition to the conventional settings).

Traditional Irish instrumental music is generally described as an 'oral' tradition, as the main stock of repertoire is transmitted orally. The orality of this tradition is constantly referenced in guides to Irish music.[3] It is often recognized in scholarly literature, however, that the definitions of 'oral' and 'literate' are too limiting. Bohlman, Feld, Finnegan, Miller and Rice have all acknowledged the difficulties in applying highly defined theories of 'orality' and 'literacy' to musical cultures.[4] The dialectic of 'oral' and 'written' is blurred to such an extent in the Irish tradition that it provides an excellent arena in which to examine the interplay of oral and literate elements in the modern world. Ireland is a highly literate society and, therefore, in the case of Irish music, even though the tradition is described as 'oral', this does not rule out literate experiences. The oral nature of the tradition pervades its many facets, from transmission to performance, and to the processes of ornamentation and variation. Irish traditional music is often described as being passed on 'by ear', through the oral, or indeed aural mode. This mode is essential in ensuring transmission in its fullest sense. Performers of traditional music never use printed scores in live performance as this would seriously deviate from any traditional performance model. The oral nature of Irish music facilitates the creation of the particular sound world that characterizes this music. It is only through oral transmission and performance that ornamentation and variation can be improvized within performance contexts. However, the long-established presence of printed sources and the recent explosion of availability of on-line printed material, forces a consideration of how 'oral' Irish music actually is. Why do we constantly refer to its orality when there is an abundance of printed material available?

Two factors problematize the concept of orality as it relates to Irish music: first, the vast amount of extant printed material and, second, the cultural context of Irish music. In addition to a 'written history',[5] printed music collections of Irish traditional music span three centuries of publication. Anthropologist Jack Goody argued that 'Oral performance in literate societies is undoubtedly influenced, to different degrees, by the presence of writing and should not be identified with the products of purely oral cultures.'[6] This is certainly the case for Irish music, but without necessarily having negative connotations. The earliest collections of traditional Irish music, such as the 1724 collection of Turlough Carolan's (1670–1738) music, were produced for commercial gain.[7] Carolan's music was still played in harpers' repertoires at that time and therefore the explicit aim of his collection was not to preserve a dying art for prosperity. By the end of the eighteenth century, however, the art of the harpers was in sharp decline.

Edward Bunting was hired to transcribe the music at the 1792 Belfast Harp Festival in order to preserve some record of this declining art. Indeed, this festival was organized by antiquarians as opposed to musicians. Bunting's collections provided the music-purchasing public with a body of tunes that was rapidly disappearing from the repertoire of Irish music. Bunting's editorial practices have elicited much criticism, yet, from a transmission point of view, he can be viewed as one of the first in a long line of great collectors. The practice of collecting and publishing traditional music has flourished since the end of the eighteenth century, with George Petrie (1790–1866), Patrick Weston Joyce (1827–1914), Francis O'Neill (1848–1936), Séamus Ennis (1919–82), Breandán Breathnach (1912–85) and many more contributing to this area. All of these collectors used staff notation to represent tunes. However, in the field of ethnomusicology it is widely acknowledged that written transcriptions cannot fully express music in its fullest sense. Sumi Gunji, for example, commented on the difficulty of notating timbre: 'Even in the most detailed notation, however, direct indication of timbre is virtually non-existent, though dynamics, tempo and artistic intention are indicated through words and/or in signs.'[8] Ruth Finnegan offers a realistic judgment on the complex relationship between oral and literate in music that aptly encapsulates the issues as they pertain to Irish music: '"Orality" or "oral tradition" can be realized in manifold different forms which cannot be predicted *a priori* but must be discovered through detailed investigation and in full appreciation of the variety and complexity inherent in oral, as in written, modes of expression and communication.'[9] Finnegan's acknowledgment of the intricacies of orality and literacy is echoed by ethnomusicologist Steven Feld who asserts that 'it is impossible to come up with a list of formal traits that *only* characterize musics of oral tradition'.[10] Both of these statements can be interpreted as calling for a case-sensitive analysis of oral traditions that acknowledges the influence of both the oral and literate on music.

The central issue with relation to orality and literacy is the impact that both of these modes have on the transmission of Irish music. To transmit is defined in the *Oxford English dictionary* as 'to pass or hand on ... communicate (ideas, emotion etc.)'.[11] What exactly is being transmitted from one musician to another, or one generation to another in Irish music? The problem of transmission in the Irish context lies not in the discrete unit being transmitted. Transmission of the 'text' (which in the instrumental context is a body of repertoire consisting primarily of dance tune types, binary in form and thirty-two bars in length) is relatively unproblematic. Transferral of a tune text alone does not equate with true stylistic transmission. Simply playing the notes of a tune does not necessarily engender an authentic traditional performance (nor does it for any type of music). What other elements are therefore required in this music type to realize a traditional performance? The nub of the problem lies in the transmission of what I have labelled the intangible elements of Irish music. These elements refer to a body of tools or components that constitute traditional style. Lawrence McCullough acknowledged that style in Irish music 'denotes the composite form of the distinctive features that identify an individual's musical performance'.[12] I propose that these intangible elements enable, through a process of interpretation, an authentic traditional style (which demonstrates stylistically appropriate interpretation of rhythm, ornamentation and variation). The central intangible facets of style are the dual processes of variation and ornamentation, and the use of a specifically 'traditional' rhythmic emphasis. I have borrowed the term 'intangible' from UNESCO as their definition of intangible cultural heritage from the Convention for the Safeguarding of the Intangible Cultural Heritage aptly expresses the role of style in traditional Irish music.

> The 'intangible cultural heritage' means the practices, representations, expressions, knowledge, skills – as well as the instruments, objects, artifacts and cultural spaces associated therewith – that communities, groups and, in some cases, individuals recognize as part of their cultural heritage. This intangible cultural heritage, transmitted from generation to generation, is constantly recreated by communities and groups in response to their environment, their interaction with nature and their history, and provides them with a sense of identity and continuity, thus promoting respect for cultural diversity and human creativity.[13]

The dual processes of variation and ornamentation are fundamental to traditional-music style. Variation incorporates ornamentation, as both the addition of ornamentation and the alteration of melody notes serve to provide variation. The essential feature of this facet of style is that it is a continuous process, or a 'generative process' to use Goody's term.[14] Seán Corcoran highlighted the importance of process in traditional Irish music when he wrote that 'the term "traditional" ... stresses the processes involved in the music, and I think that the secret of traditional music, ultimately, has to do with the processes involved in its production and creation, and it is those processes that are of a wider interest, a wider importance'.[15] Each repetition of a tune should be different from each previous rendition. Each musician is expected to express his/her unique musical style within the communally accepted framework of ornaments and variations. Hammy Hamilton echoes this sentiment by arguing that 'it is the process and not the product which defines its Irishness'.[16] The nature of this process precludes the possibility of notating variation effectively or succinctly and therefore the process of variation remains in the oral domain. Moreover, the question must be raised as to the value of a fully notated score of one particular rendition of a tune, which in reality will still fail to provide for the traditional process. Likewise, rhythm is problematic to notate. Although metre in Irish music is regular, the internal rhythmic subdivision of the bar is an idiosyncratic characteristic of the tradition. This rhythmic division is subject to both personal and idiomatic influence; generally the rhythmic distribution of notes in each bar is unequal. That is, in a jig, for example, each note is technically 'worth' a quaver; in reality, however, musicians playing in a characteristic traditional style will rarely give the full rhythmic value to each quaver but will lengthen and shorten notes to execute a stylistic traditional performance. This is impossible to notate using any available notation systems to date, but is often described verbally as a 'lilt' or a 'lift'. I would argue that rhythm is perhaps the strongest stylistic feature of traditional music. Adrian Scahill also proposes this in relation to Seán Ó Riada and Ceoltóirí Chualann:

> [Ó Riada] considered [variation] paramount in the traditional style ... However, this perception of what is the most important and valuable element of a traditional performance fails to recognize that, on a more fundamental level, the original function of the music as dance music places a greater emphasis on a player's

ability to create a satisfying rhythm, what might be described as the 'lift' in music. Without this (which for the members of Ó Riada's group was a 'given'), the whole question of variation and even ornamentation, is meaningless.[17]

Niall Keegan argues further that 'rhythm is I would argue more accurately accounted for as the underlying aesthetic to this music, naturally so as it is a dance music'.[18] The pulse of Irish music is steady and simple although the actual rhythmic patterns are quite complex as the musician expresses his/her own personal style. Rhythmic attack is almost impossible to notate in Irish music. In Western art music attack is notated to facilitate the fulfilment of a composer's musical wishes as represented in the score. On the contrary, in Irish traditional music it is considered bad practice to imitate completely another player's style. Attack is therefore a matter of personal judgment which must be made with a consideration of the 'intangibles' of traditional music in mind.

A theoretical approach

Paul van den Bos, a music educationalist, proposes a theoretical framework for the transmission of world music.[19] This framework has also been used by Huib Schippers[20] and, in relation to Irish music, by Helen O'Shea.[21] It is therefore useful to asses this model in terms of its potential for Irish music transmission. Van den Bos articulates a divide along holistic and analytic lines as opposed to along an oral/literate dichotomy. First, the holistic orientation is one whereby the repertoire is transmitted as a whole, within the natural musical context. Oral transmission is generally used in this approach. Van den Bos employs the term 'concentric' to describe the process where the music is learned first roughly in its entirety, with details added at a later stage. The opposite approach is the analytic style, whereby separate abilities, such as technique, posture and rhythm are taken as starting point. He argues that this separation of the elements divorces the music from its natural context. The following table (figure 5) summarizes van den Bos' hypothesis.

The division of methodologies into such a sharp and clear contrast is again not applicable to the nuanced situation of Irish music pedagogy. Almost all of the elements on both sides of the table correspond to various aspects of teaching that are evident in Irish music transmission today, wherein there are three main modes of transmission: (1) formal

Holistic	Analytic
'playing the music'	'playing the instrument'
music remains in natural context	music 'split up' into separate abilities , i.e. embouchure and respiration, posture, rhythmical control, playing technique, reading written music, musical theory, expression and recitation.
repertoire is starting point	separate abilities are starting point
'real' repertoire	'pedagogical' repertoire
concentric curriculum	linear curriculum
oral transmission	transmission by (staff) notation
teacher shows, student imitates	teacher guides and controls student
learning action is implicit	learning process is explicit
teacher's role passive	teacher's role active
teacher must be good musician	teacher must be good methodologist

Figure 5: Holistic and analytic teaching: van den Bos, 'Differences between Western and non-Western teaching methods in music education', p. 173

instruction; (2) transmission through text-based resources and (3) transmission via the secondary orality of audio/visual material.

The internet and Irish music

The internet serves to facilitate transmission of the Irish music tradition across geographic borders at a previously impossible rate. Online sites allow for democratic input of information. Timothy Taylor acknowledges the value of the internet for 'students of culture': 'The internet is like a giant word-of-mouth network, providing useful information of all kinds to whoever has access to it, but also allowing students of culture ways to eavesdrop on conversations by "natives" of all kinds, providing bits of virtual ethnographies'.[22] In a study of music and the internet Bart Barendgret and Wim van Zanten, focusing on music in Indonesia, noted that:

> The three music domains – the local, the national and the global – exist in Indonesia today, not in opposition but in tandem …

> People live in a world of shifting identities, as they negotiate
> themselves as members of one or more local communities and a
> national structure, and are simultaneously linked to people all over
> the world through the possibilities of the present media-scape.[23]

The same situation applies to Irish music where the local, national and
global are experienced through the medium of the internet. Moreover,
Barendgret and van Zanten correctly advise that the internet is not a
'monolithic entity ... The internet is an amalgam of interacting, co-
existing techniques and practices.'[24] Marjorie Kibby views the internet
as a place for virtual communities based on common interests. She
defines community as being 'understood in the sociological sense as
meaning a group of people who share social interaction and some
common ties between themselves and other members of the group and
who share a defined place or area for at least some of the time.'[25] I
accept the application of this definition to communities of users of online sites as, in the case of Irish music at the very least, they share a
form of social interaction. Steve Jones points to the novel ways in
which music purchasers, producers and musicians have to re-negotiate,
through the internet, established patterns of behaviour as the music
industry undergoes significant changes, and also the ways in which the
internet facilitates transnational musical experiences.[26] Arjun
Appadurai highlights the roles of imagination and media in modernity:
'there is a peculiar new force to the imagination in social life today ...
One important source of this change is the mass media, which present a
rich, ever-changing store of possible lives'.[27] Irish music transmission
has been greatly aided by technological advances in recent years, not
least of which include Bryan Duggan's 'Tunepal'.[28] All of the above
scholars point to the importance of change that the internet has
brought to the daily lives of people around the globe.

The foundation of Comhaltas Ceoltóirí Éireann in 1951 stimulated
the now extensive network of group instrumental classes. The sheer
number of students learning Irish music in the past fifty years led to the
introduction into classes of notation as a memory aid. Two systems of
notation have emerged in popular usage: staff notation and ABC
notation. Both have numerous inherent difficulties for the transmission
of the traditional repertoire as neither can effectively notate accent,
personal style or the intangible processes of variation and rhythmic
subtleties. Figure 6 shows both staff and ABC notation:

D   E   F#   G   A   B   C#   D'

Figure 6: Staff and ABC Notation

The use of 'ABC' or letter notation relates to the letter names of the scale as written out alphabetically, not on the stave, and does not require the reader to have the ability to sight-read.

Many tune databases utilize ABC notation such as Henrik Norbeck's site.[29] Norbeck has amassed a collection of over 1600 traditional tunes, all notated in ABC notation. The index at the top left of the screen gives important details about the tune such as name(s), tune type, discography, meter or time signature and key. Midi files are also available for each tune. The designation 'Key G' implies that all Fs are sharp, unless otherwise notated. Within the tune text, each note is taken to be worth a quaver. A '~' implies a crotchet and a '3' denotes a three-note ornament. Notes in the higher register are written in lower case letters. This method effectively expresses the notes and approximate time value of the tune. It allows no possibility for rhythmic emphasis, ornamentation, stylistic variation or phrasing. In terms of transmission this very popular type of medium offers dubious advantages. Furthermore, the notation is quite difficult to interpret and the audio offers little or no similarity to a stylistic interpretation of a traditional version.

The problem of authority also arises with relation to tune databases. The entire concept of tune notation in an oral tradition is problematic given that tunes are constantly subject to change and variation. To publish a notated version of a tune implies that it is somehow more valid or correct than any other version and thus there is a value judgment contained within each tune text. Francis O'Neill, the great collector in Chicago, commented on this difficulty: 'it all depends on individual taste as to which version of a tune is the most meritorious; and as it has been transmitted orally … variants and diversity of settings have naturally multiplied.'[30] This issue was also expressed succinctly by Bohlman: 'To think of the piece as somehow "authentic" or even archetypal is to treat it as a text in the most restricted sense, that is, as isolated from performance and tradition.'[31] Despite Kiri Miller's criticism[32] of Jack Goody's work on the impact of the written word on oral culture, he does make a valid point when he argues that:

The version that was first written down gets invested with the authority of the ancestors who recited it, giving rise to the notion of an orthodox version from which others have strayed. But it might equally be maintained that in an oral culture the genuine version is that produced by one's contemporaries, not the oldest but the youngest, since this will reflect the influence of present interests rather than past concerns.[33]

Goody emphasizes the living and ever-changing nature of the tradition. The very processes that characterize Irish music, namely variation and ornamentation, demand that tune texts continuously undergo some form of change. Therefore, it is impossible to designate a 'definitive' version of a tune in the Irish context. In practice, the community of practitioners generally decide what is admitted into the music by choosing to play or ignore certain tunes. The community of users of internet tune databases generally self-monitor the quality of tune transcriptions posted. However, transcriptions of questionable authority can often be found.

The website www.thesession.org is one of the most popular internet sites for both tune texts and discussion. There are over 12,000 tunes on this site, with name, type and mode posted for each. Common problems include flawed transcriptions, an observation that can only be noted by a viewer who is already familiar with the tunes. While websites such as these offer a great service to traditional music, the obvious shortcomings of transcription of an oral tradition coupled with questionable authority must be borne in mind.

One of the most groundbreaking developments in terms of Irish music transmission lies in the area of audio visual recordings. Audio visual sites provide an online equivalent for CDs and DVDs. Viewers have a great level of control when perusing music in this context. Jones comments that such practices 'involve a concomitant social reshaping by shifting the sites of hearing and listening and of buying music.'[34] There is an abundance of historical and contemporary recordings freely available on the internet on sites such as YouTube and MySpace. The ability to watch and listen to musicians brings us a step closer to the music, despite our spatially-remote location. Material, such as a clip of piper Séamus Ennis, greatly enables transmission. This clip is freely available on YouTube. In this instance we can watch and listen to Séamus Ennis explain the history of the tune that he plays, referencing his father and the particular set of circumstances that led to the composition of this tune. Ennis learned this tune from a manuscript but had direct access to the composer of the tune:

> There's a reel I'd like to play for you, a reel composed by my father in 1913 or 1914. I found his manuscript at home and I learned the reel from the manuscript and he was delighted to hear me playing it. He called it 'The Morning Thrush' and he entered it for a competition in the Feis Ceoil I think, at that time, and won the competition. And he was inspired by a thrush which used to sing in the morning in a tree outside his bedroom window. And nowadays, I can hear the thrush at home and I can get some of the phrases of the tune from the thrush as I hear it. This is the way it goes, 'The Morning Thrush'.[35]

Ennis gives the above introduction before playing the tune. On listening to the clip it is clearly evident that Ennis incorporates variation, ornamentation and traditional rhythmic emphasis into his playing. The internet gives the viewer instant access to great traditional music such as this. This brings the viewer a step closer to the performer as they can see posture and technique in addition to experiencing the auditory reception of the music. Sites such as Youtube offer access to important historic recordings of the tradition and a move towards digitization and dissemination of material generally can be observed by several leading archive sources including the ITMA, CCÉ and the CMC. However, despite the increased reach and range provided through the internet, the static state of recorded music remains an issue for Irish music. The process of continuous variation becomes an impossibility with recorded music. The only context within which this is possible is live performance.

Discussion sites are similarly important in the transmission of ideas about Irish music. Transnational discussion on sites such as www.thesession.org and the various listserves devoted to Irish music bring a once localized music into a global network. Discussion sites serve to form virtual communities of participants. The social interaction is the discourse of Irish music which functions as a common tie between all members. Memory and place are also important markers of identity in such fora, as questions arise regarding regional styles, festivals (in defined places), and localized music events. These issues pervade Irish music performance, as argued by Sally Sommers Smith:

> A traditional performer can be relied upon to add a personal stamp to the performance of the tune, but the musician from

whom the tune was learned will also be recalled and named when the tune is played in public. A portion of the social fabric that bound the tune as it was played in the past is thus transmitted as well in the traditional process.[36]

Patricia Sheehan Campbell also argues this point:

> The making of music strongly reflects how it has been learned, and is informed by the particulars of its transmission – the what, who, why, when, where, and how of music's teaching. Teachers of music in cultures across the globe are wrapped up into the musical content itself and are connected to the lineage of musicians and teachers from whom they come, the meaning and value of the musical expressions, and the time, place, and function of the musical events within their culture. Such particulars vary from one setting to the next, so that the music's transmission as well as the sound of it will reflect the cultural ways in which the teacher-musicians and their students live.[37]

Moreover, the discussion of Irish music via the internet may serve to transmit perceptions about Irish music. Irish traditional music can be imagined, evoked and to some extent experienced within the context of the most up-to-date processes of modern communication. Discussions about Irish music in internet contexts emancipate that tradition from the localized setting of music lesson or session and allow partial transmission to take place in any location, time or space. The internet facilitates memory in Irish music as historical recordings, audio files and images become instantly available.

In 1998 Michael Tubridy described the traditional teaching process to Kari Veblen as follows:

> The way I teach is I play a little bit. I teach by ear rather than by music. I think that that's the way the music did come down in the past, and I prefer to hand it on the same way ... I pick a particular tune and I play a little phrase of it. And then everyone in the group plays it after me ... We carry on alternately like that until I feel ... most people know that phrase. And then I would play that phrase plus the next phrase ... And we carry on like that until we get the whole tune covered.[38]

Tubridy explains the basic process of traditional transmission but he does not acknowledge a very important element of this action, that is, the person-to-person contact that occurs in such a setting. Timothy Rice formulates an important mode for transmission that brings us a step closer to full transmission. He uses the term visual-aural-kinaesthetic as a three-dimensional term that fulfils the requirements of oral tradition.[39] In addition to listening to and seeing a performance, the student must also engage in the act of performance to fully experience music trans-mission. Live performance and transmission, therefore, go hand in hand. Tubridy outlined a version of this method, whereby the tune text is trans-mitted as are the intangible elements of traditional music: rhythm, variation and ornamentation. This person-to-person contact is essential for the musically meaningful transmission of traditional music. The live verbal, aural and musical interaction between musicians ensures that traditional music is performed and, therefore, transmitted in its fullest sense. Hamilton remarked on this notion of 'traditionality':

> this whole notion of 'traditionality' was indeed ... central not only to the verbal exchanges among musicians but by extension to their musical behaviour as well. Further thought made me realize that the kernel of this idea is the way in which musicians [and by extension the consumers of their music] appreciate music.[40]

Despite the store of opportunities for dissemination and transmission of music and ideas through the internet, a final cautionary note must be sounded. Sommers Smith rightly argued that:

> On-line groups, for all their knowledge and devotion to the music, cannot serve as organizations to teach music to the uninitiated ... They cannot ... supply the necessary personal response to that first half of the equation: listening, practicing, and finding one's own voice in the community of Irish traditional players. For that, the novice or the learning musician must rely on the personal contact, conversation, and encouragement that only an actual community ... can provide.[41]

To return then to the question of transmission, how does an assessment of the internet further an enquiry into transmission of Irish music? The internet's function can be described as a conglomeration of substitutes for tune books, CDs, DVDs, photographs, music shops and networking. However, without interpersonal contact and live performance, some elements of the tradition remain in the imaginary domain. There is no substitute for live improvised variation and rhythmic emphasis and these processes are clearly present in the case study that I will now draw upon.

Case study: fieldwork at Scoil Éigse, 2007

I conducted this fieldwork in 2007 at the annual week-long Scoil Éigse summer school that takes place the week before the All-Ireland Fleadh Cheoil (the most respected music competition for traditional instrumental music) run by the Irish music organization Comhaltas Ceoltóirí Éireann. Scoil Éigse generally employs teachers who are deemed to be excellent teachers and performers and who exhibit a traditional style. Many teachers at Scoil Éigse will have graduated from the Comhaltas-run teacher-training course TTCT (Teastas Teagaisc Ceolta Tíre, Teaching Certificate in Traditional Music) and may also have performed on Comhaltas tours. Musicians who qualify in first or second place in the provincial finals under the age of eighteen are awarded scholarships to Scoil Éigse. The general age profile for harp classes is from age ten up to eighteen, however, this is a guideline only as younger and older harp students often participate. In 1992 I first attended the Scoil Éigse harp classes as a novice harper, when there was only one harp class at the festival. In 2007 there were three harp classes, taught by Janet Harbison, Gráinne Hambly and Eileen Gannon and over twenty-three harp students, none of whom was a beginner. I decided to carry out my fieldwork here as Scoil Éigse presented an excellent opportunity to research harp classes in a very highly-motivated environment with some of the foremost teachers and performers of Irish harp gathered in the same venue. Scoil Éigse classes act as a microcosm of weekly classes and are an excellent example of the most common method of harp music transmission.

    The fieldwork took place on 22 August 2007 at the Sacred Heart Secondary School in Tullamore, County Offaly. The classes began at 10.00 a.m. and each was one hour long. At lunchtime students could attend concerts and workshops. In each class the teacher sat at the back of the class with all students sitting around in a semi-circle. This allowed both students and teacher to see and hear each other effectively.

In Gráinne Hambly's class students were exposed to and interacted with one of the finest harpers actively playing traditional music today. Hambly is an experienced performer and teacher, steeped in the traditional style. Her approach facilitated individual music expression (a fundamental aspect of the tradition) in an oral environment. She blended Rice's visual-aural-kinaesthetic mode with the approaches outlined by van den Bos. Hambly's verbal and musical interaction with the class served to expertly impart the intangible elements of Irish music in a palatable manner. In fact, it is doubtful that the students would even be aware that these processes are at work in their music.

Janet Harbison's class consisted of the most advanced group at the harp classes. She opened the class with a discussion of ornamentation:

> When you are going to do a tune the first thing you need to think is tune, ornamentation, variation. So the idea is that the tune needs to be by far and away the 'diva' of what you are doing. And the chording comes way, way down the list. Now the first thing I would do when I teach a tune, I'll start of with 'Banish Misfortune', do any of you play that tune?

Harbison played the tune melody twice for the class, utilizing plenty of ornamentation throughout and incorporated the left-hand accompaniment and variation into the second round of the tune. Harbison moved to the blackboard where she wrote some key terms for the students. 'Let's have a look what we're calling, as the parts of a tune, just so as you understand.' Harbison compared the concept of a tune with that of a poem and drew the following table on the board based on answers elicited from the students.

Tune	Poem
Part	Verse/Stanza
Phrase	Lines
Shapes (groups of notes)	Words
Notes	Letters

Harbison called out the fingering for the class as she played the first phrase of the tune. This group were the most advanced harp class at Scoil Éigse and picked up the music quickly. The group played this 'shape' several times. Harbison offered a more 'classical' fingering alternative to the students and left the decision with them as to which they would continue to use.

In order to aid the fingering process Harbison demonstrated two fingering shapes by playing them as chords. This is a common feature of concert harping whereby arpeggios are played as block chords for practice.

Musical Example 20: Block chords

The class played the two shapes together as one phrase. Harbison continued with the melody and immediately added ornamentation. She informed students that she would concentrate on ornamentation at a later stage and just worked on one ornament for this section. Again on fingering Harbison referred to the fingering patters. 'Now you are going to have a couple of stepping up patterns. Skip and step.'

Musical Example 21: 'Skip and step'

Harbison commented: 'down the line you've got a lot of options in terms of dressing up the tune and embellishing but for now we're going to stick to a good solid version of the bones of the tune.' The class then played the phrases they had learned thus far:

Musical Example 22: First three phrases of 'Banish Misfortune'

Harbison completed the first part of the tune with the part ending. She called out a fingering pattern for the students while playing this and pointed to the turns A, G, A and D, C, D in the penultimate and final bars. The first part was then played several times by the class:

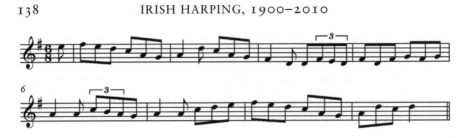

Musical Example 23: 'Banish Misfortune'

On the topic of fingering Harbison noted the need for consistency in fingering. 'It's the same thing as learning the words of a song. If you're not going to be consistent you are always going to be nebulous about trying to remember it. It will never sink in properly, because you're not allowing it to sink in if you're being too erratic.' She also spoke at length in the class about technique:

> Generally what I'm hearing is a lot more tension than you actually need in your hands [speaking to the entire group, not one individual], and I know there are some harp techniques that have your elbows out and your fingers working underneath; for Irish harping or for Celtic harping you don't need that amount of strength. So keep it comfortable but make sure there is a good punch to the rhythm, which doesn't have to be blasted out. The shaping of your phrasing as well is something to keep light and airy. Airy and effortless, but that doesn't mean that it's not under control; it's absolutely under control.

The class played the first part again after a count in to set the rhythm by Harbison. After the second playing, Harbison told the students to add in a bass drone of a D octave. Before moving to the second part of the tune, Harbison discussed ornamentation with the class, by asking them about the names that are given to various harp ornaments. Triplets, cuts, rolls were suggested by the students. Harbison clarified the last ornament by mentioning to the students that there are different types of rolls: four-note (short note, start note is excluded), five-note (long roll, start note is included), cut and tip rolls. Harbison noted that while the triplet roll is easier and more fluid the cut and tip roll was actually the proper roll. Harbison performed the first phrase with two alternative types of ornamentation. The first was with a cut and tip roll and the second, with a five-note roll.

Musical Example 24: Use of cut and tip roll

Musical Example 25: Five-note roll

When playing these rolls Harbison advised the students to dampen the lower neighbour notes so that they would not ring out longer than the desired time.

Harbison continued to discuss trebles (three notes in the time of two on one string), explaining that these could be done using fingers 1, 2, 1 (thumb, index finger and thumb) or with fingers 4, 3, 2. When the note preceding the treble was also on the same note, Harbison advised the use of 3, 4, 3, 2. The fingering pattern 2, 1, 2 could also be utilized. Each of these three alternatives gave a slightly different rhythmic attack and tone. Harbison allowed the class time to practice each of these before instructing the students to close their eyes and identify aurally which one of the three treble types she was playing (4, 3, 2/ 2, 1, 2/ 1, 2, 1). The students correctly distinguished between the treble types. She warned, however, that 'You're not going to turn cartwheels in your hands to do things when it's just not convenient, convenience is everything! But, variety is also everything. So, getting stuck into a set arrangement is a no, no, as far as I'm concerned, because that's where the creative thing just stops ... The idea is to embrace and incorporate these into your playing.' This emphasis on ornamentation and variation is characteristic of Hamilton's notion of 'traditionality'.

The group learned the second part extremely quickly; having worked with Harbison since the early morning, they were now very familiar with her process. The group easily played through this part twice before Harbison moved to the third part. Again, this was taught in much larger sections than the first.

Musical Example 26: Part 3, 'Banish Misfortune'

Harbison then demonstrated two alternate variants of the part.

Musical Example 27: Variant 1

Musical Example 28: Variant 2

Harbison played two further variants using a combination of rolls and triplets to demonstrate to the possibilities for ornamentation in this phrase and she then warned the group 'Don't ever get fixed! Is there any reason for you guys to get fixed into an edition of something?'

The group performed the basic version together three times, after which Harbison gave the students an opportunity to play the version twice through and to experiment with ornamentation. After learning the remainder of the part, Harbison discussed variation with the class:

> So there's no bit of any one tune that has to stay the same twice. And that's part of the skill of playing traditional music ... There are another couple of steps that I teach when I am teaching arranging. You really focus on the tune first because that's what relates to everybody else. That is what all of the other instruments are doing. And that's what they are going to be hearing you doing. If you're going to be doing an interesting and messy accompaniment they're not going to hear anything other than a mess. If it's complementary then it will probably be quite minimal.

A student asked Harbison to play the tune once more so that it could be recorded. As with the other groups, most students took the opportunity to record the tune as a memory aid for later. Harbison played a fast, lively and highly skilful rendition of the tune, demonstrating the processes of ornamentation and variation about which she was speaking to the group.

The case study presented in this chapter gives practical examples of the concerns of practitioners of Irish traditional music when transmitting music. Several factors are important in transmission: tune text; the traditional processes of ornamentation and variation; rhythm; and notions of 'traditionality'. Harbison's class combined all of these elements, with a significant amount of time devoted to discussing ideas about transmission and the tradition. Similarly, the internet offers a further medium of study as it presents a microcosm of the traditional music community, where the discourse of Irish music remains important.

CHAPTER 8

Gender and identity

The harp, in its Irish, Celtic or concert-harp form, has a particularly strong female association, perhaps more so than any other instrument. For example, a study by Griswold and Chroback showed the harp as rating the 'most' feminine in a sex-stereotyping of musical instruments survey.[1] The harp on the world stage has historically been gendered as female, particularly since the growth in popularity of the concert harp in eighteenth-century France. The changing gender associations of the harp in Ireland (from predominantly male up until the eighteenth century to predominantly female from the twentieth century on), in addition to the now popular association of the 'female' with 'harp', demands that Irish harping is examined as a gendered discourse, rather than solely in terms of a historical narrative. Marcia Herndon argues that 'the study of music and gender, then, is not simply a matter of describing male and female domains, styles, and performance types. The focus on gender and sex, biology and culture, adds depth to the analytical understanding of issues and problems'.[2] What is significant about the changing gender associations of the Irish harp is the extent to which it became (for the majority of the twentieth century) conflated with female identity and female music making, in terms of both the aural sound world and visual imagery. If the harp is a 'female' gendered instrument, are the implications then that it is representative of feminine attributes? This chapter will look at the relationship of music, gender, identity and the harp (as instrument and icon) through an analysis of a gendered history of the instrument; song texts; visual imagery; and identity and the representation of culture.

A gendered history

The history of the Irish harp during the seventeenth and eighteenth centuries has been particularly well documented, especially when compared with the written accounts of other Irish instruments at the time. Partly because of their high social status and partly through memoirs and written accounts (such as those by Arthur O'Neill and Edward Bunting) we have access to biographical, social and musical information about many of the most prominent harpers of those two centuries. The lifestyle of the travelling harper was an arduous one, which involved a significant amount of travel both in Ireland and Britain, usually on horseback, in all conditions.[3] Many travelling harpers were blind, and took up the harp as a means to pursuing one of the few career options open to a blind person at that time. Both Turlough Carolan and Denis Hempson were taught by females: 'at twelve years old he [Hempson] began to learn the harp under Bridget O'Cahan; "for", as he said, "in these old time, *women* as well as men were taught the Irish harp in the best families, and every old Irish family had harps in plenty"'.[4] While fewer performers were female, the role of teaching, even in the seventeenth century, was one that was considered appropriate for women. None of the most prolific and well-known harper composers from the fifteenth to nineteenth centuries (such as Cornelius Lyons, Piarais Ferriter, John and Harry Scott, Cearbhall Ó Dálaigh, Nicholas Dall Pierce, Ruaidhrí Dall Ó Chatháin and Arthur O'Neill) is female. However, by the twentieth century, the Irish harp had become almost completely associated with females, with two notable exceptions – Derek Bell and Michael Rooney. The revival of the wire-strung harp represents a more balanced gender divide, perhaps because of its lack of a gendered association with females in the twentieth century.[5] Women have had a steady, if limited, representation throughout the history of the Irish harp. At the harp festivals in Granard female representation varied. In 1781, one out of seven competitors was female; in 1782, there were two out of nine, as was the case in 1783. They were all competing for monetary prizes in a competition run by James Dungan in an effort to promote and restore the Irish harp tradition.[6] Likewise, in the Belfast Harp Festival of 1792, there was one female competitor (Rose Mooney), who incidentally had been third-place prize winner in all of the Granard festivals and was again at the Belfast Harp Festival. Her achievement at competition shows that her standard of playing must have been compa-rable to that of her male counterparts, if not quite as good as Charles Fanning or Arthur O'Neill.

The history of the harp in the nineteenth century is less well documented than in the seventeenth and eighteenth centuries. This is most likely due to the fact that despite efforts to maintain the harping tradition in its traditional form, the socio-musical climate had changed to such an extent that this was no longer feasible. Furthermore, the pervasive influence of the European concert harp was beginning to be felt in four main areas, namely musical style, gender associations, performer respectability and harp construction. The feminization of the Irish harp coincided with both the European feminization of the instrument and the dramatic decline in popularity of the Irish harp in Ireland at the end of the eighteenth century. The Granard and Belfast harp festivals and the subsequent harp schools in Dublin (1809–12), Belfast (1819–39) and Drogheda (1842–5) ultimately failed to reignite widespread demand for harping as it had previously been known. Moreover, when the harp was taken up by musicians in the nineteenth century, they operated in a vastly different social context to harpers of a century earlier. The antiquarian efforts of the late eighteenth and early nineteenth century (such as the work by Bunting, Petrie and Joyce among others) served to glorify and romanticize the Irish harp as an instrument of Gaelic antiquity. By the nineteenth century, the context of music-making had changed significantly. Harpers up to the eighteenth century found employment by travelling from house to house entertaining. However, in the nineteenth century, music making was often provided by members of the house themselves in the form of chamber music or 'drawing-room' entertainment. Thus, as William H. Grattan Flood explains:

> Between the years 1803 and 1823 the harp was taken up as a 'fad' by many titled dames, and hence a passing popularity. Lady Morgan tells us that she treated herself to an Irish harp, made by John Egan in May, 1805, 'as the first fruits of her literary earnings by the publication of the *Novice*' ... In 1809 the Marchioness of Abercorn and Lady Aberdeen purchased harps from Egan, and in 1811 there were further orders for the national instrument. Finally in 1822, Charles Egan published a *Harp Primer*, 'being a familiar introduction to the study of the harp', which was reprinted in 1829. He also issued *The Royal Harp Director* in 1827.[7]

When Egan began producing his Irish harps, he was catering to a very different market, in which the harp was being used as a drawing room instrument, often as accompaniment to song. The intricate designs and colour schemes of these harps (while far removed from the robust wire-strung harps) further situated the harp as the instrumental manifestation of Irishness. Egan's introduction of ditals allowed for the introduction of chromaticism to the harp, which facilitated a shift in the musical styles associated with the harp (see plates 17 and 18).[8]

The musical needs of this new drawing room audience for harp music were met by publications that were adaptable for both harp and piano, such as those by Thomas Moore. Flood laments the diminishing efforts of the harp societies in the mid-nineteenth century and notes that when the harp next came to prominence it was as a symbol of the Irish Ireland movement: 'Then came the Famine, and alas! the harp was allowed to become neglected till [sic] the Irish Ireland movement, inaugurated by the Gaelic League, and fostered by the Celtic Literary Society and kindred associations, again galvanized the national instrument into life'.[9]

The new popularity of the Irish harp as a drawing room instrument gave an element of bourgeois respectability to the instrument and also furthered its reputation as an instrument for music making in the home. It was considered to be a ladylike instrument. This was not unique to Ireland, as the concert harp had already a century-long identity as a 'respectable' instrument for women to play. An English conduct book of 1811 described the suitability of the harp:

> The shape of the instrument [the harp] is calculated, in every respect, to show a fine figure to advantage. The contour of the whole form, the turn and polish of a beautiful hand and arm, the richly slippered and well-made foot on the pedal stops, the gentle motion of a lovely neck, and, above all, the sweetly-tempered expression of an intelligent countenance; these are shown at one glance, when the fair performer is seated unaffectedly, yet grace-fully, at the harp.[10]

The respectability now associated with the harp was perpetuated through a new form of transmission that matched that of the piano, compared to the traditional oral methods of transmission by the harper composers and travelling harpers. Catholic convent schools, which catered exclusively for Catholic girls, run by nuns of various orders, became, from the end of the nineteenth century, the main vehicle through which the harp was taught. This intense feminization of the instrument, through female teachers (mostly nuns) to female students, ensured an ever-increasing feminization of the harp into the twentieth century. This

feminization of the instrument was a result of a confluence of circumstances. The suitability of the harp for convent students helped to
popularize it in convent schools; the existence of nuns teaching the harp
further cemented its feminine associations; and, almost all public
performances (such as competition and Celtic Congress performances)
were by females. This feminization was almost a self-fulfilling prophecy;
the harp was taught by women to girls. The cycle continued in this
manner for most of the twentieth century.

The teaching of harp through convent schools, therefore, propagated
a female-dominated tradition. The implication for the harping tradition
was immense: at the end of the eighteenth century the harp was
considered a male-dominated musical expression of Gaelic culture, by
the nineteenth century its association was with middle-class drawing
rooms and by the twentieth century it was perceived as a 'female'
tradition associated primarily with Catholic convent schools. The legacy
of the nineteenth century resulted in a female-dominated tradition
throughout the twentieth century. The role of convent schools and their
preoccupation with socially acceptable behaviour had a direct effect on
the style of Irish harping in Ireland until around the 1960s. Harpists
were encouraged to sit to the side of their harps as this was considered to
be more ladylike. Mary O'Hara, for example, consistently adopted this
posture throughout her playing career. Laoise Kelly also noted that she
was expected to play using this posture when she first commenced harp
lessons: 'The first year I learned I sat to the side of the harp. The two legs
to the side of the harp. It was lady-like'.[11] Therefore, even the posture
adopted by many harpists during the twentieth century served to
reinforce the association of the harp with women.[12]

Song texts

Alan Merriam argued that the 'expression of general cultural values
revealed in song texts can be carried further to a study of the underlying
psychological set or "ethos" of a particular culture'.[13] From the
perspective of a gendered history, song texts convey clear meanings
which can be 'read' by audiences and music consumers. The song repertoire associated with the Irish harp belongs mainly to the 1950s revival
period when the harp served as an accompaniment to the voice. The
particular songs popularized at this time clearly demonstrate an idyllic
vision of an Irish Ireland, thus further romanticizing the image of the

harp. Philip Bohlman argues that music plays a vital role in the construction of perceptions and ideologies of the nation state:

> Music helps make the nation by altering our perception of time. More skilfully and subtly than other forms of artistic expression, music finds its way into the temporal boundaries where the myth and history of the nation overlap and create complex myths about what we want a nation to be and what it is.[14]

The song repertoire in this era portrayed a mythical interpretation of Irishness and Irish life. Stylized interpretation of the female in song texts served to strengthen the notion of the harp as a female instrument. Indeed, the song texts (when analysed for gender content) did not embrace contemporary feminist ideals of the modern female, but instead harked back to an imagined, innocent Ireland. These song texts were much at odds with the sociocultural climate in Ireland during the period from the 1950s to the 1970s. Historian Terence Brown described the rapidly changing decades in Irish history during which these harpists made their careers. The 'stagnant' 1950s gave way to a rapidly changing society in the following decade:

> The 1960s and 1970s were therefore to be decades of rapid social and economic change, which stimulated much debate and controversy in the country. Indeed, those two decades of Irish intellectual and cultural life were notable, as we shall see, for reassessments and revisionism, for artistic and literary efforts to adapt to change, and for an increased public involvement in an informed Irish self-awareness.[15]

Irish society witnessed widespread urbanization in these decades, with the general population experiencing a different lifestyle to that of their parents' generation. As my analysis will show, the song/harp combination that emerged in the 1950s (and thrived into the 1960s) did not musically mirror the sociocultural context of the day. Neither was it aligned with mainstream traditional music. Four elements served to distinguish the harpists of this era from other Irish traditional musicians. First, the song texts recalled a romanticized notion of Irishness; second, the song style used, while popular in its day, was quite theatrical at times as opposed to following a 'traditional' or 'sean nós' style. Third, harpists

adopted an intentionally ladylike posture, which was not done for any
other instrument; and fourth, the transmission of harping through
convent schools served to consolidate its association with females and
produced a highly stylized musical fashion. For example, the song 'Kitty
of Coleraine', popularized by Mary O'Hara, tells the story of young
Kitty dropping her pails of buttermilk on the way back from the market.
Although the love interest element remains timeless in the song, the
remainder of the text and even the vocabulary used reinforce a stylized
interpretation that implies a rural life filled with innocence.

> *Kitty of Coleraine*
> As beautiful Kitty one morning was tripping
> With a pitcher of milk from the fair of Coleraine
> When she saw me she stumbled
> The pitcher down tumbled
> And all the sweet buttermilk
> Watered the plain
> 'Oh what shall I do now?
> 'Twas looking at you now
> Sure sure such a pitcher I'll ne'er meet again
> 'Twas the pride of my dairy
> Oh! Barney McCleary
> You're sent as the plague to the girls of Coleraine'

The pastoral love song portrays a young girl happily carrying her pail of
buttermilk home from the fair, when at the first sign of a man she is
incapable of even keeping her balance or continuing on with the job she
had set out to do. A similarly popular song among harpists was 'The
Spinning Wheel', which depicts an idyllic pastoral love scene where two
young lovers trick the girl's grandmother. The chorus describes the girl's
joyful immersion in the domestic act of spinning the spinning wheel.

> *The Spinning Wheel*[16]
>
> Verse 1
> Mellow the moonlight to shine is beginning
> Close by the window young Eileen is spinning
> Bent o'er the fire her blind grandmother is sitting
> Is crooning and moaning and drowsily knitting.

Chorus:
Merrily, cheerily, noisily, whirring,
Spins the wheel, swings the wheel, while the foot's stirring.
Spritely and lightly and airily ringing,
Sounds the sweet voice of the young maiden singing.

Verse 2
'Eily, a chara, I hear someone tapping'
''Tis the ivy dear granny against the glass flapping'
'Eily, I surely hear somebody sighing'
''Tis the sound mother dear of the autumn winds dying.'

Chorus

Verse 3
There's a form at the casement, the form of her true love.
And he whispers with face bent: 'I'm waiting for you love
'Get up on the stool, th'o' the lattice step lightly
And we'll rove in the grove while the moon's shining brightly.'

Chorus

Verse 4
Slower and slower and slower the wheel swings,
Lower and lower and lower the reel rings
Ere the wheel and the reel stopped their spinning and moving
Through the grove the young lovers by moonlight are roving.

Once again, this song text portrays a happy and innocent pastoral scene. Mary O'Hara and Deirdre Ní Fhloinn were two of the most popular singer/harpists and therefore the songs popularized by them became inextricably linked with the harping tradition. The gender bias described in the songs above demonstrates how the song texts were not a reflection of the ordinary lives of Irish women, but a romanticized interpretation of an idyllic Irish life, accompanied by the ultimate symbol of Ireland. Bohlman further describes the use of folk song as a symbol of an imagined or ideal past:

> Folk songs thus become evocative symbols of the past, and they legitimize the traditionality of a contemporary context by virtue of their symbolic value. It is not important (or possible) that a specific historical moment and place be represented; nor is there any

awareness that musical styles, genres, and repertories are juxta-
posed in ways uncharacteristic of any past. Rather, folk music,
because of its new timelessness, carries the weight of continuity
and tradition.[17]

The 'ideal' symbol of the past is represented by the charming females
both in and singing these songs.

The Irish language song texts popularized for harp accompaniment
created a further slant towards a female bias in the songs. One example of
this is Deirdre Ní Fhloinn's 1958 album, *Irish traditional songs*.[18] Out of
twenty-one tracks on this album ten are love songs, three are lullabies, five
are either pastoral or domestic with the remaining three divided between
comic and political. The role of women as culture bearers in post-colonial
contexts has been the subject of academic debate. In two contrasting
cultures, Ireland and India, studies have highlighted the importance of
women in the promotion of a nationalist ideal or, in the Irish case, 'Irish
Ireland'. The legacy of the Irish Ireland movement that began during the
era of colonialism had lasting effects into post-colonial Ireland. The ideas
laid down by this movement were still quite prevalent in the early decades
of the Irish Free State and the subsequent Republic. Frank A. Biletz
describes the work of Mary Butler in the promotion of 'domestic nationalism' at the turn of the nineteenth century:

> An article titled 'Irishwomen's Work', which appeared in one of
> the first issues of the *United Irishman* in March, 1899, suggests the
> way in which the prevailing 'separate spheres' conception of
> gender relations could be adapted to provide a significant role for
> women in nation-building. Its author, 'Máire', addressed both the
> mothers and 'maidens' of Ireland, arguing that in working for the
> national cause women did not need to clamor for 'our rights' nor
> to 'thrust ourselves into the position of men'. Rather, she
> maintained, 'we can be womanly and pure as our own blessed Ida,
> and yet help to keep first what Erin has not yet lost – her nation-
> ality.' In order to bind 'the sacred ties of Mother and Motherland',
> 'Máire' urged the women of Ireland to teach patriotism to their
> sons along with their nursery songs ... Combining the new ideas
> of cultural nationalism with the prejudices of social conserva-
> tivism, 'Máire' told her fellow Irish women that they could play a
> vital part, without stepping outside their traditional role, in the

movement to transform their country. 'Mother, sister, wife and maiden', she exhorted, 'you can work well for Ireland, each in your own sphere'.[19]

A similar argument was presented in the Indian case with regards to the role of the mother in the promotion of nationalism

> The mother of the nineteenth century was now identified with the 'motherland' or *Bharat mata*. Literally translated *Bharat mata* means 'mother India' ... The idea of *Bharat mata* was propagated through poetry, literature and the movies. Invariably, the image was of a crowned and beautiful woman in 'shackles' weeping 'tears of blood', or of the same woman holding aloft a trident and leading her countless sons and daughters to battle.[20]

In this case it is the mother's role in the home to promote nationalism through cultural products. The gendering of India as female also relates to the Irish context. The long tradition of *aislingí* in Irish poetry is comparable here, where 'Ireland' appears in a vision to the poet as a young woman. The song 'Róisín Dubh' is perhaps the most well-known of these. The prevalence of lullabies, pastoral songs and idyllic love songs on Ní Fhloinn's album represents a musical manifestation of this promotion of a suitable 'Irish' culture.

Visual imagery and the Irish harp

One of the most striking features of the harp as a visual image is its beauty in terms of shape and decoration. From the earliest extant examples of Irish harps (such as the Trinity College harp), the instruments have been decorated and, at times, bejewelled. For example, a nineteenth-century concert harp manual described the appropriateness of the harp for a young female: '[The shape of the harp] is so elegant, and the appearance of the harpist is so graceful, that it only seems suitable for a woman when she is young and beautiful'.[21] During the eighteenth century the Irish harp was appropriated as a symbol for Irish nationalism, an association that lasted up through the twentieth century.

With the foundation of the Irish Free state in 1922 (and subsequently the Irish republic in 1937), the Irish harp was adopted as the official emblem of the Irish state. The Irish harp then carries with it a long history of symbolism and associations not just of the feminine but of Irishness also. When harpists began to release harp recordings in the 1950s the image was often central to the overall record design. Visual depictions of the Irish harp on album covers offer telling insights into how the harp is both perceived and promoted. Keith Negus, in writing about album artwork, argues that: 'The visual image is often the first signal to a potential customer that an artist exists and immediately connotes a type of music, an attitude and a lifestyle; it denotes the artist as a particular type'.[22] Negus further elaborates on this point by bringing all of the album artwork into the equation:

> The cover of an album defines an artist in a specific way, locating them as a particular type of human being and as a product placed within the market categories of the music industry. The artwork and iconography is there to seduce the consumer to purchase the product. But album sleeves also explain how the music contained within them should be understood, interpreted and appropriated. Here album sleeves can enjoy a degree of independence from their specifically commercial function.[23]

Negus' arguments are both relevant and applicable to the Irish harp tradition. Album covers draw attention to the music type initially, as these are often the first point of contact for any potential music consumer. When album sleeves contain more than just texts, the artist offers further interpretation and presentation of their work.

Mary O'Hara has been the most prolific recording artist on the Irish harp to date. She has released over twenty albums as a solo artist and also features on many compilation CDs. O'Hara was the first solo artist to produce an Irish harp and voice record, in 1956 (followed shortly afterwards by Deirdre Ní Fhloinn and Caitlín Watkins). A sample of O'Hara's album covers are described as they illustrate Negus' arguments in relation to the role and function of album covers within the Irish harping tradition. O'Hara's 1956 album *Songs of Erin* depicts a smiling O'Hara sitting to the side of her harp on an old wooden chair. The chair evokes an Irish country kitchen or cottage. O'Hara's femininity is emphasized through an off-the-shoulder top, underneath a woollen shawl. This type of woollen shawl is specifically feminine and Irish, much as is the instrument she is playing. The second album cover, *Love songs of Ireland*, does not include a picture of O'Hara but of a pastoral scene of an Irish whitewashed cottage. Here, the Irishness of the music is identified, rather than the gender of the harpist. However, as argued previously, the song types also portray a gender-stylized interpretation of the Irish female. O'Hara's 1958 album, *Songs of Ireland*, emphasizes the Irishness of the music and musician through O'Hara's green clothing (and red hair), matched by the green-coloured background of the album. Here, the curved shape of the harp complements O'Hara's side-profile. Her position in the right foreground, looking down, with her hair tied back, emphasizes the curve of her neck and side facial profile. *Mary O'Hara's Ireland* is perhaps the most feminine of all these five album covers. Her gentle posture at the harp, in a drawing-room setting, recalls the nineteenth- and early twentieth-century respectability associated with the instrument. She is dressed in a formal peach-red coloured gown that reinforces the drawing-room image. Again, her posture to the side of the harp is ladylike. On O'Hara's album, *Recital*, she is pictured at the front of a serene lake scene, resting her arms on the harp. This image captures both the feminine (through O'Hara's presence) and idyllic Ireland (with the lake scene) in one picture. This encapsulates the strong associations of the Irish harp with both of these elements. [24]

Deirdre Ní Fhloinn's 1958 recording, *Irish traditional songs*, has an illustration of Patrick Street, Cork, by artist Ronald Clyne, on the front cover. This illustration appears to be of a late nineteenth-century scene, with horse and carts, pedestrians and horse-drawn carriages travelling on Patrick Street. While the front cover (where the harpist's name is mispelt Ní Fhloinn displays an urban scene, it is an antiquated image. The inside sleeve notes show rural-based images, thus maintaining a link with the notions of 'traditional' lifestyle. There is no apparent gender bias in the cover image; however, the sleeve notes (which contain all of the song texts in Irish with English translations) include four further pictures. One is of Ní Fhlionn playing her harp, one is of an unnamed harbour, and one is of a countryside scene with mountains and a bog. The last picture is of a woman sitting outside a whitewashed cottage spinning at her wooden spinning wheel. This presents a stereotypical image of an Irish woman, at domestic labour in the home. The woman is smiling in the picture and looks quite content at her work, a common theme in the songs popularized by harpists of this era. [25]

Traditional-style harpists tended to move away somewhat from the extreme stereotyping evident in the above early recordings. However, the feminine associations of the harp often filtered through in more subtle ways. For example, Máire Ní Chathasaigh's 1985 recording, *The new strung harp*, while it avoids the use of green, recalls nationalist associations of the harp with a word-play on the United Irishmen's motto 'It is new strung and shall be heard'. Butterfly images on the front cover could be interpreted as female, as they are commonly used as a popular motif in young girls' jewellery and dress.

Laoise Kelly's 1999 album, *Just harp*, plays on the imagery of the harp and nature. The photo-shoot for the album was obviously taken outside, on more rugged terrain than is commonly pictured in harp scenes. It also possibly posits the west of Ireland as a source of the tradition. On the front cover Kelly is pictured laughing and facing the camera rather than gazing into the middle distance with a serene expression on her face. Musically, her approach to the repertoire challenges preconceptions about traditional-style harping as she interprets the dance music with great speed and virtuosity. A series of pictures of Kelly and other well-established musicians in the Irish music scene are included on the inside sleeve (such as piper John McSherry, one of the founding members of traditional band Lúnasa). The inclusion of these pictures references the role of the harp in traditional style as an ensemble instrument. The cartoons of Kelly throughout the sleeve notes serve to further illustrate her new and exciting approach to traditional-style harping. In Kelly's artwork, there is little in the way of gender stereotyping, as Kelly attempts to present a vibrant depiction of her harp style.

Derek Bell's artwork differs significantly from that of his contemporary female harpers. His 1975 album, *Carolan's receipt*, offers a changed perspective from that of his female counterparts. Rather than picturing the performing artist, a well-known image of Turlough Carolan (painted by Francis Bindon) is presented for the cover artwork. In doing this Bell emphasizes the historicity of the harping tradition and also references the most well-known male harper in the Irish tradition. Bell in this case seems to justify himself as a male harper in a female-dominated tradition. His 1989 recording, *Ancient music for the Irish harp*, for example, draws on the male harping tradition of the seventeenth and eighteenth centuries. The front cover of this album is a close-up picture of the Downhill harp. This harp, which was made in 1702 by Cormac O'Kelly, is now owned by Guinness. The Downhill harp is one of the finest extant examples of an eighteenth-century harp and was the harp played by Dennis Hempson, the last harper at the 1792 Belfast Harp Festival to use the fingernail technique of playing.

Album artwork represents a form of communication between artist and audience; however, not all visual imagery of harpers falls into that category. In order to assess gender associations of the Irish harp from a different perspective, I have analyzed the journal of CCÉ, *Treoir*, over a thirty-year period from 1972 to 2004.[26] The statistics reflect a general perspective towards the harp as a female instrument over that time. It is clear that there is a bias towards including pictures of female harpers (in either a solo or a group context) rather than male harpers. The Comhaltas practice of using costumes for their Irish, British and American tours is clearly seen in these pictures as many of them were taken from official tour group photo shoots. Moreover, Comhaltas consistently endeavours to include a harp in the tour group ensemble. The musical role of the harp player (the majority of whom are female) is to provide harmonic accompaniment to the ensemble in addition to playing a selection of solo numbers.[27] Comhaltas also favours including the harp and harper in smaller group pictures of concert tour groups. Comhaltas' visual representation of male harpers differs significantly from their representation of females. First, 48% of male images were of well-known historical harpers. As observed regarding Derek Bell's artwork, this reinforces the maleness of the tradition. Furthermore, where living harpers were pictured, the majority of these were either Derek Bell or Michael Rooney.[28] The following statistics were drawn from the overall analysis:

Total number of pictures of harps/harpers: 220
- Female: 192
- Male: 21
- Harps: 7

Female pictures
- 163 are of female harpists in a group setting. This is equal to 85% of the total number of pictures with female harpists featured in them.
- 4 were publicity shots.
- 25 Solo pictures.

Male pictures
- 10 are historical = 48% of total number of 'male' pictures;
    - Of those ten, Turlough Carolan features in 40%, others 60%.
    - Of total male pictures, Turlough Carolan features in 19%.

- 8 living harpers = 52% of total number of 'male' pictures;
  - Michael Rooney, 45%
  - Derek Bell, 10%
  - other = 45%

When female harpers are pictured, they are often in CCÉ concert tour costumes. However, male harpers are mostly pictured in their own clothes. These costumes rarely challenge gender stereotypes, as they are usually full length with luxurious materials and often with elements of eighteenth- to nineteenth-century design. The costumes serve to reinforce the historical nature of the Irish tradition, but also reference a form of middle- or upper-class dress that was not always historically associated with Irish traditional music. Harpers are not singled out for special dress for the concert tours all female tour members are required to wear similar style costumes (see plate 19).

Solo female harpists are occasionally pictured (11.3% of all pictures). These tend to emphasize the femininity of the harpist. It is notable that within the date range used for this study, a very narrow range of 'Irish' musicians has appeared in the pictures that feature the harp. A relatively small number of harpists appear, but they are used frequently for a series of pictures. Most are young girls (late teens to early twenties) who represent an unchallenging interpretation of an 'Irish' musician in addition to an unchallenging depiction of the female.

Where pictures of male harpers do appear they tend to be dressed more informally than do their female counterparts. For example, an image of Michael Rooney playing solo harp (most likely taken at a Fleadh concert), from *Treoir*, 29:1 (1997), depicts him 'in action' rather than posing for a picture with the harp. The harp in this context is also the primary music-making instrument in the image, rather than an accompaniment to ensemble.

The other type of male picture used is the historical-harper type. Carolan, as the most well-known of all historical harpers, features in four out of a total number of ten pictures with historical harpers. These images are usually accompanied by an information article about the historical harp tradition. These serve to reference the historical nature of the harp tradition, but in its male guise.

Issues of gender remain pertinent to the Irish harp at present. They have informed the discourse of Irish harping for the past two centuries and have had a direct impact on the harping repertoire and presentation of the harp in media. Despite the growing number of male harpers in the Irish tradition, it remains impossible to pass judgment as to whether the gender imbalance of the twentieth century will recede in the present century. The harp's potency as a symbol of Ireland has most likely reinforced the gender stereotypes of the instrument due to its usage in stage Irish contexts and in the promotion of Irish culture. The reproduction of uncritical presentations in publicity material and album artwork has not challenged gender stereotypes associated with the harp to date. However, a decline in the extreme feminization of the instrument from the mid-twentieth century to the present day has been observed, and thus holds promise for a future rebalancing of the gender divide in Irish harping.

Identity

Martin Stokes' important volume *Ethnicity, identity and music* offers some relevant and applicable insights on music and identity for the Irish harping tradition. He argues that music is an important identifier of place and that: 'The musical event, from collective dances to the act of putting a cassette or CD into a machine, evokes and organizes collective memories and present experiences of place with an intensity, power and simplicity unmatched by any other social activity.'[29] Stokes is certainly not the only commentator to argue for the identification of music and place; however, his concise introduction is useful here.[30] The identification of music and place is an important function of the harping tradition, as both visually and aurally it has served to identify music with Ireland: as a visual symbol and emblem of Ireland; and in its role through its musical interpretation of the music of Ireland (in all of the styles possible on the Irish harp). Stokes interprets music as generative rather than reflective of meaning: 'music is socially meaningful not entirely but largely because it provides means by which people recognize identities and places, and the boundaries which separate them.'[31] The association of place and identities with music is a crucial aspect of diasporic music making and consumption. The harp's identity as a symbol of Ireland has aided its musical popularity in the key centres of Irish diaspora, namely Britain and North America. Stokes' assertion that music generates meanings allows for the meanings and identities of music to change over time, as has been the case with the Irish harping tradition. Musical meanings have been readily adopted and interpreted by nation states and governments throughout the world: 'Music is intensely involved in the propagation of dominant classifications and has been a tool in the hands of new states in the developing world, or rather, of those classes which have the highest stake in these new social formations.'[32] Ireland is no exception to this. While the Irish government has often been criticized for a lack of state support for 'music in Ireland' in the broadest sense of the term, it has frequently drawn on the visual/aural symbol of the harp for the promotion of the state.[33] The harp has generated multiple identities over the past century and continues to be interpreted in a variety of musical and extra-musical meanings. These multiple identities of the harp, in its various art, traditional, revivalist and wire-strung guises, complicate the notion of a single 'identity' for the Irish harp.

John Baily's contribution to Stokes' volume further stresses the importance of music as an expression of identity. Before discussing the Afghan case in detail he argues in more general terms that: 'The point is surely that music is itself a *potent* symbol of identity, like language (and attributes of language such as accent and dialect), it is one of those aspects of culture which can, when the need to assert 'ethnic identity' arises, most readily serve this purpose.'[34] If music is a potent symbol of identity then the harp is doubly potent given that it has been used as the official emblem of Ireland since the late fifteenth century when King Richard III used the harp on his crest.[35] Hélène La Rue points out that musical instruments have long been employed to identify status and gender, and that 'perhaps one of the most familiar instruments denoting national identity is the Irish harp ... The link of the small harp and Ireland ... [grows] from the use of this type of harp as an important cultural unifier and tool'.[36] While some of La Rue's analysis of the harping tradition is overly generalized, she correctly recognizes the inextricable link between the harp and Ireland. This type of broad identity is relevant although it does not necessarily respond to discrete styles and musical practices now evident in the harping tradition. John O'Flynn's recent book *The Irishness of Irish music* attempts to articulate the variety of ways in which musical styles are perceived as 'Irish'. He proposes that:

> Perceptions of Irishness in music come to be mediated through style in a number of ways. First, the general style category of Irish

traditional music is imbricated in most Irish people's conceptions of Irish music, though what is understood by 'traditional' and 'Irish' can vary considerably between and among different groups and individuals, depending on a range of social contexts and values (this is particularly the case with traditional-derived hybrids). Second, style, as it becomes linked to beliefs about musical authenticity, operates as a central articulatory principle when specific musical acts and/or musicians are appraised in terms of their potential Irishness *and* their musicality.[37]

A plurality of perceptions in relation to Irish music can be seen from this qoute. First, a broad definition of 'Irish music' is applicable to a wide range of musical styles, genres and contexts; the harp responds to a number of these in its various contexts. Second, O'Flynn points to the more discrete labelling of specific genres and styles by musical practioners. Notions of authenticity regarding the harping tradition were, in the early stages of revival, used as a means *not* to identify with the harp tradition. Comments made by Seán Ó Riada (as previously mentioned) in particular, attempted to demonstrate that what was happening in the harping tradition was not authentic and therefore not identifiably traditional. However, it is impossible now to argue that the Irish harp is not identified, through traditional-music style harping at the very least, as a traditional instrument. O'Flynn's interpretation of identity grapples with large-scale issues of national identity and music: 'What I wish to emphasize ... is the two-sided face of identity, and the variety of ways that this dialectic operates in positive and negative articulations of Irishness and Irish music.'[38] Perhaps a 'multi-sided' face of identity would be more appropriate than a dialectical approach. Nevertheless, O'Flynn's argument that divisions of music style are key elements in the formation of musical identity remains relevant.

Fintan Vallely argues that identity and music are more complex and discrete and that broad labels (such as 'traditional') cannot encapsulate the music of an entire grouping of people. Vallely problematizes over-generalized definitions of identity by arguing that:

Selected comments show that while the ascription 'Traditional music is Catholic music' may be popular political pragmatism, the notion is substantially superficial and uninformed: Traditional music is simply the music that was played commonly and 'popularly' on the island of Ireland by the lower classes (who had the opportunity or need, or who so desired), most strongly prior to the intervention of recording, cinema, radio and television.[39]

Valley's book serves to show that 'identity' as it applies to one music (Irish traditional music) cannot be generalized and that issues of age, gender, geography, religion, politics and musical style all affect the notion of identity and music.

The identity of the harp, then, can only be considered as a multi-dimensional identity both through musical styles and sociocultural perspectives. The long history of the harp as a symbol of Ireland has guaranteed its place as simultaneously representative of Ireland, Irish culture and, at times, nationalism: 'At their first meeting in October 1791 the United Irishmen adopted the harp with the motto "It is new strung and shall be heard" as their official insignia, and references to the harp abound in their imagery and songs.'[40] The use of the harp as a symbol of nationalism (alongside other popular symbols, including shamrock) has been comprehensively detailed by Barra Boydell.[41] The Irish Free State's decision to continue the use of the harp as its emblem guaranteed political and national associations of the harp as an identifier of Ireland. No other instrument in the tradition is so readily referenced for its extra-musical associations. In an article on Irish-American material culture Stephanie Rains argues that the commodification of symbols and their subsequent accessibility are essential for mass production of tourist souvenirs.

> Firstly, the objects require the levels of familiarity and stylization described by Lloyd ... twentieth-century tourist and diaspora objects require the same high degree of stylization in order to function as representative figurations of a culture that is otherwise distant or unknown ... they must display their markers of both ethnicity and experience vividly and in such a way that they will be recognizable with a minimum of cultural 'work' or prior knowledge on the part of consumers ... For by its very nature, diasporic material culture must, above all else, be mobile.[42]

The harp as an image or object easily fulfils these requirements. It is readily understood as a symbol of Ireland and miniature replicas have been made and sold by many Irish companies that cater to the Irish-

American market, such as Waterford Crystal and Belleek China. Rains further argues that:

> One of their most frequent design characteristics is a heavy reliance upon overtly kitsch markers of Irishness such as shamrocks, harps, leprechauns and generalized 'Celtic' images. As was discussed earlier, one of the functions of such design for a diasporic market is its overtness and 'over-performance' of ethnic identity. It is this very 'over performance' of ethnicity, which is the catalyst for the censure received by the objects and their consumers, which is in fact necessary for the function of such material culture.[43]

The kitsch or over-performance of ethnic identity is evident where the harp has been used as an iconographic symbol of Ireland on such tourist souvenirs.

Boydell makes the point that the use of a winged-maiden figure on harp symbols in the eighteenth and nineteenth centuries reflected a lack of familiarity with the harp in popular society: 'The use of this unrealistic, symbolic harp also reflects the fact that the harp-playing tradition was declining in the eighteenth century to the extent that close familiarity with the Irish harp, especially in urban Anglo-Irish circles, would have been the exception rather than the rule'.[44] As a reflection of Boydell's hypothesis, I propose that today, depictions of the harp represent the musical reality of the popularity of the harp. It is still relevant as a *musical* symbol of Ireland. When the harp is used in a stylized form today it often appears as structurally similar to real rather than classical-fictional Irish harps. The identity of the harp as a socio-musical symbol of Ireland remains relevant because of the rising popularity of the harp over the past fifty years. Stylization is often a necessary process of image design (depending on the context), but while representations of the harp from the late eighteenth to early twentieth centuries are unrealistic (as outlined by Boydell), more recent images show a familiarity with the instrument. The identity of the harp as a symbol of Ireland is unlikely to change in the near future, but the following three images demonstrate that it remains a viable interpretation of modernity in Ireland as opposed to a romanticized ideal.

The water feature in plate 20 is situated at the front entrance to the luxury Ritz-Carlton hotel in Powerscourt. In this water feature, water runs down along the almost-invisible strings (to create the illusion that water forms the strings). The hotel is a five-star hotel and part of the world-famous Ritz-Carlton group. Customers staying at such a hotel will expect certain standards and universal familiarities, with regional identifiers. Hotel publicity describes the hotel as:

> a Palladian estate tucked back in the woodlands of County Wicklow, on Ireland's east coast. Take an enchanting stroll amidst the gentle green hills and sparkling lakes of Powerscourt Gardens, then head into Dublin for some cosmopolitan flair. The sumptuous surroundings of our Ireland hotel combine the luxury and tranquility of country living with city chic.[45]

The placement of the harp feature emphasizes the location of the hotel, in one of the most scenic, popular tourist areas close to Dublin (within walking distance of Enniskerry). It is a realistic portrayal of a harp, based loosely on the design of the Brian Ború harp in terms of proportions and shape. This interpretation of a harp is employed at one of Ireland's most prestigious hotels. It appears here in a semi-musical context in that passers-by can actually 'pluck' the water/strings. The image is of a modern interpretation of 'Irishness' and luxury. The hotel also re-interprets the symbol of the harp by employing a concert harpist to play in the lobby of the hotel; perhaps the concert harp is viewed as more luxurious/prestigious than the Irish harp.[46]

Casalattico is a small town in the Frosinoli area of Lazio, Italy. Emigration from Casalattico and surrounding villages was intense after the Second World War, with many young people emigrating to Ireland and Britain. As a community they celebrate their dual Italian-Irish heritage through an annual 'Irish Fest' in August. This is incorporated into the festival culture of the region where each village holds an annual festival at the end of the summer. Casalattico's festival differs in that they celebrate their Irish culture by bringing Irish musicians to the festival to perform for the night. Plate 22 is a highly stylized version of a harp, with a shamrock attached to emphasize the Irishness of the music. This structure was placed at the top of the stage where the Irish band played in 2009. The use of the harp and shamrock symbols here obviously signal the Irishness of the festival, but they also give a visual pointer to the type of music, rather than ethnicity alone. The decision to choose the harp to identify the music being played asserts the musical viability of the harp.

Plate 23 shows the newly-opened Samuel Beckett Bridge over the river Liffey in Dublin city centre. Dublin City Council commissioned world-renowned architect Santiago Calatrava to build this bridge. In a press release by Dublin City Council, Calatrava described his vision for the bridge: 'I developed a deep affinity for the people of Dublin, and I wanted my next bridge to celebrate that connection. It is my sincere hope that the Samuel Beckett Bridge will serve as a monument to Dublin, honoring its past, present and future'. Furthermore, the press release describes the overt symbolism of the bridge:

> For Calatrava, his vision was a challenge; as he was faced with the task of creating a bridge that aesthetically belonged to the present, yet that also evoked a sense of the past. Envisioning the bridge as a harp, a historical and prominent symbol of Ireland, with steel cables as its strings, the architect was able to infuse modern elements with traditional significance. The result is a bridge that both functionally and artistically pays homage to Dublin and its people.[47]

The vision for this bridge was a contemporary, functional symbol that represented modern Ireland. The harp in this case offers the perfect blend of modernity and tradition and remains applicable as a cultural symbol of modern Ireland, as this latest city structure shows.

The identity of the harp is complex and multifarious and it is impossible to ascribe a single cultural or musical identity to the instrument. It remains viable as a symbol of modernity in Ireland only because of the multiple identities associated with it. The harp's reinvention and renewal several times during the course of the twentieth century and its adaptation to changing musical trends has enabled it to remain an important instrument in Irish music making. Its presence in Ireland today has manifested itself in more realistic, even 'playable', depictions and reconstructions of harps in contemporary symbols. It now represents a cosmopolitan-traditional symbol of the country. Gender identities have changed quite slowly over the past one hundred years. While it remains difficult to ascertain whether the female identification of the harp will pass, it is clear that the overt femininity of the mid-twentieth century has subsided. This promises much hope for the future gender identifications of the instrument.

CHAPTER 9

Conclusion

Five key issues permeate this book and allow a comparative study of the harp with 'Irish' music (in its broadest sense) while also placing the Irish harp within the discourse of world music. These issues are: (1) Irish harp music and the wider engagement with musical traditions; (2) music revival; (3) performance contexts; (4) modernity and Irish harping; and (5) music and identity. Throughout this book it has been argued that the harping tradition is situated within multiple musical traditions. In differing times and locations, the harp has engaged (and continues to do so) with art music, Irish traditional music, Celtic music and early music. In these multiple musical guises a study of the harp, such as this, allows a critical examination of notions of style, genre, technique and repertoire. The harp is unique in its versatility and integration into such a wide spectrum of musical traditions.

The multiple phases of revival and transformation that the harp has undergone demonstrate that the Irish harp has never operated in a social or cultural vacuum, but has consistently responded to emerging musical trends observable in other musical instruments, genres and styles. Revival theory facilitates a cross-cultural analysis of the harp with musical traditions elsewhere and asserts the importance of the Irish harp as a world music tradition. Correspondingly, by analyzing the key eras in harping utilizing revival theory, clear and coherent understanding of the differences between each era becomes possible. Performance contexts changed in conjunction with the various stages evident in Irish harping. A critique of the changing performance contexts demonstrates the versatility of the instrument and elucidates some of the reasons why the harp has been variously included and/or excluded into the mainstream of Irish traditional music and art music.

A study such as this must be, by its nature, grounded in a particular time frame. By using ethnographic techniques to document the harp tradition as it currently exists, this book is rooted in the present day, which in turn demands consideration of modernity and music. Issues including deterritorialization, diaspora, place, 'Irishness' and the use of modern technologies are relevant to Irish harping and show it to be a vibrant and robust music tradition. The concepts central to music and identity including gender, national identity and symbolic identity have also been explored in relation to the Irish harp. By scrutinizing these issues in relation to the harp, it can be viewed as belonging to and reflecting aspects of modern Irish culture.

This book focuses specifically on harping in the twentieth and twenty-first centuries. It critically examines the history of the harp during that time frame and attests to the new popularity of harping in the present day. Moreover, it advocates for the new authenticity of harping in all its guises and firmly roots the discourse of harping within traditional, art and early musics. The question of authenticity in harping relates to its long and complex history. Harping and harpers were afforded the utmost respect in Ireland until the late eighteenth century. In bardic Ireland, the harper was second only to the *file* (poet) in the Chieftain's court. Harpers adapted during times of changing social order so that in the seventeenth and eighteenth centuries the harpers' patrons were both the Anglo-Irish and Gaelic-Irish.

Significant research has been carried out on the harp up to the decline of that harping tradition. The first major work dates back to 1840 when Edward Bunting compiled his seminal publication. This book included chapters on 'Of the various efforts to revive the Irish harp'; 'Anecdotes of the more distinguished harpers of the last two centuries'; and 'Of the method of playing, and musical vocabulary of the old Irish harpers', in addition to three further chapters.[1] Bunting's work inarguably preserves much rich information on the harping tradition that would otherwise have been lost. It also shows that research carried out even in the nineteenth century attests to the decline of the once-glorious tradition. Bunting's work, although published in 1840, does not deal significantly with harping in the nineteenth century, but is more historically focused. Other work, such as key publications by Dónal Ó Sullivan, Colette Moloney, Joan Rimmer, Henry Grattan Flood and Gráinne Yeats tend to focus particularly on the harping tradition before its decline.[2]

A most noticeable point in the literature is the dearth of material relating to Irish harping in the nineteenth century. I propose that there are two reasons for this. First, while academic and performance-based research has been limited in Irish harping, the research that has been carried out has often centered on the period up to the nineteenth century. There remains a wealth of sources (including the Bunting manuscripts) relating to this era of harping. Publications (such as those listed above) analyze the harping tradition at a high point in its history. This era may also present an ideologically uncomplicated narrative of harping before the massive decline of the tradition. Second, given the limited activity on the wire-strung harp in the early nineteenth century there are few sources for the study of this tradition. Also, the new developments (such as the Egan harp and new performance contexts) changed the nature of the tradition so that by the late nineteenth century the Irish harp tradition was a vastly different one to that of one hundred years earlier. That manifestation of the tradition is only beginning to attract scholarly attention.[3]

In formulating the research questions, aims and boundaries of this study I decided to focus on the twentieth and twenty-first centuries. My impetus for initiating this research came from my experience as a harpist. Having played traditional-style harping from the beginning and encountering art-music style at university, I experienced the two traditions first hand from a performer's perspective. On further research at Master's and PhD levels it became very clear that little work has been done on harping in the twentieth century.

This book also addresses mythology and contradictions associated with the history of Irish harping. The most popular and incorrect myth is that the harping tradition died at the end of the eighteenth century. The nineteenth-century harp schools are testament alone that this is not the full truth. While sources on the nineteenth century are scant, it is without question that developments in harps (such as semi-tone levers and gut strings) followed on from at least nine centuries of changes in the instrument. The most important changes were in performance context so that by the beginning of the twentieth century the harp was in a very different guise. Furthermore, the findings of this research show that the harp was often at the forefront of performance activity throughout much of the twentieth century. In the early decades harping was included at both 'new' competitions – the Feis Ceoil and Oireachtas. In the 1950s the harp operated in revival settings and at a time when professional musicians in Ireland could barely make a living; Mary O'Hara successfully toured the world as a harpist and singer. The forward thinking of Cairde na Cruite helped to bring together the work of many Irish composers in a single publication and also instituted an instrument-specific residential summer course. The music of traditional-style harpers has brought the harp to even more audiences in new performance contexts while the wire-strung harp players now engage with early music. The harp tradition did not die out, but transformed and adapted so that now it operates in several vibrant musical contexts.

Gender associations have specific relevance in twentieth-century harping. Throughout the twentieth century women participated in musical activity through arrangement, composition, competitions, public performances, teaching and recording. Traditional Irish music was historically a male tradition in public settings; women rarely entered public houses before the 1950s and often retired from their musical careers when they had children. Moreover, the majority of high-profile traditional musicians in the twentieth century were male. The history of the harp offers a different trajectory, as women successfully subverted gender stereotypes and constructed successful professional careers as musicians. The harp, then, can be interpreted as a very positive vehicle for women's music making and expression. The historic respectability of the instrument, both in Ireland and Europe, facilitated a respectable way in which women could publicly participate in music.

Notions of respectability also tied in with Catholic ideas of women's roles in society. The harp was very much associated with convent schools for the first sixty to seventy years of the twentieth century. Associations of the harp as a prestigious icon of Irishness provided an unchallenging presentation of music and nationality. In another male-dominated institution, the harp gave an acceptable public face to the role of women in convent education. Through public representation of Ireland, women became the culture bearers not only of a musical tradition, but of a conservative and idyllic portrayal of a Catholic Ireland.

The harp is now an established and essential component in the overall fabric of Irish music. To any musicians who entered the tradition after the early 1980s, it is assumed that the harp has always been played in such performance contexts. People tend to recognize, however, that there are less harp players than players of other instruments. Similarly, the harp has been used for the performance of art music for the past fifty years and is no longer an unusual or rare instrument to encounter. The harp still carries romantic and nationalistic associations, particularly because it is the national emblem of Ireland. This book proves for harpists and non-harpists alike, that the harp is firmly embedded in multiple musical traditions in Ireland; that it can be used as a case study for music revivals and that it has functioned as an agent of both gender stereotyping and subversion in the past one hundred years.

The Irish harp occupies an important place in contemporary Irish traditional music, art music, early music and popular culture. The development of the traditions over the past one hundred years has ensured that harping has continued to adapt, change and remain relevant to contemporary music making and society. It is likely that the harp will continue to flourish within the three musical spheres (traditional, art and early music) given the institutional and educational support now evident for the instrument. The existence of dedicated societies (such as Cairde na Cruite, the HHSI, CCÉ, the ITMA) for the promotion of Irish music and the harp should prove beneficial. Institutional support (in terms of grade examinations and harp classes) at the major Dublin institutions for music education point to continued growth in the popularity of the instrument. This book aimed to provide a musical ethnography of the harp in the past 110 years. Future research could investigate the harp in the nineteenth century in terms of its musical and ideological interpretation and also further investigate Irish harping and its links to European and Celtic music traditions. The Irish harp will most certainly continue to provide opportunities for academic inquiry and musical engagement.

Appendix 1

Index of pieces in *The Irish harp book* (SLC), excluding studies and exercises

No.	Page	Title	Instrument	Type	Composer/Arranger
1	22	Eibhlín a Rún	Solo Harp	Air	Sheila Larchet Cuthbert
2	23	Cailín Ó Chois tSiúre Mé	Solo Harp	Air	Sheila Larchet Cuthbert
3	23	Caoine Phiarais Feiritéir	Solo Harp	Harper's Air	Sheila Larchet Cuthbert (Ferriter)
4	28	Tiarna Mhaigh Eó	Solo Harp	Harper's Air/ March	Sheila Larchet Cuthbert (David Murphy)
5	29	The Parting of Friends (Na Cumainn)	Solo Harp	Harper's Air	Charlotte Milligan Fox (Hempson)
6	34	The Irish Ho-Hone	Solo Harp	Fitzwilliam Virignal Bk	Transcribed by Sheila Larchet Cuthbert
7	35	Scarúint Na gCompánach	Solo Harp	Harper's Air	Sheila Larchet Cuthbert (Rory Dall Ó Catháin)
8	40	Miss Hamilton	Solo Harp	Harper's Air	Sheila Larchet Cuthbert (Cornelius Lyons)
9	41	The Gaelic Farmer	Solo Harp	Jig	Treasa Ní Chormaic (Transc. M. McGrath)
10	46	William O'Flinn	Solo Harp	Harper's Air	Sheila Larchet Cuthbert (Carolan)
11	47	Lament and Hornpipe	Solo Harp	Harper's Air	Lament: Mercedes Bolger (Bunting) Hornpipe: Mercedes Bolger (T. Ní Chormaic)
12	48	I Will Leave this Country and Go Along With You	Solo Harp	Air	Mercedes McGrath (Petrie Collection)
13	51	David Foy	Solo Harp	Air	Mercedes McGrath (Petrie Collection)
14	56	Hornpipe, Single Jig, Suantraí, Reel	Harp Trio	Suite	Anne Crowley
15	72	Maurice O'Connor	Solo Harp	Harper's Air	Sheila Larchet Cuthbert (Carolan)
16	73	For the Children, Song Without Words, Set Dance	Harp & Voice/Inst.	Suite (New)	Edgar M.Deale
17	86	An Cóitín Dearg	Solo Harp	Air	Aloys Fleischmann

No.	Page	Title	Instrument	Type	Composer/Arranger
18	90	John Kelly	Solo Harp	Harper's Air	Sheila Larchet Cuthbert (Carolan)
19	91	An Spailpín Fánach	Voice & Harp	Song	Carrie Townshend
20	93	Dilín Ó Deamhas	Voice & Harp	Song	Máirín Ní Shé
21	100	Allegro Giocoso	Solo Harp	Piece (New)	John Kinsella
22	103	Carolan's Farewell to Music	Harper's Air	Air	Sheila Larceht Cuthbert (Carolan)
23	104	Máire Ní Eidín	Voice & Harp	Song	Róisín Ní Shé
24	106	Anonn's Anall	Voice & Harp	Song	Gráinne Yeats (words: C.Ó Lochlainn)
25	115	John O'Connor	Air	Harper's Air	Sheila Larchet Cuthbert (Carolan)
26	116	Interlude	Solo Harp	Piece (New)	T.C. Kelly
27	119	An Fhallaingín Mhuimhneach	Voice & Harp	Song	Ruth Mervyn (Dr. A Patterson)
38	122	Grá Mo Chroí Thú, Éire	Voice & Harp	Song	N. Calthorpe (Words: T.A. Ó Rathaille)
39	125	Do Chuala Scéal	Voice & Harp	Song	Cian Ó hÉigeartaigh (words: Feirtéir)
40	134	Carolan's Concerto	Solo Harp	Harper's Air	Sheila Larchet Cuthbert (Carolan)
41	135	Three Pieces for Irish Harp (I, II, III)	Solo Harp	Piece (New)	Gerard Victory
42	145	Duet	Duet	Piece (New)	Joan Trimble
43	150	Tis Pretty to Be in Ballinderry	Voice & Harp	Song	Redmond Friel
44	151	Píobaire an Mhála	Voice & Harp	Song	Carl G. Hardebec
45	153	My Lagan Love	Voice & Harp	Song	Hamilton Harty (words: S. Mac Cathmhaoil)
46	161	Déirín Dí	Solo Harp	Air	Éamonn Ó Gallchobhair
47	163	Fantasia, Berceuse, Rondo	Solo Harp	Piece (New)	Daniel McNulty
48	172	Little Boats	Voice & Harp	Song	Herbert Hughes (words: H. Boulton)
49	174	A Soft Day	Voice & Harp	Song	C.V. Stanford (words: W.M. Letts)
50	177	Spanish Arch	Duet	Piece (New)	James Wilson
51	197	Étude Bitonal	Solo Harp	Piece (New)	A.J. Potter
52	199	The Small Black Rose	Voice & Harp	Song	John F. Larchet (words: D. O'Sullivan)
53	202	Dance for an Ancient Ritual No.2 of Four Pieces for Two Irish Harps	Duet	Piece (New)	Brian Boydell
54	211	Duet - Scintillae	Duet	Piece (New)	Seóirse Bodley
55	224	Quintet - A Carolan Tune	Quintet	Air/New	Havelock Nelson (arr.)

APPENDIX 2

Songs summarizing Irish history. Words by Thomas Moore (from Nancy Calthorpe collection)

Part I

1.	The Harp that Once	(From Trilogy to the Harp of Erin)
2.	Dear Harp of My Country	(From Trilogy to the Harp of Erin)
3.	The Came from a Land	Discovery of Ireland
4.	Silent O Moyle	(Pre-Christian Era)
5.	Rich & Rare	(Golden Age)
6.	The Meeting of the Waters	(Danish Invasion)
7.	Remember the Glories of B. the B.	(Clontarf 1014)
8.	The Valley Lay Smiling	(English Invasion)
9.	The Minstrel Boy	(Elizabethan Period)
10.	O Breath Not	(Robert Emmet)
11.	O Blame Not the Bard	(Spencer's Suspension [?] upon Irish Music)
12.	My Gentle Harp (Londonderry Air)	Conclusion of Trilogy to Harp

Part II Songs Summarizing Irish History Contd.
Words & Music by others since Moore's death.

13.	The Croppy Boy	(Rebellion of 1798)
14.	The Emigrants Lament	(1848)
15.	Who Fears to Speak of '98	(Young Ireland Movement 1850)
16.	God Save Ireland	The Fenian Movement 1870
17.	The West's Awake	(Munster Air) Modern Ireland
18.	Romantic Ireland is not Dead	W.B. Yeats

Part III Songs Portraying Irish Character

19.	Draherin-o-Machree	(Song to the Dead)
20.	Killarney	(Scenic Song)
21.	Cruiskeen Lawn	(Drinking Song)
22.	Gartan Mother's Lullaby	(Lullaby)
23.	The Last Rose of Summer	(Poetic Fancy)
24.	"Believe Me"	(Romantic)
25.	Kathleen Mavourneen	(Romantic)
26.	"I'll take you home"	(Romantic)
27.	Mother Machree	(American-Irish Modern Ballad)
28.	Father O'Flynn	(Humorous)
29.	The Garden Where the Praties Grow	(Humorous)
30.	Kitty of Coleraine	(Humorous)
31.	The Low-Backed Cow	(Humorous)
32.	The Wearin' of the Green	(Patriotic)
33.	Soldiers of Erin	(National Anthem)
34.	Songs of Our Land	(Poetic)

APPENDIX 3

Irish music festivals with harp classes/competitions

	Irish Music Festivals 2009	*Harp*
I	Carlingford Traditional Music Winter School	Yes
	6–8 February	
2	The Joseph Browne Spring School of Traditional Music	No
	Gort, Co. Galway and Crusheen	
3	Corofin Traditional Music Festival	Yes
	Co. Clare	
4	Cavan Arts Festival	Yes
	11–18 March	
5	Patrick Byrne Traditional Music Weekend	No
	Carrickmacross	
6	Ceardlann Earraigh	Yes
	Celbridge	
7	Granard Traditional Harp Festival	Yes
	16–19 April	
8	Ballydehob Traditional Music, Song and Dance Festival	Yes
	17–19 April	
9	Feile Chois Cuain	Yes
	Louisburgh, Co. Mayo, 1–4 May	
10	The 'Cup of Tae' Traditional Festival	No
	Ardara, Co. Donegal, 1–4 May	
11	Fleadh Nua	No
	Ennis, Co. Clare, 17–25 May	
12	Edward Bunting Harp Festival	Yes
	Armagh, 29–31 May	
13	Blas	
	University of Limerick, 22 June–3 July	Yes
14	Willie Clancy Summer School	Yes
	Miltown Malbay, 4–12 July	
15	Douglas Hyde Summer School	Yes
	Ballaghaderreen, 4–11 July	
16	South Sligo Summer School	Yes
	Tubbercurry, Co. Sligo, 12–18 July	
17	Meitheal Summer School	Yes
	Limerick, 13–17 July	
18	Joe Mooney Summer School	Yes
	Drumshanbo, Co. Leitrim, 18–25 July	
19	O'Carolan Summer School	Yes
	Keadue, Co. Roscommon, 26–31 July	
20	Scoil Acla	Yes
	Achill, Co. Mayo, 27 July–2 Aug.	
21	The World Fleadh	No
	Castlebar, 24 July–15 Aug.	

22	O'Carolan Harp and Traditional Music Festival Keadue, 31 July–3 Aug.	Yes
23	Feakle International Traditional Music Festival Co. Clare, 5–11 Aug.	Yes
24	Scoil Eigse	Yes
25	Eigse Mrs Crotty Kilrush, Co. Clare, 13–17 Aug.	Yes
26	Coleman Traditional Festival Gurteen, Co. Sligo, 29–31 Aug.	No
27	Eigse Ui Ghramhnaigh Baile Atha Bui, 28–30 Aug.	Yes
28	Tulla Traditional Music Festival Co. Clare, 11–13 Sept.	No
29	Feile Frank McGann Strokestown, Co. Roscommon, 8–11 Oct.	Yes

Notes

CHAPTER 1
Introduction

1 Throughout this book the term 'Irish harp' implies 'neo-Irish' harp. Other harp types will be referred to specifically throughout the text.

2 Tamara E. Livingston, 'Music revivals: towards a general theory', *Ethnomusicology*, 43:1 (1999), pp 66–85.

3 Scoil Éigse is an annual summer school run by Comhaltas Ceoltóirí Éireann in the week preceding the All-Ireland Fleadh.

4 I have previously argued for the use of these terms: Helen Lyons, 'Irish harping: styles, repertoire and technique', *Musicology Review*, 2 (2006), pp 125–48.

5 Kathleen Loughnane, *Harp to heart* (Galway: Reiskmore Music, 2005), back cover.

6 Timothy Rice, 'Understanding and producing the variability of oral tradition: learning from a Bulgarian bagpiper', *Journal of American Folklores*, 108:429 (1995), pp 266–76.

7 Helen Lawlor, 'Interview with Harry Bradley' (17 May 2007).

8 Helen Lawlor, 'Interview with Sheila Larchet Cuthbert' (19 November 2007).

CHAPTER 2
Irish harping, 1900–50

1 O'Donnell, 'Custodians of culture: a social, political, musicological and cultural history of the Irish harp and its patronage from 1790 to 1845'.

2 Rimmer, *The Irish harp*, pp 69–70.

3 William Henry Grattan Flood, *A history of Irish music* (Dublin, 1906), p. 323.

4 Charles Townshend, *Ireland, the 20th century* (London, 1998), p. 41.

5 Ibid., p. 46.

6 Harry White, 'The preservation of music and Irish cultural history', *International Review of the Aesthetics and Sociology of Music*, 27:2 (Dec. 1996), pp 123–38.

7 Ita Beausang, 'From national sentiment to nationalist movement, 1850–1900' in Michael Murphy and Jan Smazny (eds), *Irish musical studies 9: music in nineteenth century Ireland* (Dublin, 2007), pp 36–51.

8 John William Glover was organist of St Mary's Cathedral, Marlborough Street, Dublin; founder of the Royal Choral Institute; dedicated commemorator of Thomas Moore.

9 Beausang, 'From national sentiment to nationalist movement', p. 41.

10 *Freeman's Journal*, 2 February 1884, quoted in Beausang, 'From national sentiment to nationalist movement', p. 43

11 *Evening Telegraph*, 14 April 1897, quoted in Beausang, 'From national sentiment to nationalist movement', p. 47.

12 Barra Boydell, 'The iconography of the Irish harp as a national symbol' in Patrick F. Devine & Harry White

(eds), *Irish musical studies 5. The Maynooth International Musicological Conference 1995. Selected proceedings: part two* (Dublin, 1995), p. 55.

13 S. Shannon Millin, *The Irish harp, a lecture* (London, 1898), pp 29–30.

14 Ibid., pp 61–2.

15 Out of 123 musical instrument companies known in Ireland from the seventeenth to the nineteenth centuries, seven out of eight listed harp makers were producing harps in the first half of the eighteenth century. Thereafter, there seems to have been very little harp making activity in Ireland until the twentieth century. For further details see John Teehan, 'A list of Irish instrument makers', *The Galpin Society Journal*, 16 (1963), pp 28–32.

16 Both Coffey and O'Connor used their initials only when publishing as they were nuns and it was not considered appropriate to seek public acclaim for their work. I will therefore use their initials when referring to them.

17 Mother Attracta Coffey, *Irish melodies transcribed and arranged for the Irish harp* (London, 1902).

18 Mother Alphonsus O'Connor, *Irish airs arranged for the harp* (London, n.d.).

19 Lanier, '"It is new-strung and shan't be heard": nationalism and memory in the Irish harp tradition', p. 15.

20 Lawlor, 'Interview with Sheila Larchet Cuthbert'.

21 *Irish Times*, 18 August 1905, p. 7.

22 Rudolf Trebitsch, *Celtic recordings – Ireland, Wales, Brittany, Isle of Man, and Scotland (1907–09), sound documents from the phonogrammarchiv of the Austrian Academy of Sciences. The complete historical collections, 1899–1950*, Series 5/2 (Vienna 2003), CD booklet, p. 110.

23 *Freeman's Journal*, 13 October 1908, p. 5.

24 *Freeman's Journal*, 20 May 1909, p. 5.

25 *Freeman's Journal*, 25 July 1914, p. 6.

26 Flood, *A history of Irish music*, p. 335.

27 In bar seven the A on the last beat of the bar should actually be an A natural, as the lower A of this octave is notated as an A natural. I propose that the omission of the natural sign is an error. Viewing the octave A as two A naturals would therefore give a I6/4 chord, leading into the perfect cadence in bar eight. This makes more sense musically than any other option.

28 Lawlor, 'Interview with Sheila Larchet Cuthbert'.

29 Tom Maher, *The harp's a wonder* (Mullingar, 1991), p. 98.

30 Ibid., p. 99.

31 *Irish Times*, 11 May 1922.

32 *Irish Times*, 16 May 1925.

33 Sheila Larchet Cuthbert, *The Irish harp book* (Dublin, 1975), p. 238.

34 *Irish Times*, 4 May 1929, p. 10.

35 This type of Celtic-design embroidery was contemporaneously popular on Irish dancing costumes for females. For further information see John Cullinane, *Irish dancing costumes* (Cork, 1996).

36 *Irish Times*, 3 January 1931, p. 4.

37 *Irish Times*, 25 April 1931, p. 4.

38 Larchet Cuthbert, *The Irish harp book*, p. 237.

39 *Irish Times*, 1 November 1932, p. 5.

40 *Irish Times*, 9 May 1932, p. 4.

41 *Irish Times*, 6 July 1934, p. 4.

42 *Irish Times*, 6 July 1934, p. 4.

43 *Irish Times*, 8 July 1938, p. 3.

44 Maher, *The harp's a wonder*, p. 100.

45 *Irish Times*, 'Harp revival', 10 May 1940, p. 3.

46 *Irish Times*, 2 July 1940, p. 3.

47 *Irish Times*, 14 May 1943, p. 2.

48 *Irish Times*, 15 May 1943, p. 3.

49 *Irish Times*, 11 May 1944, p. 3.

50 *Irish Times*, 12 May 1948.

51 Maher, *The harp's a wonder*, p. 101.

CHAPTER 3
Revival

1 A version of this chapter appeared as Helen Lawlor, 'Popularity and revival: factors affecting harp reception in the 1950s and 1960s' in Thérèse Smith (ed.), *Ancestral imprints: histories of Irish traditional music and dance* (Cork, 2012).

2 Terence Brown, *Ireland, a social and cultural history* (London, 2004), pp 200–8.

3 Ibid., p. 218.

4 Aloys Fleischmann, *Music in Ireland: a symposium* (Cork, 1952).

5 Ibid., p. 34.

6 Ibid., p. 169.

7 Ibid., p. 177.

8 Ibid., p. 186.

9 Mike Cronin, 'Projecting the nation through sport and culture: Ireland, Aonach Tailteann and the Irish Free State, 1924–32', *Journal of Contemporary History*, 38:3 (2003), pp 395–411.

10 Brown, *Ireland, a social and cultural history*, pp 209–10.

11 Marie McCarthy, *Passing it on, the transmission of music in Irish culture* (Cork, 1999), p. 178.

12 Brown, *Ireland, a social and cultural history*, p. 224.

13 McCarthy, *Passing it on*, pp 178–9.

14 O'Hara, *The scent of the roses*, pp 33–4.

15 Mary O'Hara, 'Travels with my harp', Paper given at the 9th World Harp Congress (UCD, Dublin, 2005).

16 Frances M. Burroughs, 'Souvenir gifts for An Tostal', *Irish Independent*, 27 January 1953.

17 O'Hara, 'Travels with my harp'.

18 www.guinness.com/global/story/history, accessed 12 December 2006.

19 The Irish harp image is used as the government emblem on all official documents including passports, driving licences and the presidential

standard, as well as on the national currency, the Irish version of the Euro coinage.

20 Accessed 12 December 2006. Image courtesy of Diageo.

21 Boydell, 'The iconography of the Irish harp as a national symbol', p. 134.

22 Mary O'Hara, *Mary O' Hara's Ireland* (Emerald Gem GES 1905, 1973).

23 L. Perry Curtis Jr, *Apes and angels: the Irishman in Victorian caricature* (London, 1997), p. xxii. See also page xxiii of the same preface for an illustration from *Fun*, in 1882, of the 'wild Irish Paddy'.

24 O'Hara, *The scent of the roses*, p. 152.

25 Aoife Nic Cormaic, 'Interview with Laoise Kelly on "Cherish the Ladies"' (Dublin, RTE, Radio 1, 25 July 2005).

26 Timothy D. Taylor, 'The commodification of music at the dawn of the era of "mechanical music"', *Ethnomusicology*, 51:2 (2007), pp 281–305.

27 Seán Ó Riada, *Our musical heritage*, ed. Thomas Kinsella and Tomás Ó Cannain (Mountrath, 1982); Breandán Breathnach, *Folk music and dances of Ireland* (Cork, 1996), pp 126–7.

28 For further reading see: Rimmer, *The Irish harp*; Lyons, 'Irish harping: styles, repertoire and technique'.

29 Michael B. Bakan, 'From oxymoron to reality: agendas of gender and the rise of Balinese women's "Gamelan Beleganjur" in Bali, Indonesia', *Asian Music*, 29:1 (1997), pp 37–85, p. 42.

30 See Lyons, 'Irish harping: styles, repertoire and technique', for a detailed description of this topic.

31 Denis Hempson played using this technique at the Belfast Harp Festival of 1792. For further details see Gráinne Yeats, *Féile na gCruitirí, Béal Feirste 1792* (Dublin, 1980).

32 The Otway harp is now housed by Trinity College Dublin; the Dalway harp is housed by the National Museum of Ireland.

33 Ó Riada, *Our musical heritage*, p. 78.

34 Breathnach, *Folk music and dances of Ireland*.

35 Colin Graham, '"Blame it on Maureen O'Hara": Ireland and the trope of authenticity', *Cultural Studies*, 15:1 (2001), p. 71.

36 Yeats, *Féile na gCruitirí, Béal Feirste 1792*, p. 25.

37 Ó Riada, *Our musical heritage*, pp 78–9.

38 Breathnach, *Folk music and dances of Ireland*, pp 126–7.

39 O'Hara, *The scent of the roses*, p. 42

40 Sr Carmel Warde, 'Personal account of the harp school in Sion Hill, 1949–1989' (2004).

41 Seán Ó Riada, Ceoltóirí Chualann, and Seán Ó Sé, *Ó Riada sa Gaeity* (Gael Linn, ORIADACD01, 2005).

42 O'Hara, *The scent of the roses*, pp 48–9.

43 Moloney, *The Irish music manuscripts of Edward Bunting (1773–1843)*, p. 86.

44 Deirdre Ní Fhloinn, *Irish traditional songs* (Washington DC: Smithsonian Folkways Records, FW 8762, 1958).

45 O'Hara, *The scent of the roses*, p. 33.

46 Glynis Casson and Cormac De Barra, 'The harp that once' (Concert at Domincan College, Sion Hill, 28 January 2007); Lyons, 'State of the harp: the Irish harp in Ireland in the twenty-first century' (M.Mus, UCD, 2005), Appendix II.

47 Cormac De Barra, *Barcó* (Barcó, 2002).

48 Frank Harte, 'Singing voices, traditional singing styles in Ireland – the singers' voices' (RTE Radio 1, 30 December 2005 (1987)).

49 John Moulden, 'Song' in Fintan Vallely (ed.), *The companion to Irish traditional music* (Cork, 1999), p. 353.

50 Julie Henigan, 'Technique (song)' in Fintan Vallely (ed.), *The companion to Irish traditional music*, 2nd edition (Cork, 2011), p. 628.

51 The difficulties associated with standard staff notation are well documented. See for example Breandán Breathnach, 'The use of notation in Irish folk music' in Seán Potts, Terry Moylan, and Liam McNulty (eds), *The man and his music* (Dublin, 1996); Niall Keegan, 'Literacy as a transmission tool in Irish traditional music' in Patrick F. Devine & Harry White (eds), *Irish musical studies 4. The Maynooth International Musicological Conference 1995. Selected proceedings: part one* (Dublin, 1996); Thérèse Smith, 'The challenge of bringing oral traditions into an academic teaching environment' in Fintan Vallely, et al. (eds), *Crosbhealach an Cheoil* (Cork, 1996).

52 Transcription by Helen Lawlor from CD recording: O'Hara, *Irish traditional folk songs*.

53 Moloney, *The Irish music manuscripts of Edward Bunting (1773–1843)*.

54 Ibid., p. 75.

55 Criticism of Bunting's work frequently relates to his use of harmonic accompaniments (mostly Western-Classical in style) and his alteration of keys. See, for example, Breandán Breathnach's arguments in Breathnach, *Folk music and dances of Ireland*, pp 106–7.

56 Yeats, *Féile na gCruitirí, Béal Feirste 1792*, p. 21.

57 Edward Bunting, *The ancient music of Ireland* (Dublin, 1840), p. 73.

58 Bunting, *The ancient music of Ireland*, p. 73.

59 Moloney, *The Irish music manuscripts of Edward Bunting*, p. 73.

60 Summary of table given in Moloney,

*The Irish music manuscripts of
Edward Bunting*, p. 28.

61 Transcription by Helen Lawlor;
Gráinne Hambly, *Between the
showers* (Shamrock Records, 1050–2,
1998).

62 Ó Riada, Chualann and Sé, *Ó Riada
sa Gaeity.*

CHAPTER 4
Art music and the Irish harp

1 Livingston, 'Music revivals: towards a
general theory'.

2 Ibid., pp 80–1.

3 Bart Feintuch, 'Musical revival as
musical transformation' in Neil V.
Rosenberg (ed.), *Transforming
traditions: folk music revivals
examined* (Urbana and Chicago,
1993), p. 184.

4 Feintuch, 'Musical revival as musical
transformation', p. 187.

5 Ibid., pp 191–2.

6 Helen Lawlor, 'Interview with
Mercedes Garvey' (16 July 2008).

7 Ó Dálaigh later became Chief Justice
and then President of Ireland.

8 Lawlor, 'Interview with Sheila Larchet
Cuthbert'. Colm Ó Lochlainn was
owner of the publishing house, 'At the
Sign of the Three Candles', and was
employer to piper Séamus Ennis in the
early 1940s. For more details see Pat
Mitchell, *The dance music of Séamus
Ennis* (Dublin, 2007).

9 Cairde na Cruite,
www.cairdenacruite.com/about.html,
accessed 27 January 2012.

10 Newspaper clipping from Nancy
Calthorpe's notebook collection. No
publication date given.

11 This arrangement can be found in
Mercedes McGrath, *My gentle harp*,
ed. Elizabeth Hannon & Mercedes
Bolger (Dublin, 1992).

12 C.A., 'Cairde Na Cruite Gives a
Concert', *Irish Times*, Monday, 8
May 1961. C.A. in this case may have
been Charles Acton, music critic in
the *Irish Times* in 1961.

13 Mary MacGoris, 'Eight harpists in
Dublin concert', *Irish Independent*, 5
May 1961.

14 Lawlor, 'Interview with Mercedes
Garvey'.

15 Lawlor, 'Interview with Sheila Larchet
Cuthbert'.

16 Ibid.

17 The publication details of these
volumes are as yet unknown as there
are currently no extant copies of
either volume available.

18 For further details see chapter 2.

19 See Lyons, 'Irish harping: styles,
repertoire and technique' for further
analysis.

20 All graphs compiled from material in
Larchet Cuthbert, *The Irish harp
book*.

21 Lawlor, 'Interview with Sheila Larchet
Cuthbert'.

22 See Appendix 1 for a full listing of
titles and composers/arrangers in 'The
Irish harp book'.

23 Lawlor, 'Interview with Sheila Larchet
Cuthbert'.

24 Charles Acton, 'The Irish harp for
players', *Irish Times*, 3 December
1975, p. 8.

25 Lawlor, 'Interview with Mercedes
Garvey'.

26 Ralph Vaughan Williams, quoted in:
Michael Broken, *The British folk
revival* (Aldershot, 2003), p. 8.

27 In 'The Irish harp book', Irish
language translations are given for the
parts of the harp (p. 13) and
intermittently through the text, (pp 5,
245, for example). On my fieldwork
at An Chúirt Cruitireachta,
Termonfeckin in June 2008 I noted
the regular integration of the Irish
language in a variety of contexts, such
as concert introductions and general
instructions to students. Furthermore,
the summer school hosted sean-nós
singer Seosaimhín Ní Bheaglaoich as
singer in residence. All of the songs
taught by Seosaimhín were in the Irish
language.

28　See chapter 2 for more details. Coffey, *Irish melodies transcribed and arranged for the Irish harp.*

29　Evelyn Hearns, 'Nancy Calthorpe: the arranger' (BA thesis, NUIM, 2001), p. 1.

30　Hearns, 'Nancy Calthorpe', p. 2.

31　Ibid.

32　See bibliography for a full publication list.

33　Hearns, 'Nancy Calthorpe', p. 3.

34　Flood, *A history of Irish music*, p. 76.

35　The annual Feis Ceoil in Dublin awards two prizes annually in her honour: the Nancy Calthorpe Cup and the Nancy Calthorpe Memorial Prize.

36　Nancy Calthorpe, 'Copy Book 6' (Úna McSweeney Collection).

37　Calthorpe had a deep understanding of Irish song and a strong familiarity with the repertoire. Appendix 2 is taken from one of her copybooks (No. 6). It is a list of songs, divided into three sections by Calthorpe: songs by Thomas Moore that summarize Irish history; songs that summarize Irish history since the death of Thomas Moore; and, songs that express an Irish character. This list gives a further insight into her breadth of knowledge of songs and their subject matter.

38　See chapter 2 for a detailed description of these styles.

39　For further details see Clement Mac Manuis, 'Eamonn Ó Gallchobhair (1900–1982): an annotated catalogue of works' (MA dissertation, Dundalk Institute of Technology, 2009).

40　O'Donnell, 'It is new strung and it shall be heard: a study of the Irish harp in the twentieth century', p. 96.

41　Ibid., p. 73.

42　Unsigned, *Irish Times*, 1 October 1971, p. 10.

43　Berghout was founder of the World Harp Congress. Kortinska (based in London) was teacher to Denise Kelly (who now teaches concert and Irish harp in the DIT Conservatory of Music and Drama). Mercedes Bolger and Gráinne Yeats were invited to perform at a concert at one of the harp weeks in Holland (Lawlor, 'Interview with Mercedes Garvey').

44　Lawlor, 'Interview with Mercedes Garvey'.

45　Ibid.

46　Geraldine Collins, 'School again for harpists', *Irish Independent*, 24 July 1989.

47　I attended the festival in June 2008 as part of my PhD research. Yeats made these comments in the closing session of the summer school. 2008 was the first time that the festival had a resident singer.

48　Collins, 'School again for harpists'.

49　The teachers were: Cormac De Barra, Máire Ní Chathasaigh, Helen Davies, Dearbhail Finnegan, Kim Flemming, Gráinne Hambly, Kathleen Loughnane, Anne-Marie O'Farrell, Catríona Yeats (concert harp), Deirdre O'Brien-Vaughan and Seosaimhín Ní Bheaglaoich (song).

50　Lyons, 'Interview with Mercedes Garvey'.

51　McGrath, *My gentle harp*; Larchet Cuthbert, *The Irish harp book*; Mercedes Bolger and Gráinne Yeats, *Sounding harps, Books 1–4* (Dublin, 1990–8).

52　See Dawn Finnerty's MA thesis for a full analysis and catalogue of works for the Irish harp, Dawn Finnerty, 'Irish contemporary harp music' (MA, DkIT, 2011).

CHAPTER 5
*Style and context:
traditional Irish harping*

1　Bruno Nettl, *The study of ethnomusicology: thirty-one issues and concepts* (Urbana, 2005 (1983)), p. 179.

2 Janet Harbison, 'Harpists, harpers or harpees?' in Fintan Vallely et al. (eds), *Crossbhealach an Cheoil. The crossroads conference* (Cork, 1996), pp 94–100.

3 Mairéad Sullivan, *Celtic women in music* (Kingston, 1999), p. 135.

4 Philip V. Bohlman, *The study of folk music in the modern world* (Bloomington, 1988), pp 126–7.

5 Máire Ní Chathasaigh, *The new strung harp* (Temple Records, COMCD 2019, 1985).

6 Sabina McCague, 'An overview of the Irish harping tradition' (B.Mus, DIT Conservatory of Music and Drama, 2007), appendix E, p. 2.

7 Helen Lawlor, 'Interview with Kathleen Loughnane' (2005).

8 Niall Keegan, 'The verbal context of style in traditional Irish music' in Thérèse Smith and Mícheál Ó Súílleabháin (eds), *Blas, the local accent in Irish traditional music* (Limerick, 1997), p. 121.

9 Keegan, 'The verbal context of style in Irish traditional music'.

10 Ibid., p. 117.

11 Mark Slobin, *Subcultural sounds: micromusics of the West* (London, 1993), p. 11.

12 The existence of an oral tradition is commonly identified when attempting to define Irish traditional music. This does not necessarily deny the existence of written texts but rather, privileges oral transmission.

13 Slobin, *Subcultural sounds: micromusics of the West*, p. 33.

14 Niall Keegan's recent article (Niall Keegan, 'The parameters of style in Irish traditional music', *Inbhear* 1:1 (2010), available at http://www.irishworldacademy.ie//inbhear/, accessed 31 January 2012) offers thirteen parameters of style in Irish traditional music. This article develops some ideas further and offers detailed musical analysis that is useful in terms of describing ornamentation and variation types.

15 Lawrence E. McCullough, 'Style in Irish traditional music', *Ethnomusicology*, 21:1 (1977), pp 85–97.

16 Ibid., p. 85.

17 ITMA, 'What is Irish traditional music', http://www.itma.ie/Publications/What IsLeaflet.html, accessed 13 July 2009.

18 Michael Rooney, *Harp tunes, volume 1* (Sligo, 2006), p. 23.

19 Gráinne Hambly, *Traditional Irish music arranged for harp* (Claremorris, 2001), p. 4.

20 Breathnach, *Folk music and dances of Ireland*; Tomás Ó Canainn, *Traditional music of Ireland* (London, 1978); Fintan Vallely, *The companion to Irish traditional music* (Cork, 1999).

21 Hambly, *Traditional Irish music arranged for harp*, p. 6.

22 Rooney, *Harp tunes, volume 1*, p. iv.

23 Kathleen Loughnane, *Affairs of the harp* (Galway, 2002), p. iv.

24 Máire Ní Chathasaigh, *The Irish harper, volume 1* (Ilkely, 1991), p. 3.

25 Hambly, *Traditional Irish music arranged for harp*, p. 4.

26 Loughnane, *Affairs of the harp*, p. iv.

27 Hambly, *Traditional Irish music arranged for harp*, p. 7.

28 Rooney, *Harp tunes, volume 1*, p. v.

29 Hambly, *Traditional Irish music arranged for harp*, p. 7.

30 Ibid., p. 16.

31 Some composers of Irish music have witnessed the integration of some of their tunes into the repertory in their lifetimes, most notably Charlie Lennon, Tommy Peoples, Brendan Tonra and Paddy Ryan.

32 For a detailed analysis of the growth in harping at the All-Ireland Fleadh,

see Lyons, 'State of the harp: the Irish harp in Ireland in the twenty-first century'. Competitors in the All-Ireland Fleadh must first qualify from their county and province. Only two competitors may progress from each province, thus eight competitors may enter the All-Ireland from Ireland. The remaining six qualify from the All-Britain and US fleadhs.

33 John Tomlinson, *Globalization and culture* (Cambridge, 2000 (1999)), p. 27.

34 Tomlinson, *Globalization and culture*, p. 108.

35 Helen Lawlor, 'Interview with Hammy Hamilton' (11 June 2007).

36 Lawlor, 'Interview with Hammy Hamilton'.

37 Philip V. Bohlman, *World music: a very short introduction* (Oxford, 2002), p. 115.

38 James Porter, 'Introduction: locating Celtic music (and song)', *Western Folklore*, 57:4 (1998), p. 208.

39 Ibid., p. 210.

40 Ibid., p. 216.

41 Malcolm Chapman, 'Thoughts on Celtic music' in Martin Stokes (ed.), *Ethnicity, identity and music: the musical construction of place* (Oxford, 1994), p. 41.

42 Bohlman, *World music: a very short introduction*, p. 80.

43 Ibid.

CHAPTER 6
The early-Irish harp in its modern context

1 Simon Chadwick, 'The early Irish harp', *Early Music*, 36:4 (2008), p. 521.

2 Moloney, *The Irish music manuscripts of Edward Bunting (1773–1843)*.

3 Rimmer, *The Irish harp*.

4 Ann Heymann, *Secrets of the Gaelic harp* (Minneapolis, 1988).

5 Yeats, *Féile na gCruitirí, Béal Feirste 1792*.

6 Armstrong, *The Irish and Highland harps*.

7 For example, Bill Taylor's website header describes him as a: 'Specialist in the performance of ancient harp music from Ireland, Scotland, and Wales', http://www.billtaylor.eu, accessed 5 May 2010.

8 See Simon Chadwick's informative website for more details about extant harps: http://www.earlygaelicharp.info/.

9 Chadwick, 'The early Irish harp', p. 522.

10 Ibid., pp 522–3.

11 Helen Lawlor, 'Interview with Siobhan Armstrong' (2009).

12 Ann Heymann, 'Harp' in Fintan Vallely (ed.), *The companion to Irish traditional music* (Cork, 1999).

13 Helen Lawlor, 'Ann Heymann Workshop' (Dundalk Institute of Technology, 2009).

14 Nollaig Brolly, *Banríon an Cheoil (Queen of Music)* (Lugh Films and Gallan Films, funded by Northern Ireland Screen Irish Language Broadcast Fund (ILBF) and TG4, Broadcast 3 May 2010 (TG4)), Television Documentary.

15 http://www.kortier.com/, accessed 6 May 2010.

16 Anne Marie O'Farrell demonstrated one of these harps at the 2007 'Musical journeys with the Flight of the Earls' symposium at DIT, 3 February 2007. For further details see Wolfgang Marx, 'Conference review: "musical journeys with the Flight of the Earls", DIT Conservatory of Music and Drama', *Musicology Review*, 3 (2007), pp 279–81.

17 Lawlor, 'Ann Heymann Workshop'.

18 Chadwick, 'The early Irish harp', p. 528.

19 Francis Collinson, *The traditional and national music of Scotland* (London, 1966), p. 249.

20 http://www.clarsachsociety.co.uk/, accessed 6 May 2010.

21 Alison Kinnaird, *The harp key, crann nan teud* (Temple Records COMD1001, 1995 (1978)).

22 See, for example, her collaboration with Ann Heymann: Alison Kinnaird & Ann Heymann, *The harper's land* (Temple Records COMD 2012, 1983).

23 Stephen D. Winick, 'Breton folk music, Breton identity, and Alan Stivell's *Again*', *Journal of American Folklore*, 108:429 (1995), p. 336.

24 Alan Stivell, *Renaissance de la harp celtique* (Fontana 6325 302, 1972).

25 Winick, 'Breton folk music, Breton identity, and Alan Stivell's *Again*', p. 345.

26 Sullivan, *Celtic women in music*, p. 242.

27 Gráinne Yeats, 'Some thoughts on Irish harp music', *Ceol*, 4:2 (1973), pp 37–50; Gráinne Yeats, 'Lost chords', *Ceol*, 7:1 & 2 (1984), pp 14–19; Yeats, *Féile na gCruitirí, Béal Feirste 1792*.

28 Gráinne Yeats, *Belfast Harp Festival* (Dublin: Gael Linn, 1992), CD.

29 http://www.pauldooley.com/the%20harp/index.html, accessed 6 May 2010.

30 British Library Additional MS 14905.

31 Paul Dooley, *Rip the calico* (PDCD 001, 1996).

32 Paul Dooley, *Music from the Robert Ap Huw Manuscript* (PDCD 002, 2004).

33 Heymann, *Secrets of the Gaelic harp*.

34 Chadwick, 'The early Irish harp', p. 528.

35 Lawlor, 'Ann Heymann Workshop'.

36 Ann Heymann, *Queen of harps* (Temple Records, COMD2057, 1994), sleevenotes, p. 2.

37 Personal communication.

38 Lawlor, 'Interview with Siobhán Armstrong'.

39 Ibid.

40 Her most notable contribution to early-Irish harping is her 2004 recording: Siobhán Armstrong, *Cláirseach na Héireann, the harp of Ireland* (May Recordings MCD0401 DDD, 2004). See also http://www.siobhanarmstrong.com/recordings.htm for full details of her recording credits.

41 Bunting manuscript 33(1) p. 62, (f31v), housed at Queen's University Belfast. http://www.earlygaelicharp.info/tutor/fairmolly.htm, accessed 5 May 2010.

42 Lawlor, 'Ann Heymann Workshop'.

43 Lawlor, 'Interview with Siobhán Armstrong'.

44 Harper Ruaidhrí Dall Ó Catháin, (1546–1653) spent some time in Scotland. One of his compositions, 'Rory Dall's Port', can also be found in the 1627 Straloch Manuscript, National Library of Scotland, Adv. MS 5.2.18.

45 Brolly, *Banríon an cheoil (Queen of music)*. See also: http://www.northernirelandscreen.co.uk/newspage.asp?id=143&storyID=2586, accessed 6 May 2010 and http://live.tg4.ie/main.aspx?level=Faisneis&content=85439560705, accessed 6 May 2010.

CHAPTER 7
Transmission and Irish harping

1 Henry Kingsbury, *Music, talent & performance: a conservatory cultural system* (Philadelphia, 1988).

2 Ibid., p. 101.

3 See, for example, the definition published by the Irish Traditional Music Archives, http://www.itma.ie/publications/whatisleaflet.html; McCullough, 'Style in traditional Irish music'.

4 Philip V. Bohlman, *The study of folk music in the modern world* (Bloomington, 1988); Bohlman, 'World music at the "end of history"',

Ethnomusicology, 46:1 (2002), pp 1–32; Steven Feld, 'Orality and consciousness' in Yosihiko Tokumaru and Osamu Yamaguti (eds), *The oral and the literate in music* (1986); Ruth Finnegan, *Literacy and orality* (Oxford, 1988); Kiri Miller, '"First sing the notes": oral and written traditions in sacred harp transmission', *American Music*, 22:4 (2004), pp 475–501 and Timothy Rice, 'Understanding and producing the variability of oral tradition: learning from a Bulgarian bagpiper', *Journal of American Folklore*, 108:429 (1995), pp 266–76.

5 Walter J. Ong, *Orality and literacy: the technologizing of the world* (London, 1993), p. 15.

6 Jack Goody, *The power of the written tradition* (London, 2000), p. 26.

7 Nicholas Carolan, *A collection of the most celebrated Irish tunes proper for the violin, German flute or Hautboy: Dublin 1724 / [Compiled by] John & William Neal; facsimile edition* (Dublin 1986).

8 Sumi Gunji, 'Indication of timbre in orally transmitted music' in Yosihiko Tokumaru and Osamu Yamaguti (eds), *The oral and the literate in music* (Tokyo, 1986), p. 173.

9 Ruth Finnegan, *Studies in the technology* (Oxford, 1988), p. 126.

10 Feld, 'Orality and conciousness', p. 22.

11 J.M. Hawkins and R. Allen, *The Oxford encyclopedic English dictionary* (Oxford, 1991), p. 1534.

12 McCullough, 'Style in traditional Irish music', p. 85.

13 UNESCO, http://www.unesco.org/culture/ich/index.php?pg=00022&Art=Art2#Art2, accessed 29 June 2007.

14 Goody, *The power of the written tradition*, p. 40.

15 Sean Corcoran, 'What is traditional music?' in Peter McNamee (ed.), *Traditional music: whose music?* (1991), p. 7.

16 Hammy Hamilton, 'Innovation, conservatism, and the aesthetics of Irish traditonal music' in Hammy Hamilton, Eithne Vallely and Liz Doherty (eds), *Crosbhealach an Cheoil* (Cork, 1996), p. 83.

17 Scahill, 'The knotted chord: harmonic accompaniment in printed and recorded sources of Irish traditional music', p. 440.

18 Keegan, 'The parameters of style in Irish traditional music', p. 28.

19 Paul van den Bos, 'Differences between Western and non-Western teaching methods in music education. How can both methods supplement each other?' in Margot Lieth-Philipp and Andreas Gutzwiller (eds), *Teaching musics of the world* (Basel, 1993).

20 Huib Schippers, 'Taking distance and getting up close: the seven continuum transmission model (Sctm)' in Patricia Sheehan Campbell (ed.), *Cultural diversity in music education* (Brisbane, 2005).

21 Helen O'Shea, 'Reinventing the reel: learning choices among adult players of Irish traditional music', conference paper given at ICTM World Conference (Vienna, 2007).

22 Timothy D. Taylor, *Global pop. World music, world markets* (New York, 1997), p. xvii.

23 Bart Barendregt and Wim van Zanten, 'Popular music in Indonesia since 1998, in particular fusion, indie and Islamic music on video compact discs and the internet', *Yearbook for Traditional Music*, 34 (2002), p. 101.

24 Ibid., p. 97.

25 Marjorie D. Kibby, 'Home on the page: a virtual place of music community', *Popular Music*, 19:1 (2000), p. 96.

26 Steve Jones, 'Music and the internet',

Popular Music, 19:2 (2000), pp 217–30.

27 Arjun Appadurai, *Modernity at large* (Minneapolis, 2006), p. 53.

28 Bryan Duggan, 'Content based music information retrieval: query-by-playing systems for traditional Irish music', LAP LAMBERT Academic Publishing (Saarbrücken, 2010). Bryan Duggan, 'Tunepal: The traditional musician's toolbox', eHeritage 2010: Proceedings of the second workshop on eHeritage and digital art preservation (New York, 2010), pp 25–30.

29 Henrik Norbeck, http://www.norbeck.nu/abc/, accessed 22 April 2010.

30 Nicholas Carolan, *A harvest saved. Francis O'Neill and Irish music in Chicago* (Cork, 1997), p. 43.

31 Bohlman, *The study of folk music in the modern world*, p. 17.

32 Kiri Miller, '"First sing the notes": oral and written traditions in sacred harp transmission', p. 480.

33 Goody, *The power of the written tradition*, p. 45.

34 Jones, 'Music and the internet', p. 218.

35 Séamus Ennis, http://ie.Youtube.Com/Watch?V=Lle9etqoiwq.

36 Sally K. Sommers Smith, 'Irish traditional music in a modern world', *New Hibernia Review*, 5:2 (2001), p. 112.

37 Patricia Sheehan Campbell, *Teaching music globally: experiencing music, expressing culture* (Oxford, 2004).

38 Kari Veblen, 'The teacher's role in transmission of Irish traditional music', *International Journal of Music Education*, 24 (1994), p. 26.

39 Rice, 'Understanding and producing the variability of oral tradition: learning from a Bulgarian bagpiper', p. 268.

40 Hamilton, 'Innovation, conservatism,

and the aesthetics of Irish traditonal music', p. 82.

41 Sommers Smith, 'Irish traditional music in a modern world', pp 123–4.

CHAPTER 8
Gender and identity

1 Philip A. Griswold and Denise A. Chroback, 'Sex-role associations of music instruments and occupations by gender and major', *Journal of Research in Music Education*, 29:1 (1981), p. 58.

2 Marcia Herndon, 'Biology and culture: music, gender, power, and ambiguity' in Marcia Herndon and Susanne Ziegler (eds), *Music, gender, and culture* (Wilhelmshaven, 1990), p. 26.

3 For further reading see Dónal Ó Sullivan, *Carolan: the life, times and music of an Irish harper* (London, 1958); Bunting, *The ancient music of Ireland*.

4 Bunting, *The ancient music of Ireland*, p. 74.

5 For a fuller discussion of the early-Irish harp revival see chapter 6.

6 For further reading see Flood, *A history of Irish music*.

7 Ibid., p. 322.

8 The ditals were positioned along the inside of the forepillar. They allowed for one semi-tonal movement, thus opening up the potential key range of a harp from Ab major to E major (inclusive), and their natural and harmonic minors. Each lever changes approximately four strings at a time (for example, the C dital changes every C string simultaneously). The mechanism allows for a semitonal change of one semitone. Ditals operated using a similar mechanism to a single-action concert harp. Movement can be made, for example, from D natural to D sharp or from D natural to D flat but not from D flat to natural to sharp as this would

require an entirely different system (as exists on a fully-chromatic concert harp). See details of photographs above.

9 Flood, *A history of Irish music*, p. 323.

10 *The mirror of the Graces* (London 1811), p. 195, cited in Robert Anderson and Jacqueline Letzter, '"For a woman when she is young a beautiful": the harp in eighteenth-century France' in Annette Kreutziger-Herr and Katrin Losleben (eds), *History/Herstory, Alternative Musikgeschichten* (Köln, 2009), pp 321–2.

11 Nic Cormaic, 'Interview with Laoise Kelly on "Cherish the Ladies"'.

12 It must be noted, however, that harpists playing in the art-music style generally did not sit to the side of the harp as they were drawing on the posture and technique of concert harp.

13 Alan P. Merriam, *The anthropology of music* (Evanston, 1964), p. 205.

14 Philip V. Bohlman, *The music of European nationalism* (Oxford, 2004), p. 23.

15 Brown, *Ireland, a social and cultural history*, p. 202.

16 O'Hara, *Travels with my harp*, pp 4–5.

17 Bohlman, *The study of folk music in the modern world*, p. 130.

18 Ní Fhloinn, *Irish traditional songs*.

19 Frank A. Biletz, 'Women and Irish-Ireland: the domestic nationalism of Mary Butler', *New Hibernia Review*, 6:1 (2002), p. 64.

20 Suruchi Thapar, 'Women as activists; women as symbols: a study of the Indian nationalist movement', *Feminist Review*, 44 (1993), p. 88.

21 Anderson and Letzter, '"For a woman when she is young and beautiful"', p. 314.

22 Keith Negus, 'Sinéad O'Connor – musical mother' in Sheila Whiteley (ed.), *Sexing the groove: popular music and gender* (London, 1997).

23 Ibid., p. 186.

24 Mary O'Hara, *Songs of Erin* (LP, Decca Belatona IEP49, 1956), Mary O'Hara, *Love songs of Ireland* (LP, Decca Belatona LBE 20, 1957), Mary O'Hara, *Songs of Ireland* (LP, Tradition Records TLP 1024, 1958), Mary O'Hara, *Mary O'Hara's Ireland* (LP, Emerald GES 1095, 1973), Mary O'Hara, *Mary O'Hara's Scotland* (LP, Emerald GES 1116, 1974), Mary O'Hara, *Recital* (LP, Boot BOS 7237, 1983).

25 Ní Fhloinn, *Irish traditional songs*.

26 With kind permission of Comhaltas Ceoltóirí Éireann.

27 See, for example, the following Comhaltas live clips: Edel Fox (concertina) and Shauna Davey (harp) playing on the 2004 Comhaltas tour of North America: (http://comhaltas. ie/music/detail/comhaltaslive_285_5_e del_fox_and_shauna_davey/) and Nadia Markey (harp) playing (solo) on the 2007 Comhaltas tour of North America: (http://comhaltas.ie/music/ detail/comhaltaslive_235_2_nadia_ma rkey_on_harp/).

28 The pictures of Bell were published while he was alive.

29 Martin Stokes, 'Introduction: ethnicity, identity and music' in Martin Stokes (ed.), *Ethnicity, identity and music: the musical construction of place* (Oxford, 1997), p. 3.

30 See, for example, the following: Louise Wrazen, 'Relocating the Tatras: place and music in Górale identity and imagination,' *Ethnomusicology*, 51:2 (2007), pp 185–204; May McCann, 'Music and politics in Ireland: the specificity of the folk revival in Belfast', *British Journal of Ethnomusicology*, 4 (1995), pp 51–75; Fintan Vallely, *Tuned out. Traditional music and identity in Northern Ireland* (Cork, 2008); John

O'Flynn, *The Irishness of Irish music* (Surrey, 2009); Daithí Kearney, 'Crossing the river: exploring the geography of Irish traditional music', *Journal of the Society for Musicology in Ireland*, 3 (2007–8).

31 Stokes, 'Introduction: ethnicity, identity and music', p. 5.

32 Ibid., p. 10.

33 For example, the 1952 An Tostal festival used harpists as part of the festival promotion. Furthermore, Áras an Uachtaráin frequently book Irish harpists to play at functions in the Áras.

34 John Baily, 'The role of music in the creation of an Afghan national identity' in Martin Stokes (ed.), *Ethnicity, identity and music*, p. 48.

35 Boydell, 'The iconography of the Irish harp as a national symbol', p. 132.

36 Hélène La Rue, 'Music, literature and etiquette: musical instruments and social identity from Castiglione to Austen' in Martin Stokes (ed.), *Ethnicity, identity and music*, p. 189.

37 O'Flynn, *The Irishness of Irish music*, p. 195.

38 Ibid., p. 199.

39 Vallely, *Tuned out. Traditional music and identity in Northern Ireland*, p. 4.

40 Boydell, 'The iconography of the Irish harp as a national symbol', p. 139.

41 Ibid.; Barra Boydell, 'The Irish harp on glass', *Irish Arts Review Yearbook*, 12 (1996), pp 110–14; Barra Boydell, 'Female figures on Irish and European harps', *Galpin Society Journal*, 50 (1997), p. 306.

42 Stephanie Rains, 'Celtic kitsch: Irish-America and Irish material culture', *Circa*, 107 (2004), pp 53–4.

43 Ibid., p. 57.

44 Boydell, 'The iconography of the Irish harp as a national symbol', p. 137.

45 http://www.ritzcarlton.com/en/Properties/Powerscourt/Information/Default.htm.

46 There is no required repertoire for such occasions, during which the concert harp is used to provide background music for hotel guests.

47 http://www.dublincity.ie/RoadsandTraffic/MajorTransportProjects/Samuel%20Beckett%20Bridge/Pages/default.aspx, accessed 24 July 2009.

CHAPTER 9
Conclusion

1 Bunting, *The ancient music of Ireland*.

2 Ó Sullivan, *Carolan: the life, times and music of an Irish harper*; Moloney, *The Irish music manuscripts of Edward Bunting (1773–1843)*; Rimmer, *The Irish harp*; Flood, *A history of Irish music*; Yeats, *Féile na gCruitirí, Béal Feirste 1792*.

3 Ita Beausang mentions some harping activity in her 2007 article: Beausang, 'From national sentiment to nationalist movement, 1850–1900'. Also, Mary-Louise O'Donnell gave a paper at the 2010 Women and Music in Ireland Conference in Maynooth: Mary-Louise O'Donnell, '"Ireland's only harpist" – Miss Emilie Glover and the grand harp and vocal concerts of 1869'.

Bibliography

Printed sources

Anderson, Robert and Jacqueline Letzter, '"For a woman when she is young and beautiful": the harp in eighteenth-century France' in Annette Kreutziger-Herr and Katrin Losleben (eds), *History/Herstory, Alternative Musikgeschichten* (Köln Weimar Wien, 2009), pp 321–2.

Appadurai, Arjun, *Modernity at large* (Minneapolis, 2006).

Armstrong, Robert Bruce, *The Irish and Highland harps* (Shannon, (1904), rpr. 1969).

Baily, John, 'The role of music in the creation of an Afghan national identity' in Martin Stokes (ed.), *Ethnicity, identity and music the musical construction of place* (Oxford, 1997), pp 85–98.

Barendregt, Bart and Wim van Zanten, 'Popular music in Indonesia since 1998, in particular fusion, indie and Islamic music on video compact discs and the internet', *Yearbook for Traditional Music*, 34 (2002), pp 67–113.

Beausang, Ita, 'From national sentiment to nationalist movement, 1850–1900' in Michael Murphy and Jan Smazny (eds), *Irish musical studies 9: music in nineteenth century Ireland* (Dublin, 2007), pp 36–51.

Biletz, Frank A., 'Women and Irish-Ireland: the domestic nationalism of Mary Butler', *New Hibernia Review*, 6:1 (2002), pp 59–72.

Bohlman Philip V., *The study of folk music in the modern world* (Bloomington, 1988).

——, 'World music at the "end of history"', *Ethnomusicology*, 46:1 (2002), pp 1–32.

——, *World music: a very short introduction* (Oxford, 2002).

——, *The music of European nationalism* (Oxford, 2004).

Boydell, Barra, 'Female figures on Irish and European harps', *The Galpin Society Journal*, 50 (1997), p. 306.

——, 'The iconography of the Irish harp as a national symbol' in Patrick F. Devine & Harry White (eds), *Irish musical studies 5. The Maynooth International Musicological Conference 1995. Selected proceedings: part two* (Dublin,1995).

——, 'The Irish harp on glass', *Irish Arts Review Yearbook*, 12 (1996), pp 110–14.

Breathnach, Breandán 'The use of notation in Irish folk music' in Seán Potts, Terry Moylan, and Liam McNulty (eds), *The man and his music* (Dublin, 1996).

——, *Folk music and dances of Ireland* (Cork, 1996).

Broken, Michael, *The British folk revival* (Aldershot, 2003).

Brown, Terence, *Ireland, a social and cultural history* (London, 2004).

Bunting, Edward, *The ancient music of Ireland* (Dublin, 1840).

Calthorpe, Nancy, *Copy Book collection, Copy 1* (Úna McSweeney Collection).

——, *Copy Book 6* (Úna McSweeney Collection).

Carolan, Nicholas, *A collection of the most celebrated Irish tunes proper for the violin,*

German flute or Hautboy: Dublin 1724 / [compiled by] John & William Neal, facsimile edition (Dublin, 1986).

——, *A harvest saved. Francis O'Neill and Irish music in Chicago* (Cork, 1997).

Casson, Glynis and Cormac De Barra, 'The harp that once' (Concert at Domincan College, Sion Hill, 28 January 2007).

Chadwick, Simon, 'The early Irish harp', *Early Music,* 36:4 (2008), pp 521–31.

Chapman, Malcolm, 'Thoughts on Celtic music' in Martin Stokes (ed.), *Ethnicity, identity and music: the musical construction of place* (Oxford, 1994), pp 29–44.

Clark, Nora Joan, *The story of the Irish harp* (Lynnwood, 2003).

Coffey, Mother Attracta, *Irish melodies transcribed and arranged for the Irish harp* (London, 1902).

Collinson, Francis, *The traditional and national music of Scotland* (London, 1966).

Corcoran, Sean, 'What is traditional music?' in Peter McNamee (ed.), *Traditional music: whose music?* (1991).

Cullinane, John, *Irish dancing costumes* (Cork, 1996).

Duggan, Bryan, 'Content based music information retrieval: query-by-playing systems for traditional Irish music', *LAP LAMBERT* Academic Publishing (2010).

——, 'Tunepal: the traditional musician's toolbox', *eHeritage 2010*: 2nd ACM Workshop on eHeritage and Digital Art Preservation, 25 October 2010, Firenze, Italy (2010)

Feintuch, Bart, 'Musical revival as musical transformation' in Neil V. Rosenberg (ed.), *Transforming traditions* (Urbana and Chicago, 1993).

Feld, Steven, 'Orality and consciousness' in Yosihiko Tokumaru and Osamu Yamaguti (eds), *The oral and the literate in music* (Tokyo, 1986).

Finnegan Ruth, *Studies in the technology* (Oxford, 1988).

——, *Literacy and orality* (Oxford, 1988)

Finnerty, Dawn, 'Irish contemporary harp music' (MA, DkIT, 2011).

Fleischmann, Aloys, *Music in Ireland a symposium* (Cork, 1952).

Goody, Jack, *The power of the written tradition*, ed. William L. Merrill and Ivan Karp, Smithsonian Series in Ethnographic Inquiry (London, 2000).

Graham, Colin, '"Blame it on Maureen O'Hara": Ireland and the trope of authenticity', *Cultural Studies*, 15:1 (2001).

Grattan Flood, William Henry, *A history of Irish music* (Dublin, 1906).

Griswold, Philip A. and Denise A. Chroback, 'Sex-role associations of music instruments and occupations by gender and major', *Journal of Research in Music Education*, 29:1 (1981), pp 57–62.

Gunji, Sumi, 'Indication of timbre in orally transmitted music' in Yosihiko Tokumaru and Osamu Yamaguti (eds), *The oral and the literate in music* (Tokyo, 1986).

Hamilton, Hammy, 'Innovation, conservatism, and the aesthetics of Irish traditonal music', in Hammy Hamilton, Eithne Vallely and Liz Doherty (eds), *Crosbhealach an Cheoil* (Cork, 1996).

Harbison, Janet, 'Harpists, harpers or harpees?' in Hammy Hamilton, Eithne Vallely and Liz Doherty (eds), *Crosbhealach an Cheoil* (Cork, 1996).

Hawkins, J.M. and R. Allen (eds), *The Oxford encyclopedic English dictionary* (Oxford, 1991).

Hearns, Evelyn, 'Nancy Calthorpe: the arranger' (BA, NUIM, 2001).

Henigan, Julie, 'Technique (Song)' in Fintan Vallely (ed.), *The companion to Irish traditional music*, 2nd edition (Cork, 2011).

Herndon, Marcia, 'Biology and culture: music, gender, power, and ambiguity' in Marcia

Herndon and Susanne Ziegler (eds), *Music, gender, and culture* (Wilhelmshaven, 1990).

Heymann, Ann, 'Harp' in Fintan Vallely (ed.), *The companion to Irish traditional music*, (Cork, 1999).

Jones, Steve, 'Music and the internet', *Popular Music,* 19:2 (2000), pp 217–30.

Kearney, Daithí , 'Crossing the river: exploring the geography of Irish traditional music' *Journal of the Society of Musicology in Ireland,* 3 (2007–8).

Keegan, Niall, 'Literacy as a transmission tool in Irish traditional music' in Patrick F. Devine & Harry White (eds), *Irish musical studies 4. The Maynooth International Musicological Conference 1995. Selected proceedings: part one* (Dublin, 1996),

——, 'The verbal context of style in traditional Irish music' in Thérèse Smith and Mícheál Ó Súilleabháin (eds), *Blas, the local accent in Irish traditional music* (Limerick, 1997).

Kibby, Marjorie D., 'Home on the page: a virtual place of music community', *Popular Music,* 19:1 (2000), pp 91–100.

Kingsbury, Henry, *Music, talent & performance* (Philadelphia, 1988).

La Rue, Hélène, 'Music, literature and etiquette: musical instruments and social identity from Castiglione to Austen' in *Ethnicity, identity and music*, ed. Martin Stokes (Oxford, 1997).

Lanier, S.C., '"It is new-strung and shan't be heard": nationalism and memory in the Irish harp tradition', *British Journal of Ethnomusicology* 8 (1999), pp 1–26.

Larchet Cuthbert, Sheila, *The Irish harp book* (Dublin, 1975).

Lawlor, Helen, 'Ann Heymann workshop' (Dundalk Institute of Technology, 2009).

——, 'Interview with Harry Bradley' (17 May 2007).

——, 'Interview with Mercedes Garvey' (16 July 2008).

——, 'Interview with Sheila Larchet Cuthbert' (19 November 2007).

——, 'Popularity and revival: factors affecting harp reception in the 1950s and 1960s', *Ancestral imprints: histories of Irish traditional music and dance*, ed. Thérèse Smith (Cork, 2012).

Livingston, Tamara E., 'Music revivals: towards a general theory', *Ethnomusicology,* 43:1 (1999), pp 66–85.

Lyons, Helen 'State of the harp: the Irish harp in Ireland in the twenty-first century' (M.Mus Thesis, UCD, 2005).

Lyons, Helen, 'Irish harping: styles, repertoire and technique', *The Musicology Review,* 2, pp 125–48.

Maher, Tom, *The harp's a wonder* (Mullingar, 1991).

Marx, Wolfgang, 'Conference review: "Musical journeys with the Flight of the Earls", Dit Conservatory of Music and Drama', *The Musicology Review,* 3 (2007), pp 279–81.

McCague, Sabina, 'An overview of the Irish harping tradition' (B.Mus, DIT Conservatory of Music and Drama, 2007).

McCann, May, 'Music and politics in Ireland: the specificity of the folk revival in Belfast', *British Journal of Ethnomusicology,* 4 (1995), pp 51–75.

McCarthy, Marie, *Passing it on: the transmission of music in Irish culture* (Cork, 1999).

Merriam, Alan P., *The anthropology of music* (Evanston, 1964).

Miller, Kiri, '"First sing the notes": oral and written traditions in sacred harp transmission', *American Music,* 22:4 (2004), pp 475–501.

Millin, S. Shannon, *The Irish harp, a lecture* (London, 1898).

Mitchell, Pat, *The dance music of Séamus Ennis* (Dublin, 2007).

Moloney, Colette, *The Irish music manuscripts of Edward Bunting (1773–1843)* (Dublin, 2000).

Moulden, John, 'Song' in *The companion to Irish traditional music*, ed. Fintan Vallely (Cork, 1999).

Negus, Keith, 'Sinéad O'Connor – musical mother' in *Sexing the groove: popular music and gender*, ed. Sheila Whiteley (London, 1997).

Nettl, Bruno, *The study of ethnomusicology: thirty-one issues and concepts* (Urbana, 2005 (1983)).

Ó Canainn, Tomás, *Traditional music of Ireland* (London, 1978).

Ó Riada, Seán, *Our musical heritage*, ed. Kinsella and Ó Cannain (Mountrath, 1982).

Ó Sullivan, Dónal, *Carolan: the life, times and music of an Irish harper* (London, 1958).

O'Donnell, Mary, 'Custodians of culture: a social, political, musicological and cultural history of the Irish harp and its patronage from 1790 to 1845' (PhD, UL, 2008).

——, 'The Anglicization of the Irish harp. A history of the Irish harp from 1800 to the present day' (MA, UCD, 1999).

O'Donnell, Teresa, 'It is new strung and it shall be heard: a study of the Irish harp in the twentieth century' (MA, NUIM, 2000).

O'Connor, Mother Alphonsus, *Irish airs arranged for the harp* (London, nd).

O'Donnell, Mary-Louise, '"Ireland's only harpist" – Miss Emilie Glover and the grand harp and vocal concerts of 1869', paper given at: Women and Music in Ireland Conference (NUI Maynooth, 2010).

John O'Flynn, *The Irishness of Irish music* (Surrey, 2009).

O'Hara, Mary, 'Travels with my harp', paper given at the 9th World Harp Congress (UCD, Dublin, 2005).

——, *The scent of the roses* (London, 1980).

Ong, Walter J., *Orality and literacy* (London, 1993).

O'Shea, Helen, 'Reinventing the reel: learning choices among adult players of Irish traditional music', conference paper given at ICTM World Conference (Vienna, 2007).

Perry Curtis, L. Jr., *Apes and angels: the Irishman in Victorian caricature* (London, 1997).

Porter, James, 'Introduction: locating Celtic music (and song)', *Western Folklore*, 57:4 (1998), pp 205–24.

Rice, Timothy, 'Understanding and producing the variability of oral tradition: learning from a Bulgarian bagpiper', *Journal of American Folklore*, 108:429 (1995), pp 266–76.

Rimmer, Joan, *The Irish harp* (Dublin, 1984).

Scahill, Adrian, 'The knotted chord: harmonic accompaniment in printed and recorded sources of Irish traditional music' (PhD, UCD, 2004).

Schippers, Huib, 'Taking distance and getting up close: the seven continuum transmission model (Sctm)' in *Cultural diversity in music education*, ed. Patricia Sheehan Campbell (Brisbane, 2005).

Sheehan Campbell, Patricia, *Teaching music globally, experiencing music, expressing culture* (Oxford, 2004).

Slobin, Mark, *Subcultural sounds: micromusics of the west* (London, 1993).

Smith, Thérèse, 'The challenge of bringing oral traditions into an academic teaching environment' in *Crosbhealach an Cheoil*, ed. Fintan Vallely, et al. (Cork, 1996).

Sommers Smith, Sally K., 'Irish traditional music in a modern world', *New Hibernia Review*, 5:2 (2001), p. 112.

Stokes, Martin, 'Introduction: ethnicity, identity and music' in *Ethnicity, identity and music*, ed. Martin Stokes (Oxford, 1997).

Sullivan, Mairéad, *Celtic women in music* (Kingston, 1999).

Taylor, Timothy D., *Global pop: world music, world markets* (New York, 1997).

——, 'The commodification of music at the dawn of the era of "mechanical music"', *Ethnomusicology*, 51:2 (2007), pp 281–305.

Teehan, John, 'A list of Irish instrument makers', *The Galpin Society Journal*, 16 (1963), pp 28–32.

Thapar, Suruchi, 'Women as activists; women as symbols: a study of the Indian nationalist movement', *Feminist Review*, 44 (1993), p. 88.

Tomlinson, John, *Globalization and culture* (Cambridge, 2000 (1999)), p. 27.

Townshend, Charles, *Ireland, the 20th century* (London, 1998).

Vallely, Fintan, *The companion to Irish traditional music*, 2nd edition (Cork, 2011).

——, *The companion to Irish traditional music* (Cork, 1999).

——, *Tuned out. Traditional music and identity in Northern Ireland* (Cork, 2008).

Van den Bos, Paul, 'Differences between Western and non-Western teaching methods in music education. How can both methods supplement each other?' in *Teaching musics of the world*, ed. Margot Lieth-Philipp and Andreas Gutzwiller (Basel, 1993).

Veblen, Kari, 'The teacher's role in transmission of Irish traditional music', *International Journal of Music Education,* 24 (1994), p. 26.

White, Harry, 'The preservation of music and Irish cultural history', *International Review of the Aesthetics and Sociology of Music*, 27:2 (Dec. 1996), pp 123–38.

Winick, Stephen D., 'Breton folk music, Breton identity, and Alan Stivell's *Again*', *Journal of American Folklore*, 108:429 (1995), p. 336.

Wrazen, Louise, 'Relocating the Tatras: place and music in Górale identity and imagination', *Ethnomusicology*, 51:2 (2007), pp 185–204.

Yeats, Gráinne, 'Lost Chords', *Ceol*, 7:1 & 2 (1984).

Yeats, Gráinne, 'Some thoughts on Irish harp music', *Ceol*, 4:2 (1973).

Yeats, Gráinne, *Féile na gCruitirí, Béal Feirste 1792* (Dublin, 1980).

Scores

Hambly, Gráinne, *Traditional Irish music arranged for harp* (Claremorris, 2001).

Heymann, Ann, *Secrets of the Gaelic harp* (Minneapolis, 1988).

Loughnane, Kathleen, *Affairs of the harp* (Galway, 2002).

McGrath, Mercedes, *My gentle harp*, ed. Elizabeth Hannon & Mercedes Bolger (Dublin, 1992).

Ní Chathasaigh, Máire, *The Irish harper, volume 1* (Ilkely, 1991).

Mary O'Hara, *Travels with my harp, volume 1* (self published: 2008).

Michael Rooney, *Harp tunes, volume 1* (Sligo, 2006).

Discography

Armstrong, Siobhán, *Cláirseach na hÉireann, The harp of Ireland* (May Recordings MCD0401 DDD, 2004).

De Barra, Cormac, *Barcó* (Barcó, 2002).

Dooley, Paul, *Music from the Robert Ap Huw Manuscript* (PDCD 002, 2004).

Dooley, Paul, *Rip the calico* (PDCD 001, 1996).

Hambly, Gráinne, *Between the showers* (Shamrock Records, 1050–2, 1998).

Harte, Frank, 'Singing voices, traditional singing styles in Ireland – the singers' voices' (RTE Radio 1, 30 December 2005 (1987)).

Heymann, Ann, *Queen of harps* (Temple Records, COMD2057, 1994).

Kelly, Laoise, *Just harp* (LK001, 1999).

Kinnaird, Alison & Ann Heymann, *The harper's land* (Temple Records COMD 2012, 1983).

Kinnaird, Alison, *The harp key, crann nan teud* (Temple Records COMD1001, 1995 (1978)).

Loughnane, Kathleen, *Harp to heart* (Galway: Reiskmore Music, 2005).

Ní Chathasaigh, Máire, *The new strung harp* (Temple Records, COMCD 2019, 1985).

Ní Fhloinn, Deirdre, *Irish traditional songs* (Washington DC: Smithsonian Folkways Records, FW 8762, 1958).

Nic Cormaic, Aoife, 'Interview with Laoise Kelly on "Cherish the Ladies"' (Dublin, RTE, Radio 1: 25 July 2005).

Ó Riada, Seán, Ceoltóirí Chualann and Seán Ó Sé, *Ó Riada sa Gaeity* (Gael Linn, ORIADACD01, 2005).

O'Hara Mary, *Songs of Erin* (LP, Decca Belatona IEP49, 1956)

O'Hara, Mary, *Irish traditional folk songs* (Beverly Hills: Legacy International, CD 333, 1993).

O'Hara, Mary, *Mary O'Hara's Scotland* (LP, Emerald GES 1116, 1974).

O'Hara, Mary, *Love songs of Ireland* (LP, Decca Belatona LBE 20, 1957).

O'Hara, Mary, *Mary O'Hara's Ireland* (LP, Emerald GES 1095, 1973).

O'Hara, Mary, *Recital* (LP, Boot BOS 7237, 1983).

O'Hara, Mary, *Songs of Ireland* (LP, Tradition Records TLP 1024 , 1958).

O'Hara, Mary, *Mary O'Hara's Ireland* (Emerald Gem GES 1905, 1973).

O'Hara, Mary, *Focus on Mary O' Hara* (London: Decca FOS 49/50, 1958).

Stivell, Alan, *Renaissance De La Harp Celtique* (Fontana 6325 302, 1972).

Trebitsch, Rudolf, *The collections of Rudolf Trebitsch. Celtic recordings – Ireland,* Rudolf Trebitsch, Celtic Recordings – Ireland, Wales, Brittany, Isle of Man, and Scotland (1907–09), Sound Documents from the Phonogrammarchiv of the Austrian Academy of Sciences. The complete historical collections, 1899–1950, Series 5/2, (Vienna, 2003).

Yeats, Gráinne, *Féile na gCruitirí, Béal Feirste 1792* (Dublin: Gael Linn, 1980).

Internet sources

http://grainne.harp.net/

http://www.myspace.com/laoisekelly

http://www.billtaylor.eu

www.cairdenacruite.com/about.html,

http://www.clarsachsociety.co.uk/

www.comhaltas.ie

http://www.dublincity.ie/RoadsandTraffic/MajorTransportProjects/Samuel%20Beckett%20Bridge/Pages/default.aspx

www.draiochtmusic.com

http://www.earlygaelicharp.info/

http://www.guinness.com/ie_en/ads/classic/1970sPress/1970a/guinness.com+-+the+ads+-+classic+ads+-+press+ads.htm

www.irishharper.com

http://www.itma.ie/publications/whatisleaflet.html

http://www.janetharbison.com/ImageGallery/HARP%20COLLEGE%202008.pdf

http://www.kortier.com/
http://live.tg4.ie/main.aspx?level=Faisneis&content=85439560705
http://www.norbeck.nu/abc/
http://www.northernirelandscreen.co.uk/newspage.asp?id=143&storyID=2586,
http://www.pauldooley.com/the%20harp/index.htm
http://www.ritzcarlton.com/en/Properties/Powerscourt/Information/Default.htm
http://www.siobhanarmstrong.com/recordings.htm
http://www.unesco.org/culture/ich/index.php?pg=00022&Art=Art2#Art2.

Index